MW00799538

SSSP

Springer
Series in
Social
Psychology

SSSP

Richard E. Petty
John T. Cacioppo

Communication and Persuasion
Central and Peripheral Routes
to Attitude Change

87

Springer-Verlag New York Berlin Heidelberg
London Paris Tokyo

Richard E. Petty
Department of Psychology
University of Missouri
Columbia, Missouri 65211
U.S.A.

John T. Cacioppo
Department of Psychology
University of Iowa
Iowa City, Iowa 52242
U.S.A.

With 40 Illustrations

Library of Congress Cataloging in Publication Data
Petty, Richard E.
  Communication and persuasion.
  (Springer series in social psychology)
  Bibliography: p.
  Includes index.
  1. Persuasion (Psychology) 2. Attitude change.
3. Communication—Psychological aspects. I. Cacioppo,
John T. II. Title. III. Series.
BF637.P4P47 1986   302.2'4   86-11822

Typeset by Ampersand Publisher Services, Rutland, Vermont.
Printed and bound by R.R. Donnelley & Sons, Harrisonburg, Virginia.
Printed in the United States of America.

9 8 7 6 5 4 3 2 1

ISBN 0-387-96344-8 Springer-Verlag New York Berlin Heidelberg
ISBN 3-540-96344-8 Springer-Verlag Berlin Heidelberg New York

To Lynn and Barbara

Preface

It has been over 10 years since we initiated work on our first series of collaborative experiments. As graduate students, we had great fun planning, conducting, and writing this research (Petty & Cacioppo, 1977). We enjoyed arguing with each other at our initial meeting in 1973 and have subsequently become best friends, but neither of us suspected at the time that we would or could actively maintain a research collaboration over the next decade, or that we would now find ourselves in a position to write this monograph.

As we note in Chapter 1, we began our studies of persuasion at a time when social psychology was in "crisis," and interest in research on attitude change in particular was declining. As we write this, we are aware of six new volumes on persuasion that are in press or in preparation and that should appear over the next few years. In retrospect, it is not so surprising that research on attitudes and persuasion would reemerge as a central concern of social psychology. We believe that human feelings, beliefs, and behaviors, whether in the domain of interpersonal relations (e.g., marriage, aggression), politics (e.g., voting, revolution), health (e.g., following a medical regimen), or economics (e.g., consumer purchases) are greatly influenced by the evaluations people have of other people, objects, and issues. Furthermore, evaluations (attitudes) are influenced by affect, cognition, and behavior. Because of this reciprocal interdependence and the general importance of the attitude construct for many disciplines, attitude theory, perhaps more than any other field of inquiry in social psychology, has the potential to provide one of the general theories for the social sciences.

In this monograph we present a general framework for understanding the attitude changes that result from exposure to persuasive communications. This theory, which we have called the Elaboration Likelihood Model (ELM), outlines two "routes to persuasion." One route is based on a careful and thoughtful assessment of the central merits of the position advocated (central route). The other is based on some cognitive, affective, or behavioral cue in the persuasion context which becomes attached to the advocacy or allows a relatively simple inference as to the merits of the position advocated (peripheral route). Similar amounts of attitude change can be produced via either route. However, the changes induced via the central route require more cogitation and are postulated to be more persistent, resistant to counterpersuasion, and predictive of behavior. We believe that these two routes to persuasion are applicable to the full range of situations in which people are influenced by persuasive communications. For example, we believe the model holds promise for explaining a variety of effects of interest to social scientists ranging from (a) the conditions under which people will vote for candidates based on relatively simple cues such as political party or physical attractiveness rather than their issue positions, to (b) the situations in which attitude changes induced by advertisements will and will not lead to changes in purchase intentions, to (c) the extent to which belief changes induced by a therapist will prove resistant to countervailing forces. Despite our optimistic view regarding the potential applicability of the model, our focus here is on the initial basic research designed to test and validate the framework. We hope that the body of this book will be of some general interest to all scholars and students of the psychology of persuasion. As such, the material should be appropriate for segments of courses on attitude change and may provide useful supplementary material for graduate courses on topics for which the psychology of influence is a central focus (such as influence processes in counseling, psychology of advertising and consumer behavior, etc.).

Although the major purpose of this monograph is to present the ELM and our own program of research on persuasion which examines various features of the model, we also present the work of others when it provides evidence that is directly relevant to our conceptualization of persuasion. It is important to note that there are many studies that can be viewed as consistent (or inconsistent) with the ELM that we have chosen *not* to cover here. One difficulty in analyzing previous work is that most persuasion studies have not paid much attention to the content of the persuasive messages employed in the research or to background variables (such as prior knowledge) that might determine the extent and/or direction of message elaboration. This poses a great difficulty for reinterpretation because, as we explain in the text, the ELM may make *opposite* predictions for the effect of some variable on persuasion depending upon whether the message employed in the experiment was generally strong and likely to elicit favorable cognitions, or generally weak and likely to elicit unfavorable thoughts. Furthermore, the ELM may make different predictions for one variable depending upon the level of another factor that was not manipulated in the study (e.g., is the message topic one of high, low, or uncertain personal relevance). Because of these complexities, we have focused our attention on those studies conducted by others that have the necessary features (e.g., a manipulation of argument quality, a manipulation of personal relevance) that permit relatively unambiguous interpretation. One desirable feature of the ELM, we think, is that it may encourage future persuasion researchers to consider message quality and important background variables (such as personal relevance) in order to more definitively pin down the processes mediating the impact of the variables under study.

Acknowledgments

It is difficult to write a book like this without the support and assistance of many people. First and foremost, we owe a continuing debt to our wives, Lynn and Barbara, who have put up with us and our work habits for many years. We love them dearly and would be lost without them. Our families are also a source of persistent encouragement, and we are very grateful for this.

We have been fortunate over the years to have worked with many talented social psychologists including Tim Brock, Robert Cialdini, Tony Greenwald, John Harvey, Steve Harkins, Bibb Latané, Tom Ostrom, Kip Williams, and Gary Wells. Our contact with them has enhanced the quality of this volume (though they should not be blamed for any flaws found!). It is important to note that many of the studies reported in this book would not have been conducted were it not for the efforts of a group of dedicated and ambitious graduate students and postdoctoral and Fulbright fellows. These people—Cheri Christensen, Rachel Goldman, Curt Haugtvedt, Martin Heesacker, Chuan Feng Kao, Jeff Kasmer, Hai Sook Kim, Mary Losch, Beverly Marshall-Goodell, Kathy Morris, Rik Pieters, Jim Puckett, Leo Quintanar, Greg Rennier, David Schumann, Joe Sidera, Cal Stoltenberg, and Lou Tassinary—were and are a pleasure to work with and make academic life fulfilling. We are also indebted to the thousands of undergraduates who provided the data for the studies that we report here and the many students with whom we have worked as experimenters and research assistants. Their talents were very valuable, and we are pleased that many have gone on to distinguished careers ranging from law (Charlotte Lowell) to acting (Kate Capshaw). Some have even decided to become social psychologists (Tom Geen, Alan Strathman)!

Finally, we owe a debt of gratitude to those colleagues who commented on various portions of the manuscript (Icek Ajzen, Bob Cialdini, Marty Heesacker, Chet Insko, Wolfgang Stroebe, and Abe Tesser), to the National Science Foundation for providing support for our research program over the past decade, and to the professionals at Springer-Verlag who were a joy to work with over the long course of preparing this volume.

Columbia, Missouri   Richard E. Petty
Iowa City, Iowa   John T. Cacioppo

Contents

Chapter 1

The Elaboration Likelihood Model of Persuasion

Introduction

On New Year's Day, 1986, U.S. President Ronald Reagan and U.S.S.R. Premier Mikhail Gorbachev appeared on television in each other's countries. It was the first time that American and Russian leaders had exchanged messages that were simultaneously televised. Reagan's message, broadcast without warning during the popular Soviet evening news, spoke of world peace and called for the development of new defensive weapons. Gorbachev's message, which appeared while many Americans were watching coverage of the traditional Tournament of Roses parade, also spoke of peace but decried seeking security with new weaponry. How effective were these messages likely to be? What would be the major determinant of effectiveness—the substance of the messages, or the appearance and demeanor of the speakers? If the messages produced attitude changes, would these changes last and would they lead to changes in behavior?

Social psychologists have been concerned with questions such as these ever since the discipline began (Allport, 1935; Ross, 1908; see McGuire, 1985). The study of influence has also long been at the heart of many applied psychological fields such as consumer behavior (Bettman, 1986; Kassarjian, 1982; Poffenberger, 1925; Strong, 1925) and clinical and counseling psychology (cf., Frank, 1963; Heppner & Dixon, 1981; Strong, 1968). Nevertheless, after a considerable flourishing of research and theory from the 1920s through the 1960s, interest in the psychology of persuasion began to wane. Two factors were largely responsible for this. First, the utility of the attitude construct itself was questioned as researchers wondered whether atttitudes were capable of predicting behavior. Some reasoned that if attitudes did not influence behavior, then it might be time to abandon the attitude concept (Abelson, 1972; Wicker, 1971). Second, so much conflicting research and theory had developed that it had become clear that "after several decades of research, there (were) few simple and direct empirical generalizations that (could) be made concerning how to change attitudes" (Himmelfarb & Eagly, 1974, p. 594).

Reviewers of the attitudes literature during the early 1970s lamented this sorry state of affairs. For example, in their 1972 *Annual Review of Psychology* chapter on attitudes, Fishbein and Ajzen wrote: "the attitude area is characterized by a great deal of conceptual ambiguities and methodological deficiencies . . . It is painfully obvious that what is required at this point in time . . . is . . . a rather serious reconsideration of basic assumptions and thoughtful theoretical reanalyses of problems confronting the field" (p. 531–532). Kiesler and Munson concluded their 1975 *Annual Review* chapter by noting that "attitude change is not the thriving field it once was and will be again" (p. 443).

By the late 1970s, considerable progress had been made in addressing important methodological and theoretical issues regarding the first substantive problem plaguing the field—the consistency between attitudes and behaviors. Conditions under which attitudes would and would not predict behavior were specified (e.g., Ajzen & Fishbein, 1977, 1980; Fazio & Zanna, 1981), and researchers began to explore the processes underlying attitude-behavior correspondence (Sherman & Fazio, 1983; Fazio, 1985). The attitude change problem was slower to be addressed, however. In 1977, Muzifer Sherif posed the question: "What is the yield in the way of established principles in regard to attitude change?" His answer was that there was a "reigning confusion in the area" and a "scanty yield in spite of (a) tremendously thriving output" (p. 370). In a 1978 review that generally heralded the arrival of a new optimism in the attitudes field, Eagly and Himmelfarb noted that "ambiguities and unknowns still abound" (p. 544; for even more optimistic reviews see Cialdini, Petty, & Cacioppo, 1981; Cooper & Croyle, 1984; Eagly, in press).

As we noted above, the major problem facing persuasion researchers was that after accumulating a vast quantity of data and an impressive number of theories, perhaps more data and theory than on any other single topic in the soical sciences (see McGuire, 1985), there was surprisingly little agreement concerning if, when, and how the traditional source, message, recipient, and channel variables (cf., Hovland, Janis, & Kelley, 1953; McGuire, 1969; Smith, Lasswell, & Casey, 1946) affected attitude change. Existing literature supported the view that nearly every independent variable studied increased persuasion in some situations, had no effect in others, and decreased persuasion in still other contexts. This diversity of results was even apparent for variables that on the surface, at least, appeared to be quite simple. For example, although it might seem reasonable to propose that by associating a message with an expert source, agreement could be increased (e.g., see Aristotle's *Rhetoric*), the accumulated contemporary research literature suggested that expertise effects were considerably more complicated than this (Eagly & Himmelfarb, 1974; Hass, 1981). Sometimes expert sources had the expected effects (e.g., Kelman & Hovland, 1953), sometimes no effects were obtained (e.g., Rhine & Severance, 1970), and sometimes reverse effects were noted (e.g., Sternthal, Dholakia, & Leavitt, 1978). Unfortunately, the conditions under which each of these effects could be obtained and the processes involved in producing these effects were not at all apparent.

Our primary goal in this monograph is to outline and provide evidence for a general theory of attitude change, called the Elaboration Likelihood Model (ELM; Petty & Cacioppo, 1981a), which we believe provides a fairly comprehensive framework for organizing, categorizing, and understanding the basic processes underlying the effectiveness of persuasive com-munications. Importantly, the ELM attempts to integrate the many seemingly conflicting research findings and theoretical orientations under one conceptual umbrella. The ELM began in our attempts to account for the differential persistence of communication-induced attitude change. After reviewing the literature on attitude persistence, we concluded that the many different empirical findings and theories in the field might profitably be viewed as emphasizing one of just two relatively distinct "routes to persuasion" (Petty, 1977; Petty & Cacioppo, 1978). The first type of persuasion was that which likely occurred as a result of a person's careful and thoughtful consideration of the true merits of the information presented in support of an advocacy (central route). The other type of persuasion, however, was that which more likely occurred as a result of some simple cue in the persuasion context (e.g., an attractive source) that induced change without necessitating scrutiny of the central merits of the issue-relevant information presented (peripheral route). In the accumulated literature, the first kind of persuasion appeared to be more enduring than the latter (see Petty, 1977, and Cook & Flay, 1978, for reviews; see Chapter 7 for a comparison of the ELM with previous models of attitude persistence).

Following our initial speculation about the two routes to persuasion and the implications for attitudinal persistence, we have developed, researched, and refined a more general theory of persuasion, the ELM, which is based on these two routes. The two routes to persuasion and the ELM were first presented schematically as depicted in Figure 1-1 (Petty, 1977; Petty & Cacioppo, 1978, 1981a), but we have subsequently formalized the ELM in seven postulates that make the major principles of the model more explicit (Petty & Cacioppo, 1986; see Table 1-1). We will present these postulates shortly. In addition, we have addressed the various applications of the model to such fields as psychotherapy and counseling (Cacioppo, Petty, & Stoltenberg, 1985; Petty, Cacioppo, & Heesacker, 1984) and mass media advertising and selling (Cacioppo & Petty, 1985; Petty & Cacioppo, 1983a, 1984b; Petty, Cacioppo, & Schumann, 1984).

The ELM deals explicitly with exposure to persuasive communications, but as we note elsewhere in this volume, the basic principles of the ELM may be applied to other attitude change situations. In the remainder of this chapter we will outline the seven postulates of the ELM. In the next chapter we will provide a methodology for testing the underlying processes outlined

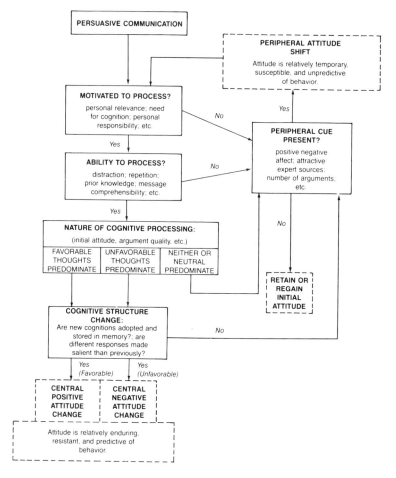

Figure 1-1. Schematic depiction of the two routes to persuasion. This diagram depicts the possible endpoints after exposure to a persuasive communication according to the Elaboration Likelihood Model (i.e., central attitude change, peripheral shift, no change) (adapted from Petty, 1977; Petty & Cacioppo, 1981a, 1986).

by the ELM, and in the remaining chapters in this book we will review our program of research and other relevant studies that address the validity of the major principles of the ELM.

Before presenting the ELM postulates, however, it is important to define our use of the term *attitude* and the terms *influence* and *persuasion*. Consistent with the positions of other attitude theorists (e.g., Thurstone, 1928), we regard attitudes as general evaluations people hold in regard to themselves, other people, objects, and issues. We will use *influence* as a very general term that refers to any change in these evaluations. We will use

Table 1-1. Postulates of the Elaboration Likelihood Model of Persuasion

1. People are motivated to hold correct attitudes.

2. Although people want to hold correct attitudes, the amount and nature of issue-relevant elaboration in which they are willing or able to engage to evaluate a message vary with individual and situational factors.

3. Variables can affect the amount and direction of attitude change by (a) serving as persuasive arguments, (b) serving as peripheral cues, and/or (c) affecting the extent or direction of issue and argument elaboration.

4. Variables affecting motivation and/or ability to process a message in a relatively objective manner can do so by either enhancing or reducing argument scrutiny.

5. Variables affecting message processing in a relatively biased manner can produce either a positive (favorable) or negative (unfavorable) motivational and/or ability bias to the issue-relevant thoughts attempted.

6. As motivation and/or ability to process arguments is decreased, peripheral cues become relatively more important determinants of persuasion. Conversely, as argument scrutiny is increased, peripheral cues become relatively less important determinants of persuasion.

7. Attitude changes that result mostly from processing issue-relevant arguments (central route) will show greater temporal persistence, greater prediction of behavior, and greater resistance to counterpersuasion than attitude changes that result mostly from peripheral cues.

persuasion more specifically to refer to any change in attitudes that results from exposure to a communication. A person's general evaluations or attitudes can be based on a variety of behavioral, affective, and cognitive experiences and are capable of guiding behavioral, affective, and cognitive processes. Thus, a person may come to like a new political candidate because she just donated $100 dollars to the campaign (behavior-initiated change), because the theme music in a recently heard commercial induced a general pleasantness (affect-initiated change), or because the person was impressed with the candidate's issue positions (cognitive-initiated change). Similarly, if a person already likes a political candidate he may agree to donate money to the campaign (behavioral influence), may feel happiness upon meeting the candidate (affective influence), and may selectively encode the candidate's issue positions (cognitive influence).

Postulates of the ELM

Postulate on Underlying Motivation

Our first postulate and an important guiding principle in the ELM agrees with Festinger's (1950) statement that:

People are motivated to hold correct attitudes.

Incorrect or improper attitudes are generally maladaptive and can have deleterious behavioral, affective, and cognitive consequences. As Festinger (1954) noted,"the behavioral implication of ... such a drive is that we would expect to observe behavior on the part of persons which enables them to ascertain whether or not their opinions are correct" (p. 118). Of course, as Festinger noted, attitudes or evaluations cannot be correct in any *absolute* sense. Instead, perceptions of which attitudes are right and which are wrong are necessarily subjective. Attitudes must be judged against some standard. In his influential theory of social comparison processes, Festinger focused on how people evaluated the "correctness" of their opinions by comparing them to the opinions of others. When other people are perceived to hold similar attitudes, one's confidence in the validity of one's own attitude is increased (Holtz & Miller, 1985). As Hovland, Janis, and Kelley (1953) noted, a sense of "rightness" accompanies holding opinions similar to others (p. 137).

In Chapters 4 and 8 we address how the ELM accounts for attitude changes induced by exposure to the opinions of varying numbers of other people. For now, it is important to note that the ELM does not exclusively link a person's subjective assessment of the correctness of an attitude to the number of others who hold this opinion (although as we note later, this may be used in some situations). Instead, there are a variety of standards people might use to determine which attitudes are correct for them. Furthermore, the standards used to judge what is right and what is wrong may differ among people (cf., Kohlberg, 1963), and different standards may be applied in different situations. Ultimately, we suspect that attitudes are seen as correct or proper to the extent that they are viewed as beneficial for the physical or psychological well-being of the person. Before discussing some of the different standards that might be applied, however, we need to outline our next postulate.

Postulate on Variations in Elaboration

Our second postulate states:

> **Although people want to hold correct attitudes, the amount and nature of issue-relevant elaboration in which they are willing or able to engage to evaluate a message vary with individual and situational factors.**

Postulate 2 recognizes that even though people want to hold correct attitudes, the amount of effort they are willing or able to engage in to hold these attitudes varies widely. Consider a person who is exposed to a message from the Secretary of the Treasury advocating a tax increase/reform package. At one extreme, a person may go to the library to do research, consult tax attorneys, rework his taxes under the new system, and list and consider all of the personal and national pros and cons in an attempt to determine the desirability of the tax proposal. At the other extreme, a person may favor the proposal based largely on the credibility of the proposer or may reject the proposal based simply on its position (i.e., any tax increase is deemed unacceptable). It may even be possible for a person's attitude to be changed without his awareness if motivation and ability to process are very low and a strong positive or negative affective event becomes associated with the advocacy. The first person in our example has expended considerable cognitive (and physical) effort to evaluate the message, whereas the latter people have expended little effort.

Miller and his colleagues (1975) noted that: "It may be irrational to scrutinize the plethora of counterattitudinal messages received daily. To the extent that one possesses only a limited amount of information processing time and capacity, such scrutiny would disengage the thought processes from the exigencies of daily life" (p. 623). People must therefore choose which messages to scrutinize and which to process as "lazy organisms" (McGuire, 1969) or "cognitive misers" (Taylor, 1981). We assume that the more important it is to hold a correct attitude, the more effort people will be willing to expend in order to evaluate an advocacy. Importantly, even if a person is highly motivated to scrutinize a message, if ability is lacking the person may be forced to rely on simple cues such as source credibility in order to evaluate the message.

The Elaboration Continuum
Implicit in Postulate 2 is the notion that one of the best ways for people to form veridical attitudes is to carefully *elaborate* the information that is perceived relevant to the central merits of the advocacy. By elaboration, we mean the extent to which a person carefully thinks about issue-relevant information. In a persuasion context, elaboration refers to the extent to which a person scrutinizes the issue-relevant arguments contained in the persuasive communication. When conditions foster people's motivation and ability to engage in issue-relevant thinking, the "elaboration likelihood" is said to be high. This means that people are likely to attend to the appeal; attempt to access relevant information from both external and internal sources; scrutinize and make inferences about the message arguments in light of any other pertinent information available; draw conclusions about the merits of the arguments for the recommendation based upon their analyses; and consequently derive an overall evaluation of, or attitude toward, the recommendation. This conceptualization suggests that when the elaboration likelihood is high, there should be evidence for the allocation of considerable cognitive resources to the advocacy. Issue-relevant elaboration will typically result in the new arguments, or one's personal translations of them, being integrated into the underlying belief structure (schema) for the attitude object (Cacioppo & Petty, 1984a). As we will note shortly, sometimes this issue-relevant elaboration proceeds in a relatively objective manner and is governed mostly by the issue-relevant arguments presented, but at other

times this elaboration is more biased and may be guided more by the person's initial attitude.

We view the extent of elaboration recieved by a message as a continuum going from no thought about the issue-relevant information presented, to complete elaboration of every argument, and complete integration of these elaborations into the person's attitude schema. The likelihood of elaboration will be determined by a person's motivation and ability to evaluate the communication presented (see Figure 1-1). In the ELM, motivational variables are those that affect a person's rather conscious intentions and goals in processing a message. Features of the persuasive message itself (e.g., is the topic of high or low personal relevance?), the persuasion context (e.g., is a forewarning of persuasive intent provided?), and the message recipient (e.g., is the person high or low in "need for cognition"?) can all affect the intensity with which a person chooses to process a message and the direction of that processing (see further discussion of motivational variables in Chapters 4 and 5). Ability variables in the ELM are those that affect the extent or direction of message scrutiny without the necessary intervention of conscious intent. Features of the message itself (e.g., is it understandable?), the persuasion context (e.g., is external distraction present?), and the message recipient (e.g., how much topic-relevant knowledge does the person have?) can all determine whether or not the person is capable of elaborating upon the message (see further discussion of ability variables in Chapter 3). Our conceptualization of motivation and ability therefore has parallels to Heider's (1958) concept of "trying" (motivation) and "can" (ability; see Chapter 9 for further discussion).

In an earlier review of the attitude change literature (Petty & Cacioppo, 1981a), we suggested that the many theories of attitude change could be roughly placed along an elaboration likelihood continuum (cf., Palmerino, Langer, & McGillis, 1984). At the high end of this continuum are theoretical orientations such as inoculation theory (McGuire, 1964), cognitive response theory (Greenwald, 1968; Petty, Ostrom & Brock, 1981a), information integration theory (Anderson, 1981), and the theory of reasoned action (Ajzen & Fishbein, 1980; Fishbein, 1980), which make the assumption that people typically attempt to evaluate carefully (though not always successfully) the information presented in a message and integrate this information into a coherent position. Researchers within this tradition have emphasized the need to examine what kinds of arguments are persuasive and how variables affect the comprehension, elaboration, learning, integration, and retention of issue-relevant information (McGuire, 1985).

Other persuasion theories do not place much credence on the arguments in a message or issue-relevant thinking. Instead, they focus on how simple affective processes influence attitudes without much conscious thought or on how people can employ various rules, inferences, or heuristics to judge their own attitudes or the acceptability of an attitudinal position. Although in most laboratory studies of attitude change, subjects will have some motivation and/or ability to form at least a reasonable opinion either by scrutinizing arguments or making an inference about the acceptability of the message based on cues in the context, there are circumstances in which neither arguments nor acceptance cues are present. For example, when nonsense syllables are employed (Staats & Staats, 1957) or polygons are presented subliminally (Kunst-Wilson & Zajonc, 1980), no elaboration of arguments is possible because none are presented, and validity cues may be irrelevant because there is no explicit "advocacy" to judge. Theories such as classical conditioning (Staats & Staats, 1957) and mere exposure (Zajonc, 1968; 1980), which describe evaluations of objects changing as a result of rather primitive affective and associational processes, are especially relevant under these circumstances. Although these theories have been tested and applied primarily in situations where no explicit "advocacy" is presented, they should also be applicable to situations in which an issue position is advocated, but people have virtually no ability and/or motivation to consider it. In these situations, attitudes may still be changed if the attitude object is associated with a relatively strong positive or negative affective cue, or if a weaker cue is continually paired with the attitude object.

Whether or not strong affective cues are presented, it is also possible for people to form a "reasonable" attitude without relying on scrutiny of the issue-relevant arguments presented by relying on various persuasion rules or inferences that may be either rather simple or relatively complex. For example, according to self-perception theory (Bem, 1972), people may come to like or dislike an object as a result of a simple inference based on their own behavior (e.g., if I bought it, I must like it). According to the heuristic model of persuasion (Chaiken, 1980; Eagly & Chaiken, 1984), people may evaluate messages by employing various rules that they have learned on the basis of past experience (e.g., people agree with people they like). In social judgment theory (Sherif & Sherif, 1967), it is proposed that people evaluate messages mostly on the basis of their perceived position—messages are contrasted and rejected if they appear too discrepant (fall in the latitude of rejection), but are assimilated and accepted if they appear closer to one's initial position (fall in the latitude of acceptance; Pallak, Mueller, Dollar, & Pallak, 1972). In addition to the relatively simple acceptance/rejection rules proposed by the preceding models, more complex reasoning processes such as those invoked by balance (Heider, 1946; Insko, 1984) and attribution (Kelley, 1967; Eagly, Wood, & Chaiken, 1978) theories may also be used to evaluate messages without requiring scrutiny of the issue-relevant arguments presented.[1] For example, a recipient may attribute credibility to a speaker and accept the message because the source appears to be arguing against his own best interests (e.g., Eagly, Chaiken, & Wood, 1978).

---

[1]See Insko (1981) for an extension of balance theory to include arguments processing.

Importantly, even though this attributional acceptance may require cognitive activity, the "peripheral route" to persuasion has still been followed because the cognitive activity is not spent personally evaluating the actual merits of the issue-relevant arguments presented by the speaker.

In sum, we have proposed that when either motivation or ability to process issue-relevant arguments is low, attitudes may be changed by associating an issue position with various affective cues, or people may attempt to form a reasonable opinion by making inferences about the likely correctness or desirability of a particular attitude position based on cues such as message discrepancy, one's own behavior, and the characteristics of the message source.

Developmental Trends in Elaboration
Interestingly, the attitude change processes that we have just described form an elaboration continuum that may coincide with the manner in which attitude change processes (and the subjective determination of right and wrong) develop through adulthood. Specifically, the very young child probably has little motivation to think about the true merits of people, objects, and issues, and even less ability to do so. Thus, attitudes may be affected primarily by what feels good or bad. As children mature, they become more motivated to express correct opinions on certain issues, but their ability to scrutinize issue-relevant arguments is still poor. Therefore, they may be particularly reliant on what others say and do and certain cognitive rules developed from experience such as, "My mother knows what's right," or "If I play with it, I must like it." Consistent with this reasoning, children have been shown to be more susceptible to appeals based on behavioral cues and self-perceptions than issue-relevant argumentation (e.g., Miller, Brickman, & Bolen, 1975).

Finally, as people move into adulthood, interests become more focused and the consequences of holding correct opinions on certain issues increase. In addition, as people's acquired knowledge and cognitive skills grow, this renders them more able to critically analyze issue-relevant information on certain topics and makes them less reliant than children on certain primitive heuristics (cf., Ross, 1981). As we noted earlier, of course, although people may have the requisite ability and motivation to scrutinize certain attitude issues, they will lack motivation and ability on others. Thus, simple inferences and affective cues may still produce attitude change in adults.

In sum, one's initial evaluations are likely to be largely hedonistic and because one lacks the motivation and/or ability to consider issue-relevant arguments, attitudes will be based primarily on positive and negative affective cues associated with the attitude object. As development proceeds, some attitudes may be formed on the basis of social attachments, simple inferences, and decision rules. Finally, the formation and change of some attitudes becomes a very thoughtful process in which issue-relevant information is scruninzed carefully and evaluated in terms of existing knowledge and values. Importantly, our sequence of the developmental stages of influence is consistent with other developmental models of judgment. For example, in discussing the development of moral standards of correctness, Kohlberg (1963) identifies three developmental levels. At the first level (preconventional), moral evaluations are based primarily on the affective consequences of an act. At level 2 (conventional), evaluations of acts are based primarily on socially accepted rules and laws. Finally, at level 3 (postconventional), an evaluation of an act is based on a person's idiosyncratic but well-articulated moral code. The parallels to our stages of influence are obvious.

Although we have argued that there is a continuum of message elaboration ranging from none to complete, and that different attitude change processes may operate along the continuum, it is also important to note that these different theoretical processes can be viewed in their extreme cases as specifying just two qualitatively distinct routes to persuasion. The first route, which we have called the "central route," occurs when motivation and ability to scrutinize issue-relevant arguments are relatively high. The second, or "peripheral route," occurs when motivation and/or ability are relatively low and attitudes are determined mostly by positive or negative cues in the persuasion context that either become directly associated with the message position or permit a simple inference as to the validity of the message. In short, even though one can view message elaboration as a continuum, we can distinguish persuasion that is primarily a result of issue-relevant thinking from persuasion that is primarily a result of some cue in the persuasion context that permits attitude change without argument scrutiny. In fact, we will find it useful elsewhere in this volume to talk about the elaboration likelihood continuum by referring to the prototypical processes operative at each extreme.

Additional Distinctions about the Extent of Thinking

The ELM is not unique, of course, in its view that the type or amount of cognitive effort expended by people varies from situation to situation. In fact, current research in cognitive and social psychology strongly supports the view that at times people engage in "controlled," "deep," effortful," and/or "mindful" analyses of stimuli, and at other times the analyses are better characterized as "automatic," "shallow," "heuristic," and/or "mindless" (see Craik, 1979; Eagly & Chaiken, 1984; Kahneman, Slovic, & Tversky, 1982; Langer, 1978; and Schneider & Shiffrin, 1977). Before proceeding with our other postulates, it would be instructive to briefly compare the ELM with its elaboration continuum and central and peripheral routes to persuasion with some of the more prominent processing distinctions from cognitive psychology.

Automatic versus controlled processing. Automatic and controlled processes have been proposed to distinguish between types of processing that are under the control of the person and those that are not (Laberge & Samuels, 1974; Schneider & Shiffrin, 1977; Shiffrin & Schneider, 1977). Automatic processes are characterized by effortlessness and by the absence of capacity limitations. Posner and Snyder (1975, p.55), for instance, proposed that an automatic process occurs without intention, without giving rise to conscious awareness, and without interfering with ongoing mental activity. Bargh (1984) has argued that automatic processes are those under the immediate control of the environment, requiring no conscious intervention of any kind. Controlled processing, in contrast, requires attention, gives rise to awareness, is flexible and easily adapted to the particular features of a given situation, is severely limited by the available processing capacity, and interferes with other processing.

Langer's (1975, 1978, 1982; Langer, Blank, & Chanowitz, 1978) notions of "mindlessness" and "mindfulness" embody a distinction analogous to automatic and controlled processes. Langer has argued that people progress through their social environment relying much more on habit and less on problem-solving activities than has been assumed:

> We typically have assumed that virtually all behavior other than over-learned motor acts are performed with conscious awareness. Perhaps a more efficacious strategy is one that assumes that by the time a person reaches adulthood, (s)he has achieved a state of "ignorance" whereby virtually all behavior may be performed *without awareness . . . unless forced to engage in conscious thought.* (Langer, Blank, Chanowitz, 1978, p. 48, italics added)

Recently, Langer, Chanowitz, and Blank (1985) have clarified their earlier position and distinguish between "mindful" and "mindless" cognitive activity:

> When mindful, the individual was presumed to be actively drawing distinctions, making meaning, or creating categories. When mindless, the individual was said to rely on distinctions already drawn . . . Further, mindless activity does not imply the absence of all cognitive activity—just the absence of flexible cognitive processing. Under such circumstances, individuals are neither reasoning well nor reasoning badly about the significance of the environment. *They are not reasoning at all.* (p. 605, italics added)

That is, the distinction between mindfulness and mindlessness appears to be analogous to the distinction between automatic and controlled processing.

Although traveling the central route clearly involves controlled processing, the central/peripheral distinction is not synonymous with the automatic/controlled distinction. When the elaboration likelihood is high, there should be evidence for the allocation of cognitive resources *to the issue under consideration.* Hence, central processing is a particular kind of controlled process—one directed at evaluating the merits of the arguments for a recommendation. Although automatic inputs are possible, as when one's prior knowledge influences how one interprets message-relevant information (see Chapter 5), the deliberations themselves require attention, give rise to awareness, are flexible and easily adapted to the particular features of a given situation, are severely limited by the available processing capacity, and can interfere with other processing.

As factors in the persuasion setting reduce the recipients' motivation or ability to think about an issue, there is a reduction in the likelihood that the recipients will try to evaluate the merits of the recommendation by relating the incoming information to their prior knowledge about and experiences with the attitude object. The concept is that when the "elaboration likelihood" is low, individuals will not utilize much in the way of cognitive resources, or they will expend much of their cognitive resources on another task. As we noted earlier, in peripheral processing individuals are more likely to adopt a strategy in which they attempt to derive a "reasonable" attitude based on existing schemata and superficial analyses of the veracity of the recommendation. That is, when the elaboration likelihood is low, the acceptance or rejection of the appeal is not based on the careful consideration of issue-relevant information and consequent restructuring of schemata, but rather it is based on the issue or object being associated with positive or negative cues (an association of which the individuals may or may not be aware), or with the individual's drawing a simple inference based on various cues in the persuasion context. Hence, although a peripheral route to attitude change could conceivably rely on an automatic process (e.g., frequency/liking; see Zajonc, 1980), they are not synonymous.

An analogy may help to clarify the distinction we wish to draw between the processes involved when traveling the central versus peripheral route to persuasion. Consider first the case of a student who has studied diligently for an exam. The student knows the material over which he is being tested, reads each test question and set of answers, relates this incoming information to what he remembers about the material, attempts to integrate these various data, and selects the option that is judged to be the most veridical. This manner of processing the material corresponds to the message processing that we have suggested is invoked when the elaboration likelihood is high in a persuasion context. There is no guarantee that the student's responses will be correct or that his attempts to relate the material from the test question to the prior knowledge he has about the topic will necessarily be logical or rational. However, the student's responses are more likely to be reliable (enduring) and correct than if his answers were based on a simpler, more peripheral analysis of the question. Note, too, that the student's comprehension of the question and memory of material relevant to the topic are important but distal mediators of his response to the question; these factors affect how the student interprets, elaborates upon, and evaluates the incoming information,but it is the nature of the topic-relevant thinking that is viewed here as being the proximal determinant of the student's response to the question.

The responses of this student, who went through the diligent and effortful process of evaluating the merits of the various options, can be *contrasted* to the reactions of a student who, because he either does not care (i.e., low motivation) or does not know the material (i.e., low ability), reads each question and set of answers but fails to relate the incoming information to memorial information that is related specifically to the topic in question. The responses of this student are not necessarily random or irrational, but rather they can reflect the operation of simple and sometimes specious decisional rules evoked by peripheral cues, such as the position of the answer within the set of answers (e.g., "a" is seldom the correct answer) or previous responses (e.g., "c" was marked twice previously, so I'll try "b"). Note that the incoming information may still be deliberately related to prior knowledge (i.e., may still invoke controlled processes), but this body of knowledge applies to test-taking in general and not specifically to the merits of the person's various options for a particular question. Thus, as the student's "elaboration likelihood" decreases, obvious features in the testing (or persuasion) setting that signal which option is likely to be acceptable or correct are more likely to be used to cue him regarding the option to adopt— even though all of the externally provided information may well be comprehended and recalled.

Cognitive effort. Another prominent processing distinction in cognitive psychology is between "effortful" and "effortless" information processing. Briefly, cognitive effort refers to the amount of cognitive capacity expended on a task (Tyler, Hertel, McCallum, & Ellis, 1979). This distinction, too, shares the assumption that people are neither invariantly cogitative nor universally mindless when dealing with their world. Moreover, we believe that in most natural circumstances people will expend more cognitive effort when evaluating the merits of the arguments for a recommendation (central route) rather than forming their attitudes based on prior conditioning or by using some simple decisional rule (peripheral route). However, elaboration rather than cognitive effort is the crucial dimension here. Recall that by elaboration we mean the process of relating the to-be-elaluated recommendation and arguments to other issue-relevant information in memory. Elaboration, therefore, typically results in the self-generation of information unique to the externally provided communication.[2] Cognitive

---

[2]The term "elaboration" also appears in the experimental psychological literature in discussions of encoding activities. For instance, Craik and Watkins (1973) discriminated between "maintenance rehearsal" and "elaborative operations." Maintenance rehearsal is simply repetitive rehearsal, as one might do when trying to remember a telephone number until it is dialed. The elaborative process, on the other hand, is described as a "meaningful connections strategy" wherein subjects form associations, sentences, and images when encoding a stimulus. In an illustrative study, Craik and Tulving (1975) manipulated "elaboration" by varying the amount of information expressed in stimulus sentences. For example, subjects might

effort will tend to covary with message elaboration, therefore, because one feature of message elaboration is the use of cognitive resources in evaluating the merits of a recommendation. However, message elaboration is not the only cause of cognitive effort in persuasion contexts, and hence these constructs cannot be equated. For instance, consider a hypothetical study in which half of the subjects received a personally involving counterattitudinal text in which interfering labels have been embedded, whereas half of the subjects received the same communication without interfering labels embedded. Although message processing in the former condition should require more cognitive effort (cf., Zacks, Hasher, Sanft, & Rose, 1983), the embedded labels might also interfere with subjects' attempts to evaluate the implication and merits of the message arguments and, hence, *lower* elaboration likelihood (Petty, Cacioppo, & Heesacker, 1981; Petty, Wells, & Brock, 1976).

Levels of processing. The "levels" of processing" framework was proposed by Craik and Lockhart (1972) who argued that what is remembered about a particular event will be what was attended to when the event was experienced, and semantic or meaningful features support better retention than do nonsemantic features. The distinction between the central and peripheral routes to persuasion, on the other hand, is based more on the direction than the depth of cognitive activity. Central processing pre-supposes that the persuasive communication is being processed semantically, whereas peripheral processing can be based on semantic or nonsemantic processing. Under conditions of high elaboration likelihood, however, the person's cognitive activity is directed at relating the information in a persuasive appeal to what is already known about the topic

---

be asked to state whether the noun "watch" fits into a relatively unelaborated sentence frame such as "He dropped the _____," or a more elaborated sentence frame such as "The old man hobbled across the room and picked up the valuable _____ from the mahogany table." After acquisition, participants were supplied with the sentence frames originally heard during acquisition and were tested for cued recall of the target nouns. Results revealed an increase in cued-recall as the elaborateness of the sentence frames increased—but only when the sentence frames were congruous with the target nouns. Elaboration is important in these cognitive models because of the links between elaborative encoding operations and subsequent recall of the initial stimulus. Although cognitive psychologists use elaboration to refer to any information added to the original stimulus, whether provided by the experimenter or generated by the subject, we mean more specifically information added by the subject in the process of vigilantly scrutinizing the arguments and information in memory bearing specifically on the desirability of a persuasive recommendation. Moreover, the link of interest in the ELM is not between an externally provided stimulus and recall as in cognitive psychology, but between the self-generated issue-relevant thoughts (i.e., elaborations) and attitudes.

in order to evalute the merits of a recommendation and thereby identify the most veridical position on an issue. Under conditions of low elaboration likelihood, on the other hand, the person may be engaged in a great deal or in very little cognitive activity; the person may be cognizant of searching for and selecting a simple affective cue or decisional rule with which to respond to the appeal (as illustrated in the example above of the student taking a test for which he was unprepared) or she may not. The critical feature is that a person's prior knowledge dealing specifically with the topic under consideration and the inferences one might draw from the externally provided message arguments are less likely to be considered in reponse to the persuasive appeal when the elaboration likelihood is low.

Postulate on How Variables Affect Persuasion

Now that we have reviewed our major guiding assumptions and compared the ELM processing continuum with others, we are ready to list the unique postulates that are directly relevant to persuasion. Our next postulate lists the three major ways in which variables can have an impact on attitude change.

Variables can affect the amount and direction of attitude change by (a) serving as persuasive arguments, (b) serving as peripheral cues and/or (c) affecting the extent or direction of issue and argument elaboration.

In subsequent chapters of this volume we discuss how many of the typical source, message, recipient, channel, and context variables manipulated in the accumulated persuasion literature can be understood in terms of the three-part categorization above. In the next chapter we provide further discussion of these constructs and provide a methodology for assessing them. In this section we will provide a brief conceptual overview of the constructs so that we can move on to the remaining postulates.

Argument Quality

In the ELM, arguments are viewed as bits of information contained in a communication that are relevant to a person's subjective determination of the true merits of an advocated position. Because people hold attitudes for many different reasons (Katz, 1960; Smith, Bruner, & White, 1956), people will invariably differ in the kinds of information they feel are central to the merits of any position. In discussing the application of the ELM to consumer behavior, we provided the following example:

Consider an advertisement for cigarettes that depicts a man and a woman on horseback riding through majestic mountain terrain. At the bottom of the ad is the headline, "20 REASONS WHY CALBOROS ARE BEST," along with a list of twenty statements. Will attitude changes induced because of this ad occur via the central or the peripheral route? Our framework suggests that in evaluating or designing an ad for a particular product, it is extremely important to know what information dimensions are important for people who desire to evaluate the true merits or implications of the product (in this case, cigarettes). On the one hand, to smokers over fifty, the most important information may relate to the health aspects of the brand (for example, tar content). For this group, an effective ad would likely have to present considerable information about the medical consequences of the brand if it were to be effective in inducing influence via the central route. If the twenty statements listed in the ad presented cogent information about the health aspects of Calboros over competing brands, favorable thoughts may be rehearsed, and a relatively permanent change in attitudes that had behavioral implications might result. On the other hand, for teenage smokers, who may be more concerned with impressing their peers than with their health, the major reason why they smoke may relate to the image of the particular brand (for example, "tough man," "independent woman"; see Chassin et al., 1981). For this group, the presentation of the rugged outdoor images might provide important product-relevant information that would elicit numerous favorable thoughts and enduring attitude changes with behavioral consequences. It is interesting to note that for nonsmokers over fifty (an uninvolved group), the majestic scenery might serve as a peripheral cue inducing momentary liking for the brand and that for teenage nonsmokers, the twenty statements might lead to momentary positive evaluations of the brand because of the simple belief that there are many arguments in favor of it. (Petty & Cacioppo, 1983a, pp. 21–22)

This example makes it clear that the kind of information that is relevant to evaluating the central merits of a product or issue may vary from situation to situation and from person to person. A compelling demonstration of this is provided by a recent series of studies by Snyder and DeBono (1985). These authors reasoned that people who score highly on the self-monitoring personality scale (Snyder, 1974) should be especially susceptible to advertisements employing an "image" campaign. This is because high self-monitors are very concerned with the images they convey in social situations (Snyder, 1979). Low self-monitors, on the other hand, were postulated to be less concerned with image and more concerned about the specific attributes of the product. In one test of these notions, Snyder and DeBono exposed high and low self-monitors to image or attribute ads for products. For example, one image-oriented ad depicted a man and woman smiling at each other in a candle lit room drinking coffee. The slogan read: "Make a chilly night become a cozy evening with Irish Mocha Mint." The attribute version of this ad contained the same picture but read: "Irish Mocha Mint: A delicious blend of three great flavors—coffee, chocolate, and mint." After exposure to either three image or three attribute ads, subjects were asked to indicate how much they would be willing to pay for each of the advertised products. High self-monitoring individuals were willing to pay more for the products advertised with the image campaign, but low self-monitoring individuals were willing to pay more for the products advertised with the attribute messages. Importantly, Snyder and DeBono view both high and low self-monitoring individuals as following the central route to persuasion, and we concur since both groups of subjects appear to be attempting to evalute the central merits of the product.

However, what features are believed to be central differ between high and low self-monitors. The important point is that in the ELM, the term "arguments" refers to any information contained in a message that permits a person to evaluate the message target (e.g., issue, object, person) along whatever target dimensions are central for that person.

It is important to note that in our own research presented in the remainder of this volume, we have studied attitude objects (e.g., the institution of comprehensive exams for college seniors) for which for most people, *cognitive* considerations are likely to be central to a determination of merit. For other issues, however, it is quite reasonable to suppose that *affective* or *behavioral* considerations are central to a determination of merit. The ELM recognizes that people can scrutinize or elaborate upon feelings and behaviors as well as beliefs if they are perceived central to the merits of the attitude object under consideration. In short, just as peripheral cues can be based on affective, cognitive, or behavioral factors (see Chapter 6), a person's perception of the central merits of an attitude object can be based on these domains as well. In the next chapter, we will be more specific about how we have operationalized agrument quality in our research.

Peripheral Cues
In the ELM, peripheral cues refer to stimuli in the persuasion context that can affect attitudes without necessitating processing of the message arguments. As we indicated earlier, some stimuli may influence attitudes by triggering relatively primitive affective states that become associated with the attitude object. Various reinforcing (e.g., food; Janis, Kaye, & Kirschner, 1965) and punishing (e.g., electric shock; Zanna, Kiesler, & Pilkonis, 1970) stimuli have proven effective in this regard. Other stimuli work, however, because they invoke guiding rules (e.g., balance; Heider, 1946) or inferences (e.g. self-perception, Bem, 1972). In the next chapter we will describe some methods for determining whether a stimulus is serving as a peripheral cue.

Message Elaboration
The third way in which a variable can affect persuasion is by influencing the extent or direction of message elaboration. We have already defined what we mean by "elaboration," and have noted that the extent of elaboration can range from very little to very much. In Chapter 2 we outline various procedures for gauging the extent of processing induced by a message. It is important to note, however, that in addition to the quantitative dimension of extent of processing, the ELM also makes a more qualitative distinction between elaboration that is relatively *objective* versus elaboration that is more *biased* (Petty & Cacioppo, 1981a). By relatively objective elaboration, we mean that some variable either motivates or enables people to see the strengths of cogent arguments and the flaws in specious ones, or inhibits them from doing so. By relatively biased processing, we mean that a variable either motivates or enables people to generate a particular kind of thought

(favorable or unfavorable) in response to a message, or inhibits particular thoughts. Our next two postulates deal more specifically with these two kinds of processing.

Postulates on Relatively Objective and Relatively Biased Elaboration

Variables affecting motivation and/or ability to process a message in a relatively objective manner can do so by either enhancing or reducing argument scrutiny.

Variables affecting message processing in a relatively biased manner can produce either a positive (favorable) or negative (unfavorable) motivational and/or ability bias to the issue-relevant thoughts attempted.

In the strictest sense, when a person is *motivated* to process a message in a relatively objective manner, this means that the person is trying to seek the truth wherever it might lead. This, of course, does not ensure that the person will come to the truth, only that the person is attempting to do so. When a person has the *ability* to process a message in a relatively objective manner, this means that the person has the requisite knowledge and opportunity to consider the arguments impartially. When a variable enhances argument scrutiny in a relatively objective manner, the strengths of cogent arguments should become more apparent as should the flaws in specious ones. Similarly, when a variable reduces argument scrutiny in a unbiased fashion, the strengths of cogent arguments should become less apparent as should the flaws in specious ones.

In contrast to this relatively objective processing, when a variable affects the motivation to process in a relatively biased manner, this means that the variable encourages or inhibits the generation of *either* favorable or unfavorable thoughts in particular. When a variable affects the ability to process in a relatively biased manner, this means that the person's knowledge base or situational factors make it more likely that one side will be supported over another. Our distinction between relatively objective and biased processing has certain parellels with the cognitive distinction between "bottom-up" and "top-down" processing. Specifically, objective processing has much in common with bottom-up processing because the elaboration is postulated to be relatively impartial and guided by the data (message arguments) presented. Biased processing has more in common with top-down processing because the elaboration may be governed, for example, by a relevant attitude schema that guides processing in a manner favoring the maintenance or strengthening of the original schema (cf., Bobrow & Norman, 1975; Landman & Manis, 1983).

As we will document in subsequent chapters, there are many variables that determine the extent and direction of message elaboration. For example, the motivation to process a message increases as it becomes more important or adaptive to form a correct position, such as when an advocacy portends a large number of personal consequences (Petty & Cacioppo,

1979b). This enhanced processing is likely to be largely objective when the person has relatively little investment in which particular position turns out to be the best. For example, consider a couple buying a home for the first time. They would like to obtain the best mortgage, but which particular bank is ultimately deemed best does not matter. Rather, it is obtaining the best loan that is important. Elaboration is more likely to be biased when some threat is associated with adopting one position over another (e.g. deciding if one's children are delinquents). Of course, pure cases of objective or biased processing may be rare since competing motives are likely in many situations and people may often have somewhat more information on one side of an issue than another. Nevertheless, it is possible and useful to distinguish message processing that is *relatively* objective from that which is *relatively* biased. In the next chapter we describe procedures for doing this, and in Chapters 3 to 6 we discuss some of the more important variables affecting message processing in either a relatively objective or relatively biased manner.

Postulate on Elaboration versus Peripheral Cues

We have now argued that the elaboration of a persuasive message may proceed in a relatively objective or in a relatively biased manner. However, in some persuasion contexts people may be unmotivated or unable to engage in either kind of message elaboration. Our next postulate indicates that there is a tradeoff between message elaboration and the effectiveness of peripheral cues.

> **As motivation and/or ability to process arguments is decreased, peripheral cues become relatively more important determinants of persuasion. Conversely, as argument scrutiny is increased, peripheral cues become relatively less important determinants of persuasion.**

When situational and individual factors foster a high elaboration likelihood, people will scrutinize the message, though this processing may occur in a relatively objective or in a relatively biased way. Importantly, following the central route to persuasion requires both the motivation and the ability to elaborate the message. If ability is high, but motivation is low at the time of message exposure, little argument processing will occur. Instead, if any influence occurs at all, it will be the result of simple positive or negative cues that become associated with the advocacy, or simple inferences based on cues that permit the adoption of a subjectively reasonable position while conserving cognitive resources. However, if the person subsequently becomes motivated to process the issue, attitude change may occur via the central route. Whether the argument elaboration in the later processing will be relatively objective or biased will depend on a number of factors such as the number and kind of message arguments people recall. For example, to the extent that people tend to better remember arguments on their own side of the issue, or weak rather than strong arguments that are opposed to their position, the subsequent processing of the advocacy is likely to be highly biased.

If motivation to process the message is high, but ability is low, the person will want to process the message arguments, but will be unable to do so. In this case, the person is likely to engage in whatever processing is possible and may be forced to rely on shortcut inferences about message validity based on peripheral cues in the persuasion context. Again, if ability to process the arguments is subsequently acquired and motivation remains high, attitude changes via the central route may occur. When both motivation and ability to process the message are low, any influence that occurs will be the result of peripheral cues. In short, we postulate a tradeoff between argument elaboration and the operation of peripheral cues. As argument processing is reduced, whether objective or biased, peripheral cues become more important determinants of persuasion. In Chapter 6 we review the evidence relevant to this postulate.

Postulate on Consequences of Elaboration

In the preceding postulates we have outlined how the ELM accounts for the initial attitude changes induced by persuasive communications, and we have detailed the two routes to persuasion. Our last postulate specifies the different consequences of attitude changes induced via the central and the peripheral routes.

> **Attitude changes that result mostly from processing issue-relevant arguments (central route) will show greater temporal persistence, greater prediction of behavior, and greater resistance to counterpersuasion than attitude changes that result mostly from peripheral cues.**

There are several reasons why these differential consequences would be expected. Recall that under the central route, attitude changes are based on a thoughtful consideration of issue-relevant information and an integration of that information into an overall position. Under the peripheral route, however, an attitude is based on a simple cue that provides some affective association or allows some relatively simple inference as to the acceptability of the advocacy. Thus, attitude changes induced via the central route involve considerably more cognitive work than attitude changes induced under the peripheral route. The process of elaborating issue-relevant arguments involves accessing the schema for the attitude object in order to evaluate each new argument (e.g., by comparing it to information previously stored in memory). Under the peripheral route, however, the schema may be accessed only once to incorporate the affect or inference elicited by a salient cue. Or a peripheral schema unrelated to the issue-schema may be invoked in order to evaluate the cue (e.g., Is the source credible?). Under the central route then, the issue-relevant attitude schema may be accessed, rehearsed, and manipulated more times, strengthening the interconnections among the components and rendering the schema more internally consistent, accessible, enduring and resistant than under the peripheral route (cf., Crocker, Fiske, & Taylor, 1984; Fazio, Sanbonmatsu, Powell, & Kardes, 1986; McGuire, 1981). Our analysis asumes, of course, that we are comparing subjects who have processed a message and have changed via the central route to subjects who have processed the same message and have changed to the same degree, but via the peripheral route. It may be possible to produce attitudes via the peripheral route that have some of the same characteristics (e.g., persistence, accessibility) as those produced via the central route, but more message and cue exposures should be required to achieve the same result (e.g., Johnson & Watkins, 1971; Weber, 1972).

The greater the accessibility of the information supporting an attitude, the greater the likelihood that the same attitude will be reported over time if people consider their prior knowledge before reporting their attitudes. Even if people don't scan their store of attitude-relevant information before reporting their attitudes in some circumstances (Lingle & Ostrom, 1981), the greater accessibility and endurance of the attitude itself would enhance the likelihood that the same attitude would be reported at two points in time. Also, the greater the accessibility of the information supporting the attitude and the more well organized it is, the greater the likelihood that this attitude-relevant knowledge can be used to defend the attitude from subsequent attack. Finally, the greater the accessibility of the attitude itself and the more well-orgnaized it is, the greater the likelihood that it will guide behavior (Fazio, Chen, McDonel, & Sherman, 1982; Fazio & Williams, 1985; Norman, 1975).

In sum, the greater organization and accessibility of attitudes and attitude-relevant information for persuasion occuring via the central than the peripheral route render people more *able* to report the same attitude over time, to defend their beliefs, and to act on them. A motivational factor may also be relevant, however. Specifically, the process of scrutinizing issue-relevant arguments may generally be more deliberate than the processes of affective association and the invocation of well-rehearsed (even automatic) decision rules (Cialdini, 1984, 1985). Thus, changes induced under the central route may be accompanied by the subjective perception that considerable thought accompanied opinion formation. This perception may induce more confidence in the attitude, and attitudes held with more confidence may be more likely to be reported over time, to be slower to be abandoned in the face of counterpropaganda, and to be more likely to be acted upon. In Chapter 7 we review the evidence for the differential consequences of the route to persuasion and we compare the ELM to some alternative models of attitude persistence, resistance, and attitude-behavior correspondence.

Although the consequences of attitude change via the central route are quite desirable, the ELM makes it clear that this is a difficult persuasion strategy. The recipient of the message must have both the motivation and the ability to process the information contained in the communication, and the information presented must elicit a profile of thoughts (elaborations) that is more favorable than that available prior to message exposure. In basic experimental work on persuasion which is designed to test theories, it is possible to select topics for which strong comprehensible arguments can be constructed (even if that requires fabricating information), and to select situations and contexts in which people are likely to attend to and process these arguments. In the "real world," there are often constraints on the topics, arguments, and settings that can be employed. For example, the intended audience may be able to counterargue the only arguments available; or, the arguments may be compelling, but too complex to be understood fully by the audience. In many cases, the problem in inducing attitude change via the central route is even more basic—just motivating people to attend to and think about the message presented (in Chapter 4 we discuss variables that can increase motivation to process a message).

Given the difficulty of change via the central route, it is not surprising that what we have labeled the peripheral route is a popular and potentially successful persuasion strategy when the only available arguments are weak and/or the elaboration likelihood is low. Since persuasion via this route is postulated to be short lived, however, it will be necessary to constantly remind the targeted audience of the cue or cues upon which favorable attitudes are based. These constant reminders (accomplished, for example, via advertising repetition, political posters, etc.) may be sufficient to get the audience to buy certain products or vote for certain candidates. Interestingly, once a person has made a decision and voted for a candidate or purchased a product, motivation (e.g., due to increased personal relevance or personal responsibility) and ability (e.g., due to increased knowledge) to process any subsequent information received about the attitude object may be enhanced. This of course, could ultimately lead to attitudes that are persistent, resistant, and predictive of future behavior.

Retrospective

In this chapter we have reviewed the seven postulates of the Elaboration Likelihood Model of persuasion. We have argued that people want to be "correct" in their attitudes and opinions but that they are not always willing or able to personally evaluate the merits of the issue-relevant arguments presented in support of an appeal. When people do elaborate issue-relevant arguments, this processing may proceed in either a relatively objective or in a relatively biased manner. When motivational and ability variables render the likelihood of issue-relevant elaboration as low, however, then attitudes may still be changed if simple positive or negative cues in the persuasion context either become directly associated with the advocacy or provide the basis for inferences that allow a subjective determination of the desirability of the advocacy. Attitude changes based on extensive elaboration of issue-relevant arguments (central route) are postulated to be more persistent, resistant, and predictive of behavior than attitude changes based on simple cues (peripheral route). In the next chapter we discuss methodological factors relevant to testing the ELM and in the remainder of this volume we present the empirical evidence for the ELM.

Chapter 2
Methodological Factors in the ELM

Introduction

In the preceding chapter we outlined the postulates of the Elaboration Likelihood Model. In the remainder of this volume we will review the evidence for the ELM. Before turning to this, however, it would be useful to cover some general methodological issues that arise in testing the ELM. We will first briefly address the procedures we have employed to assess attitudes and attitude change in our experiments. Then we will discuss procedures for assessing and operationalizing the three basic constructs in the ELM: argument quality, peripheral cues, and message elaboration. Finally, we discuss individual differences in the likelihood of message elaboration.

Assessing Attitudes and Persuasion

As noted in Chapter 1, we use the term "attitude" to refer to a general favorable, unfavorable, or neutral evaluation of a person, object, or issue. "Persuasion" refers to any effort to modify an individual's evaluations of people, objects, or issues by the presentation of a message. Importantly, our definitions identify the attitude concept with a general evaluative dimension rather than with specific cognitive, affective, or behavioral responses. This is not intended to diminish the importance of cognition, affect, or behavior in attitudes and persuasion, but rather these constructs are accorded independent conceptual status, so that their functions as antecedents and consequences of attitude change may be examined separately.

Ever since Thurstone (1928) introduced the first attitude scale, attitude measurement techniques have generally focused on assessing a global evaluative reaction to some stimulus. The classic scaling techniques of Thurstone (1928) and Likert (1932), techniques for measuring emotional or behavioral responses (cf., Lemon, 1973), and the more popular and straightforward semantic differential (Osgood, Suci, & Tannenbaum, 1957) and single-item rating scales (cf., Cacioppo, Harkins, & Petty, 1981) are all designed to gauge how much one likes or dislikes, or appraises favorably or unfavorably, a stimulus. In research described in the subsequent chapters, we have generally employed multi-item semantic differentials with bipolar adjectives from the evaluative dimension serving as anchors (e.g., good/bad) and/or single-item rating scales (e.g., 1 = "agree completely," 9 = "disagree completely") on which subjects respond to evaluative statements. When both types of scales have been used, the responses to each are standardized and aggregated to obtain an overall index of people's attitude toward the target stimulus (see Figure 2-1 for example).

To mitigate the effects of response sets (e.g., acquiescence, social desirability), the ends of the scales denoting positive and negative attitudes are either counterbalanced or determined randomly. Also, a cover story is employed so that subjects are unaware that the study concerns their persuasibility. In some experiments, for example, subjects are told that the psychology department is cooperating with the School of Journalism in evaluating radio editorials that were submitted by colleges and universities throughout the country (e.g., Petty, Cacioppo, & Heesacker, 1981). The subjects are instructed that their task is to assist in rating the broadcast quality of selected editorials. An important attribute of the cover story is that it not draw undue attention to the subjects' attitudes toward the persuasive

```
1.  Rate how you feel about requiring college seniors to take a comprehensive
    exam in their major as a requirement for graduation on the scales below.

                        COMPREHENSIVE EXAMS ARE:

       bad     ___  ___  ___  ___  ___  ___  ___  ___  ___      good
               -4   -3   -2   -1    0   +1   +2   +3   +4

unfavorable    ___  ___  ___  ___  ___  ___  ___  ___  ___      favorable
               -4   -3   -2   -1    0   +1   +2   +3   +4

      wise     ___  ___  ___  ___  ___  ___  ___  ___  ___      foolish
               +4   +3   +2   +1    0   -1   -2   -3   -4

beneficial     ___  ___  ___  ___  ___  ___  ___  ___  ___      harmful
               +4   +3   +2   +1    0   -1   -2   -3   -4


2.  To what extent do you agree with the proposal requiring college seniors to
    take a comprehensive exam in their major before graduating?

do not agree  ___  ___  ___  ___  ___  ___  ___  ___  ___  ___  ___   agree
   at all      1    2    3    4    5    6    7    8    9   10   11  completely
```

Figure 2-1. Example attitude scales. These were the questions used to measure attitudes toward senior comprehensive exams in the Petty & Cacioppo (1979b, Experiment 2) study depicted in Figure 4-2. Similar attitude assessments were employed for the other studies reported in this volume.

appeal as a focus of study. After hearing a specially prepared persuasive communication, subjects are told that because their personal views on the desirability of the recommendation might influence the way they rate the broadcast quality of the tapes, a measure of their own opinion on the issue is desired. Subjects then indicate their postcommunication attitude using the scales (e.g., semantic differentials) provided. This procedure supplies individuals with a justification for reporting their attitudes toward the recommendation while attenuating the biasing influences of suspicion and social desirability.

Initial Attitude Changes

In most experimental studies of persuasion, the theoretical question of interest concerns the *relative* rather than the absolute effects of various factors on attitude change. Consider, for example, an experiment designed to examine the effects of Factor-X (e.g., message repetition) on persuasion. All subjects might be exposed to the same message in the same persuasion context, but some would be assigned at random to a condition in which there is a low level of Factor-X, others to a condition in which there is a moderate level of X, and others to a condition in which there is a high level of X. Postcommunication measures of attitudes provide information about the relative effects of Factor-X, since successful random assignment to conditions assures that on average, subjects in each condition begin with the same attitudes toward the recommendation. These experimental conditions do not provide information about what levels of Factor-X led to *absolute* attitude change, however, because it is possible that one or more of the levels of X failed to elicit significant attitude change.

For instance, if the results depicted in the top panel of Figure 2-2 represent the postcommunication attitudes obtained in this hypothetical study, then one could infer that a moderate level of Factor-X elicits more support for the recommendation than low or high levels of Factor-X. However, this relative result could have occurred because: (a) low and high levels of X produced *no* change, but moderate levels produced positive change, (b) all levels of X produced positive change, but moderate levels produced the most change, (c) moderate levels of X produced no change, but low and high levels led to change *away from* the position advocated (boomerang), or (d) all levels of X produced negative change, but moderate levels produced the least negative change. When these "absolute" questions are of theoretical interest (or when subjects cannot be assigned randomly to all conditions, as when studying recipient factors), we have utilized either pretests or external-control groups. A pretest allows one to determine whether significant changes in attitudes occur between it and posttest, but pretests can have undesirable effects such as committing subjects to their initial attitudes or sensitizing subjects to the focus of the study. Separating the pretest from the experimental study and varying the appearance of the attitude measures can minimize these

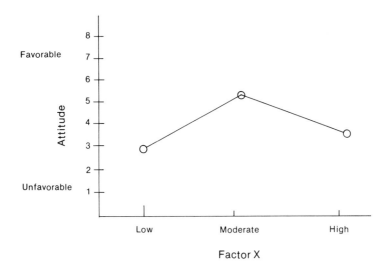

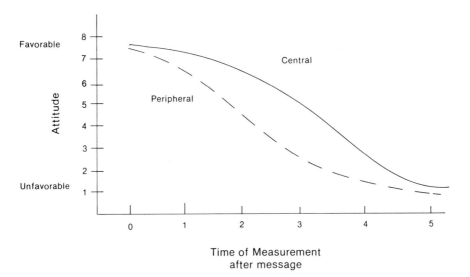

Figure 2-2. *Top panel*—effects of a hypothetical factor on attitudes (see text for discussion). *Bottom panel*—hypothetical decay functions for attitude changes induced via the central and peripheral routes (see text for discussion).

undesirable effects (Carlsmith, Ellsworth, & Aronson, 1976; Insko, 1967; Petty & Brock, 1981).

An alternative to using pretests that is less plagued by sensitization and carryover effects is to use external-control groups. For example, imagine that some subjects in our hypothetical study of Factor-X heard the experimental instructions but indicated their attitude toward the issue prior to their exposure to X. Comparisons of the attitudes expressed by these individuals with those expressed by individuals in each of the experimental conditions (e.g., using the Dunnett procedure) furnishes information regarding the absolute effects of each level of Factor-X on attitude change.

Attitude Change Over Time

Simply determining whether or not attitude change occurs does not in itself reveal whether the central or the peripheral route was traveled, since both routes can yield similar changes immediately following an individual's exposure to a persuasive communication. Recall that under the central route, recipients' susceptibility or resistance to persuasion is determined by their scrutiny and evaluation of the merits of the arguments for a recommendation. These "arguments" can be provided externally or generated internally. Thus, as noted in Chapter 1, under the central route, recipients' thinking about issue-relevant information is viewed as being the most direct determinant of the direction and amount of attitude change produced, and the attitude change induced via this route is posited to be relatively permanent, resistant to counterpersuasion, and predictive of behavior. Under the peripheral route, however, attitude change is viewed as resulting from pairing the recommendation with a simple cue that either alters recipients' moods directly, or provides them with the basis for a simple inference as to the appropriate attitude. Changes induced via this route are postulated to be relatively temporary, susceptible to counterpersuasion, and less predictive of behavior because, ceteris paribus, the attitude is associated with a cue that is more easily dissociated from the recommendation than are personally relevant beliefs and thoughts that are central to the merits of the position advocated.

It would appear then, that one way to assess whether changes are central or peripheral is to examine the consequences of the attitude changes. For example, one of the fundamental differences in the consequences of the two routes to persuasion is the temporal persistence of the induced attitude changes. It should be noted, however, that assessing this consequence may be rather difficult. Since the exact decay functions of attitude changes induced by the central versus the peripheral routes are not known, administration of one immediate and one delayed posttest does not provide a strong test. The bottom panel of Figure 2-2, which depicts hypothetical decay functions for central and peripheral attitude changes, illustrates the problem. No differences in the delayed attitude measure would be expected if the second assessment were made too early, in which case peripheral persuasion might not yet have decayed. No differences would likewise be expected if the second assessment were made too late, in which case central persuasion might have already decayed. Moreover, because researchers lose control over extraneous factors when subjects leave the laboratory, the error variance associated with follow-up attitude assessments can be large, rendering the tests insensitive. Furthermore, repeatedly assessing the same individuals' attitudes toward a recommendation can itself exert an extraneous effect, such as committing individuals to their attitudinal positions or causing them to rationalize their reported attitudes. Finally, if different groups of individuals are tested at varying points in time following the persuasive communication, the number of subjects required to conduct studies can become prohibitively large.

Many of these cautionary comments (and even additional ones) are, of course, applicable to assessing the other consequences of the route to persuasion. For example, in assessing the resistance to counterpersuasion of attitudes newly formed via the central versus peripheral routes, what kind of countermessage is optimal? If a countermessage contains both strong arguments and strong peripheral cues, both groups may retreat from their new positions, but for different reasons. Likewise, in assessing attitude-behavior consistency, what behavioral criterion is appropriate? If the behavior tested is too easy, all groups may comply. If too difficult, very few will go along. Testing multiple behaviors may be necessary (cf., Ajzen & Fishbein 1977). Because of the potential difficulties of examining in a simple and efficient manner the postulated consequences of attitude changes induced via central versus peripheral processes, an alternative assessment procedure for distinguishing these two routes is clearly desirable.

One key to the solution of this problem lies in examining the distinctive underlying *processes* postulated by these two routes. Persuasion resulting from the central, in contrast to the peripheral route, is posited to be accompanied by a more careful and cognitively demanding examination of the merits of the recommendation. This difference should be discernible during the same session that subjects are exposed to the persuasive communication. In the following sections we examine several tacts used to assess the route to persuasion.

Assessing the Basic Constructs in the ELM

As we detailed in the last chapter, the ELM holds that variables can affect the amount and direction of attitude change in one of three ways: (a) serving as persuasive arguments, (b) serving as peripheral cues, or (c) affecting the extent or direction of argument elaboration (see Postulate 3). In this section, we define in greater detail these three constructs in the ELM and we discuss operationalizations of each. As noted above, if we can distinguish attitudes that are based on argument elaboration rather than peripheral cues, we will distinguish the central and peripheral routes to persuasion. In subsequent chapters, we discuss how many of the typical source, message, recipient, channel, and context variables manipulated in the accumulated persuasion research can be understood in terms of this three-part categorization and the central and peripheral routes. In Chapter 7, we return to the postulated consequences of the two routes to persuasion.

Argument Quality

One of the least researched and least understood questions in the psychology of persuasion is: What makes an argument persuasive? As we noted in Chapter 1, literally thousands of studies and scores of theories have addressed the question of how some extra-message factor (e.g., source credibility, repetition, etc.) affects the acceptance of a particular argument, but little is known about what makes a particular argument (or message) persuasive in isolation. In fact, the typical persuasion experiment employs only one message and examines how some extra-message factor affects acceptance of the message conclusion. Furthermore, studies that do include more than one message often do so for purposes of generalizability across topics, not because the messages are proposed to differ in some theoretically meaningful way (e.g., Hovland & Weiss, 1951). There are, of course, notable exceptions to our generalization. For example, a few studies have manipulated the comprehensibility or complexity of a message (e.g., Eagly, 1974; Eagly & Warren, 1976; Regan & Cheng, 1973), mostly to test McGuire's (1968) information processing model, but even these studies were not aimed at uncovering the underlying characteristics of persuasive arguments. Perhaps the most relevant research to date is that in which subjects are asked to rate arguments or traits along dimensions such as how novel they are (Vinokur & Burnstein, 1974), or how many implications they elicit (Burstein & Schul, 1982), in order to determine what aspects of information enhance its impact. Unfortunately, this important and rare work is in its infancy. After more than 40 years of research in experimental social psychology on persuasion, Fishbein & Ajzen (1981) could accurately state that "the general neglect of the information contained in a message ... is probably the most serious problem in communication and persuasion research" (p. 359).[1]

---

[1] Notably, Fishbein and Ajzen (1975) and other expectancy-value theorists (e.g., Rosenberg, 1956) have examined argument or attribute persuasiveness from a phenomenological perspective. However, the question of *why* a particular argument or attribute is seen as more positive or negative than others is still not addressed.

In our own studies, we too have ignored the specific qualities that render some arguments cogent and others specious. Yet, for purposes of testing the ELM, it is necessary to specify arguments that people find compelling and those that are counterarguable. We have postponed the question of what specific qualities make arguments persuasive by defining argument quality in an empirical manner. In developing arguments for a topic we begin by generating a large number of arguments, both intuitively compelling and specious ones, in favor of some target issue (e.g., raising tuition). Then, members of the appropriate subject population are given these arguments to rate for persuasiveness. Based on these scores, we select arguments with high and low ratings to comprise at least one "strong" and one "weak" message. Subsequently, other subjects are given one of these messages and are told to think about and evaluate it carefully. Following examination of the message, subjects complete a "thought listing measure" (Brock, 1967; Greenwald, 1968) in which they are instructed to record the thoughts elicited by the message. These thoughts are then coded as to whether they are favorable, unfavorable, or neutral toward the position advocated (e.g., see Cacioppo & Petty, 1981c; Cacioppo, Harkins, & Petty, 1981).

We define a "strong" message as one containing arguments such that when subjects are *instructed* to think about the message, the thoughts that they generate are predominantly favorable. A "weak" message is one that is also ostensibly in favor of the advocacy. However, the arguments in a weak message are such that when subjects are instructed to think about them, the thoughts that they generate are predominantly unfavorable. A message that elicits a roughly even mixture of favorable and unfavorable thoughts would be considered an ambiguous or "mixed" message. Importantly, for positive attitude change to occur in response to a strong message, the profile of issue-relevant thoughts elicited by the arguments should be more favorable than the profile available prior to message exposure. For negative attitude change (boomerang) to occur in response to a weak message, the profile of thoughts elicited by the arguments should be less favorable than the profile available prior to message exposure.

Once the messages meet the criterion of eliciting the appropriate profile of thoughts, they are checked for other characteristics. First, a panel of subjects rates the messages for overall believability. For example, consider a message that argues that the University Chancellor wants to raise tuition so that more books can be purchased for the library. Students find this to be a strong and believable argument. Consider another message that argues that the Chancellor wants to raise tuition so that more trees and shrubs can be planted on campus. Students find this to be a weak but believable argument. Thus, although these arguments are equated in believability, they differ greatly in strength. It is, of course, possible to generate arguments that would appear even stronger or weaker but that would be completely implausible. For example, consider the argument that the Chancellor wants to raise tuition to build a 100-story monument to the university ping pong team.

Certainly a weak argument, but not one that would be taken seriously. Likewise, consider the argument that tuition should be raised because if it is, the university could improve enough in a year to become the best university in North America. Students would certainly find this consequence to be desirable, but because they wouldn't believe that it would occur, the argument would likely be derrogated. In sum, we attempt to develop arguments that are strong and weak, but that do not strain credulity (Osgood & Tannenbaum, 1955). This is not to say that our arguments are necessarily veridical—just reasonably plausible to our subjects. The Appendix at the end of this chapter provides examples of strong and weak arguments that we have used to construct the messages used in some of our studies. Importantly, since the plausibility and strength of these arguments may vary widely across different populations and times, the arguments should be pretested and adapted as necessary before usage (cf., Cacioppo, Petty, & Morris, 1983).

Finally, a panel of subjects from the relevant subject pool rates our strong and weak messages for overall comprehensibility, complexity, and familiarity. Again, our goal is to develop strong and weak messages that are roughly equivalent in their novelty and in our subjects' ability to understand them.[2] The top panel of Figure 2-3 depicts the results of a study in which a treatment variable has no effect on attitudes. In the right panel, conditions of high elaboration likelihood are shown. In this hypothetical study, only the quality of the message arguments determined the extent of attitude change. In the left panel, conditions of low elaboration likelihood are depicted. In this hypothetical study, neither the treatment nor the arguments in the message affected attitudes. This result would occur when subjects have little motivation and/or ability to process the issue-relevant arguments, and Factor-X neither serves as a peripheral cue nor affects argument processing. In subsequent sections of this chapter we compare the two simple results shown in the top panel of Figure 2-3 with the other possibilities depicted in the figure.

Peripheral Cues

According to the Elaboration Likelihood Model, one way to influence attitudes is by varying the quality of the arguments in a persuasive message. Another possibility, however, is that a simple cue in the persuasion context affects attitudes in the absence of argument processing. As we noted earlier, some cues will do this because they trigger relatively primative affective

---

[2]Although we do not detail the procedures here, it is important to note that after participation in one of our persuasion experiments, subjects recieve a thorough debriefing as to the nature of the research and any deceptions employed and their rationale.

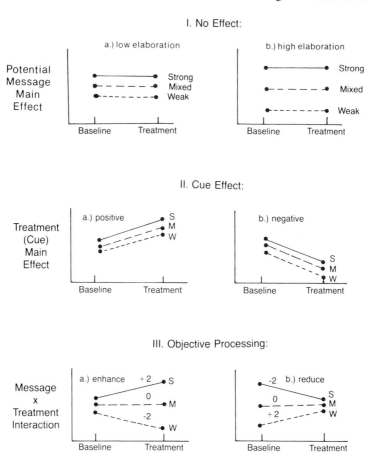

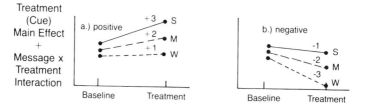

Figure 2-3. Possible effects of a treatment according to the ELM. In panel I the treatment has no effect. Instead, only an effect for argument quality is observed, at least if the elaboration likelihood is high. In Panel II, the treatment serves as a positive or negative cue affecting attitudes in the absence of much argument scrutiny. In Panel III, the treatment enhances or reduces argument scrutiny in a relatively objective manner. In Panel IV, the treatment produces either a positive or a negative bias to the message processing (adapted from Petty & Cacioppo, 1984c, 1986).

states that become associated with the attitude object. Other cues work, however, because they invoke guiding rules or inferences. (e.g., if I bought it, I must like it; Bem, 1972).

Since cues are postulated to affect attitude change without dramatically affecting argument processing, it is possible to test manipulations as potential cues by presenting them to subjects with the advocated position only (i.e., without accompanying persuasive arguments), as in prestige suggestion (see Asch, 1948). If the manipulation is a potential cue, it should have the ability to affect attitudes in the absence of any arguments. Alternatively, one could present an incomprehensible message (e.g., in a foreign language) on some topic along with the potential cue (e.g., speed of speech; Miller, Maruyama, Beaber, & Valone, 1976). Subjects could be asked to rate, for example, how likely it is that the speaker is convincing. Again, if a factor is operating as a cue it should be capable of affecting judgments even if there are no arguments to process. Finally, a simple procedure might involve merely describing various potential cues to subjects (e.g., a message with 1 vs. 10 arguments; a message from an attractive vs. an unattractive source) and asking them which would more likely be acceptable and/or persuasive. It is important to note that some cues will be difficult to uncover using the self-report procedure. For example, people may come to dislike a person more after an interaction in an uncomfortably hot than in a comfortably cool room, but may not be aware of the connection (Griffitt & Veitch, 1971). Conversely, the self-report procedure may uncover cues that people think would work, but in fact do not (Nisbett & Wilson, 1977). Furthermore, none of the procedures that we have suggested to uncover potential cues are capable of indicating *why* the cue was effective (e.g., affective association or the invocation of a simple decision rule). Nevertheless, these procedures should prove useful in suggesting whether a manipulation has the *potential* to serve as a peripheral cue.

The second panel in Figure 2-3 presents the results of a hypothetical study in which strong, weak, and mixed argument messages were presented along with a treatment that served as a peripheral cue. Note that in the pure case of cue processing, the cue affects all three kinds of messages equally. Since cues are most likely to operate when subjects are either unmotivated or unable to process issue-relevant arguments (as diagrammed in Figure 1-1), the data show a strong main effect for the cue treatment, but little effect for argument quality. In the left half of panel II in Figure 2-3 the cue is positive, and in the right half the cue is negative.

Message Elaboration

We have now described two of the key constructs in the Elaboration Likelihood Model: argument quality and peripheral cues. The third way in which a variable can affect persuasion is by determining the extent or direction of message processing. As we explained in Chapter 1, variables can affect argument processing in either a relatively objective or in a relatively biased manner (Petty & Cacioppo, 1981a). Recall that by relatively *objective* processing, we mean that the variable either motivates or enables subjects to see the strengths of cogent arguments and the flaws in specious ones, or inhibits them from doing so. By relatively *biased* processing we mean that the variable either motivates or enables subjects to generate a particular kind of thought in response to a message, or inhibits a particular kind of thought. We discuss variables that affect relatively objective processing in Chapters 3 and 4 and we discuss variables that affect relatively biased processing in Chapter 5.

Of course, in order to test the ELM, it is important to assess how much message processing subjects are engaged in (i.e., how much cognitive activity or effort is devoted to issue-relevant thinking). We have employed five different procedures to assess the extent of elaboration in our research on persuasion: (1) self-reports of effort, (2) argument recall, (3) thought-listing, (4) electrophysiological activity, and (5) manipulation of argument quality. We discuss each of these briefly below.

Self-Reported Cognitive Effort
The simplest procedure to assess the extent of thinking involves asking people directly how much effort they expended in processing the message or how much thinking they were doing about the advocacy. For instance, subjects might use a 9-point scale to respond to the following questions: (a) "To what extent were you trying hard to evaluate the communication?"; and (b) "How much effort did you put into evaluating the communication?" We have found answers to these questions to be highly interrelated (e.g., average correlation > 0.80), so each subject's average response to scales like these might serve as an index of perceived cognitive effort (e.g., Petty, Harkins, Williams, & Latane, 1977). Alternatively, subjects might be asked to rate the extent to which they generated "many thoughts" or "few thoughts" about the message (Batra & Ray, 1986). Although we have found these methods sensitive in some studies (e.g., Cacioppo, Petty, & Morris, 1983; Petty, Harkins, & Williams, 1980), in others it has not produced differences even though there were other indications of differential processing (e.g., Harkins & Petty, 1981a, 1982). The problem, of course, is that although people may sometimes be aware of how much cognitive effort they are expending, people do not always have access to their cognitive processes (Nisbett & Wilson, 1977). In addition, the measures would prove invalid indications of issue-relevant thinking to the extent that responses reflected cognitive effort or thoughts devoted to processing peripheral features of the message (e.g., the color of paper it was printed on).

In a similar vein, subjects might be asked to rate the extent to which they were trying to generate favorable or unfavorable thoughts or the extent to which it was easy or difficult to generate a particular kind of thought in an attempt to assess biased processing. Using this self-report procedure, Fukada (1986) found that subjects reported engaging in more counter-arguing during a message that followed a forewarning of persuasive intent than one that did not. This replicated the findings of previous research in which subjects actually listed their thoughts after a message with and without this type of forewarning (Petty & Cacioppo, 1979a; see further discussion in Chapter 5). Importantly, these measures suffer the same limitations as self-reports of relatively objective processing.

Argument Recall

A procedure stemming from the work on depth of processing (Craik & Lockhart, 1972) and cognitive effort (Tyler, Hertel, McCallum, & Ellis, 1979; see Chapter 1) is to give subjects five to ten minutes to list all of the arguments from the communication that they can remember. Two judges, blind to the experimental hypotheses, score the arguments recalled. An argument is counted as recalled if it correctly summarizes one of the arguments in the persuasive message. Listings of different versions of the same argument, or listings of different aspects or data used to support a given argument, are scored as a single argument correctly recalled. The interrater reliability is computed, and with few exceptions, extremely high agreement (i.e., $rs > + 0.90$) is obtained.

Among the insensitivities one can anticipate using this measure are that: (a) free recall is an imperfect measure of encoding efficacy (Eagly & Chaiken, 1984), and (b) according to the ELM, individuals in different persuasion contexts (e.g., low vs. high distraction) may be equally able to report the message arguments presented but may differ greatly in the extent to which the presentation of the arguments caused them to think about issue-relevant information and experiences (e.g., Petty, Wells, & Brock, 1976). For instance, an individual who is able but unmotivated to think about a message may have effectively encoded four of five of the arguments presented without thinking much about the personal implications of any of these arguments; an individual who is both able and motivated to think about a message, on the other hand, may have effectively encoded and elaborated on four of the five arguments. A message recall measure taken shortly after communication exposure would be unlikely to distinguish between the message processing of these individuals. In our own research, although differences between high and low elaboration likelihood con-ditions have not generally produced significant differences in the number of message arguments recalled, high elaboration likelihood has tended to be associated with more argument recall than low elaboration likelihood.

Importantly, argument recall may also prove useful in indexing the extent of biased processing. Specifically, consider two subjects who are presented with five strong arguments on each side of a controversial issue. The relative number of pro to counterattitudinal arguments recalled may index the extent to which subjects were either particularly motivated or able to process one side over another (cf., Jones & Aneshansel, 1956). Similarly, if a subject is presented with both strong and weak arguments in favor of his position, the extent to which strong arguments are recalled relative to weak ones would indicate bias. If the arguments are opposed to one's position, then biased processing would more likely favor recall of weak rather than strong arguments (cf., Jones & Kohler, 1958; Kleinhesselink & Edwards, 1975).

Thought-Listing Technique

A third procedure for assessing elaboration involves using the thought-listing technique pioneered by Brock (1967) and Greenwald (1968). In this procedure, subjects list their thoughts either in anticipation of, during, or after message exposure, and the thoughts are subsequently categorized into theoretically meaningful units (e.g., favorable and unfavorable thoughts; source-related thoughts) by the subjects or independent judges. For instance, subjects might read:

> We are now interested in what you were thinking about during the last few minutes. You might have had ideas all favorable to the recommendation, all opposed, all irrelevant to the recommendation, or a mixture of the three. Any case is fine; simply list what it was that you were thinking during the last few minutes. The next page contains the form we have prepared for you to use to record your thoughts and ideas. Simply write down the first idea that comes to mind in the first box, the second idea in the second box, etc. Please put only one idea or thought in a box. You should try to record only those ideas that you were thinking during the last few minutes. Please state your thoughts and ideas as concisely as possible . . . a phrase is sufficient. Ignore spelling, grammar, and punctuation. You will have 2.5 minutes to write your thoughts. We have deliberately provided more space than we think most people will need to ensure that everyone would have plenty of room to write the ideas they had during the message. So don't worry if you don't fill every space. Just write down whatever your thoughts were during the last few minutes. Please be completely honest and list all of the thoughts that you had. (Petty & Cacioppo, 1977)

Following these instructions, subjects are provided with boxes (e.g., created by twelve 8-inch horizontal lines each about 1 inch from the one above) in which they are to write their ideas. Subsequently, these verbal protocols are content analyzed along some dimension(s), such as *polarity,* where each listed thought is rated as being in favor of the advocated position, opposed to the advocated position, or neutral/irrelevant. A more detailed discussion of the thought-listing technique, including issues regarding the eliciting instructions, listing interval, and scoring procedures, is provided in Cacioppo and Petty (1981c) and Cacioppo, Harkins, and Petty (1981). Suffice it to say that the thought-listing technique has proven to be an important supplemental tool in tracking the amount and type of cognitive activity involved in persuasion and resistance.

Two aspects of the listed thoughts may shed light on the extent and nature of information processing. First, if Factor-A increases the total number of issue- or message-relevant thoughts subjects list in a specified period of time relative to Factor-B, then it may be reasonable to assume that Factor-A increases thinking (see Burnkrant & Howard, 1984; Brickner, Harkins & Ostrom, in press). *Issue-relevant* thoughts refer to all thoughts listed that relate to the topic of the advocacy. A subcategory of these thoughts includes those that were clearly sparked by or represent reactions to the specific message arguments presented (*message-relevant*). It might appear ideally that one would want to analyze only message-relevant thoughts to assess the extent of message processing, but this category likely underrepresents the extent of message processing. This is because many of the thoughts falling in the more global issue-relevant category may have been sparked by the message, although this cannot be definitively determined by examining the thought content. For this reason, even though it is possible to reliably code thoughts into issue- and message-relevant categories (e.g., Heesacker, Petty, & Cacioppo, 1983), it may sometimes be desirable to use the more global measure of issue-relevant thoughts to infer the extent of message processing.

Specifically, the relative *profile* of favorable and unfavorable issue-relevant thoughts listed may be used to index the extent of thinking even if there are no differences in the absolute number of thoughts listed. This follows from the fact that subjects are likely to list some issue-relevant thoughts during a postmessage thought-listing even if the specific message arguments elicited few thoughts during exposure. Importantly, issue-relevant thoughts that were not influenced by the message arguments should be guided primarily by the subject's initial attitude on the topic. Therefore, to the extent to which Factor-A elicits a profile of issue-relevant thoughts that better reflect the quality of the issue-relevant arguments presented than Factor-B, it can be assumed that Factor-A has enhanced argument processing relative to Factor-B. For example, consider a person who has not expended much effort processing a counterattitudinal message containing very strong arguments. When given 3 minutes to list thoughts about the message, this person might list 3 unfavorable and 2 favorable issue-relevant thoughts largely reflecting his or her original attitude. If the person had been given a message containing weak arguments, and the arguments were not processed, the profile of listed thoughts should be similar (i.e., 3 unfavorable, 2 favorable). Now consider a person with the same initial attitude who diligently processed a message containing cogent arguments in support of the advocacy. This person might list 4 favorable and only 1 unfavorable thought during the three-minute thought-listing task. If the strong arguments were processed, then the person should be *more* likely to list favorable thoughts but *less* likely to list unfavorable thoughts than if the message was not processed. The total number of issue-relevant thoughts might therefore be unaffected. Similarly, if this high-processing person had been exposed to a message containing weak arguments, then the profile of thoughts listed should be more likely to contain unfavorable thoughts and less likely to contain favorable thoughts than if the message was not processed. Note that both high and low processing led to the production of 5 issue-relevant thoughts. However, in the low-processing conditions, the profile of thoughts is unaffected by the manipulation of argument quality (since the thoughts are guided by the person's initial attitude), whereas in the high-processing conditions, the thoughts are affected by argument quality. The more the profile of thoughts reflects the quality of arguments presented, the more likely it is that the arguments have been processed. Finally, it is important to note that although statistical procedures have been used to show that cognitive activity (as assessed by thought-listings) mediates attitude effects in some instances (e.g., Cacioppo & Petty, 1979b; Insko, Turnbull, & Yandell, 1974; Petty & Cacioppo, 1977), thought-listings alone do not provide definitive evidence for the cognitive mediation of attitudes because the evidence is basically correlational (cf., Miller & Colman, 1981).

Electrophysiological Responses
   Cognitive activity. A fourth procedure that we have used to assess the extent and affectivity of information processing activity involves the use of psychophysiological measures. For example, we have completed several studies on perioral EMG activity and silent language processing (Cacioppo & Petty, 1979a; Cacioppo, Petty, & Marshall-Goodell, 1984; Cacioppo, Petty, & Morris, 1985). In an illustrative study, subjects participated in a 2 (Experimental replication) x 5 (Processing task) x 12 (Task replication) mixed-model factorial design, with the first factor manipulated between-subjects (Cacioppo & Petty, 1981b). Subjects were exposed to 60 trait adjectives spanning a range of likability, and each trait adjective was preceded by one of five cue-questions defining the processing task. The cue-questions were: (a) "Is the following word spoken louder than this question?" (Volume discrimination), (b) Does the following word rhyme with————?" (Rhyme), (c) "Is the following word similar in meaning to———?" (Association), (d) "Is the following word good (bad)?" (Evaluation), and (e) "Is the following word self-descriptive?" (Self-reference). Results revealed that mean recognition confidence ratings were ordered (from highest to lowest) as follows: self-reference, evaluation, association, rhyme, and volume discrimination. Importantly, all means except the last two differed significantly from each other (see left panel, Figure 2-4).
   Analyses of EMG activity in this study revealed that the mean amplitude of the EMG activity during the task over the perioral muscle region (*orbicularis oris*—which controls the pursing action of the lips) was lowest for the tasks requiring minimal associative processing (volume discrimination, rhyme), intermediate for the task of simple association, and equally high for the tasks of evaluation and self-reference. This pattern of data (see middle panel in figure 2-4) is unlikely to be due to task-induced differences in physiological arousal, because further analyses revealed that: (a) cardiac activity and the mean amplitude of EMG activity over a nonoral muscle group (i.e., the nonpreferred forearm flexors region) did not vary as a

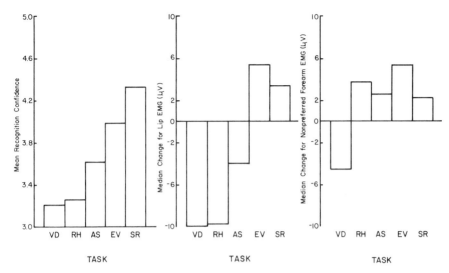

Figure 2-4. Psychophysiological assessment of extent of processing. The figure depicts the mean recognition confidence (left panel) and the median change from prestimulus levels for electromyographic activity during the processing interval for lip (middle panel) and nonpreferred forearm (right panel) as a function of orienting task. Abbreviations: VD = volume discrimination; RH = rhyme; AS = association; EV = evaluation; SR = self-reference (see text for specific orienting questions) (adapted from Cacioppo & Petty, 1981b).

function of the type of task performed (see right panel in Figure 2-4); and (b) the association between task and EMG activity over the perioral region was temporally as well as spatially specific. In other words, task-discriminating EMG activity was observed only during the period in which subjects analyzed the aurally presented trait adjectives and formulated their responses. Finally, in a follow-up study, we found that different associative tasks, such as evaluative and self-referent tasks, have discriminable effects on perioral EMG activity, although these effects are oftentimes on the form rather than the mean amplitude of the task-evoked response (Cacioppo, Petty, & Morris, 1985).

Affective reactions. Although the muscles of the lower face and perioral region are clearly involved in expressions of emotions (e.g., see Ekman & Friesen, 1978), perioral EMG activity does not appear to be related to subtle variations in the affective tone of individuals' information processing, such as those typically involved in attitude studies. For instance, some of the trait words employed in the Cacioppo and Petty (1981b) study were positive, others were neutral, and others were negative in meaning. We found no differences in perioral EMG activity as a function of word-valence, even though we have observed differential hemispheric EEG activity in response to these stimuli (Cacioppo & Petty, 1980c).

While the extent of cognitive deliberation rather than people's affective reactions has been discernible in perioral EMG activity, EMG activity over muscles controlling the movement of facial landmarks in regions ranging from the lower face (e.g., *zygomatic major,* which pulls the corners of the mouth upwards and back when forming a smile) to the upper face (e.g., *corrugator supercilii,* which draws the brows together and down in negative emotions such as anger and sadness) has been found to vary as a function of the nature and intensity of affective reactions to stimuli and the affective tone of attitudinal processing (e.g., Cacioppo & Petty, 1979a; McHugo, Lanzetta, Sullivan, Masters, & Englis, 1985; see Figure 2-5 for electrode placements). In one illustrative study, subjects were led to believe they were participating in a study on involuntary neural responses during action and imagery (Cacioppo, Petty, & Marshall-Goodell, 1984). Subjects on any given trial either lifted (action) or imagined lifting (imagery) a "light" (16 g) or "heavy" (35 g) weight, or they either silently read (action) a neutral communication as if they agreed or disagreed with its thesis, or imagined reading (imagery) an editorial with which they agreed or disagreed. Results revealed that EMG activity over the perioral region was higher during the attitudinal tasks (which involved silent language processing) than physical tasks, but perioral EMG activity was again essentially unchanged by the affective tone of the subjects' attitudinal processing. Yet whether subjects thought about the communication in a positive or negative fashion influenced EMG activity over facial muscles of emotional expression. For instance, positive attitudinal processing was associated with lower EMG

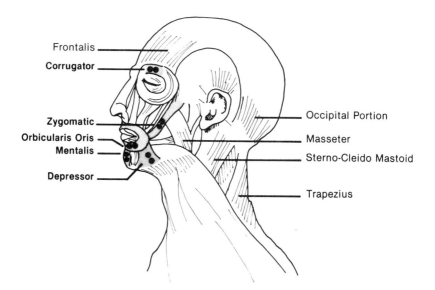

Figure 2-5. Electrode placements used for assessing extent and affectivity of processing (adapted from Cacioppo & Petty, 1981b).

activity over the corrugator region and higher EMG activity over the zygomatic region than was negative attitudinal processing. Finally, EMG activity recorded over the superficial forearm flexors did not vary as a function of the attitudinal tasks employed in this study, but it (rather than facial EMG activity) varied as a function of the simple physical tasks.

In another study (Cacioppo, Petty, Losch, & Kim, 1986), we had subjects view slides of scenes (e.g., a mountain cliff) that were mildly to moderately evocative of positive or negative affect. Pilot testing revealed that although there was consistency across individuals in their ratings of the affective valence of the scenes, there was considerable variation among individuals in terms of the rated intensity of the affect evoked by a given slide. Hence, we used the apriori classifications of *valence* as determined in pilot testing, but employed subjects' own ratings of the stimuli to determine *intensity* of the slides (i.e., which stimuli were viewed as mildly or moderately positive or negative). Electrodes were placed at appropriate locations on a subject's face (see Figure 2-5), and additional dummy electrodes were attached to the head and torso to divert attention from the face as a particular site of interest. After a period of relaxation, subjects were exposed to 16 habituation slides and then to another 32 during which data were collected. Each slide was projected for 5 seconds and after each presentation subjects used a numeric keypad to answer questions presented on a video screen before them. Subjects' faces were videotaped as they responded to the slides and subsequent analyses revealed that independent judges, blind to condition, were unable to determine from the tapes whether a positive or negative stimulus had been presented or whether a mildly or moderately intense simulus had been viewed. However, EMG activity over the corrugator, zygomatic, and orbicularis oculi regions differentiated the peasantness and intensity of individuals' affective reactions to the slides. These results suggest that gradients of EMG activity over the muscles of the face can provide objective and continuous probes of affective processes that are too subtle or fleeting to evoke expressions observable under normal conditions of social interaction (see Cacioppo & Petty, in press for further discussion).

Objective vs. biased processing. We have reviewed some evidence that electromyographic activity may be used to assess the extent and affectivity of information processing. It may also be possible to index the extent to which information processing activity is relatively objective rather than biased by assessing the extent of differential hemispheric activation during message processing. For example, in two studies we found that individuals who produced a relatively polarized profile of thoughts (unfavorable–favorable thoughts) in response to a persuasive message also demonstrated relative right hemispheric EEG activation as assessed over the parietal lobes (Cacioppo, Petty, & Quintanar, 1982; see further discussion in Chapter 5). If the EEG ratio is used in combination with measures of facial EMG, it might be possible in some situations to index both the extent and direction of elaboration. For example, a relatively high score on perioral EMG might indicate that a person was doing a lot of thinking about an issue, and a pattern of relative right hemispheric activation might indicate that this thinking was relatively one sided. Corrugator and zygomatic activity might then be used to determine the affective tone of the processing.

Summary. The physiological procedures we have described in this section have several potential advantages over self-reports of cognitive activity, argument recall, and thought-listings. For example, these measures can track psychological processes over time and may be less susceptible to artifacts (e.g., demand characteristics) and subjects' inability to recall the process or content of their thoughts. Although work on psychophysiological assessments of attitudinal processes is in its early stages, it holds considerable promise for tracking and marking the underlying mediation of persuasion and resistance (for further information, see Cacioppo & Petty, 1981a, in press; Petty & Cacioppo, 1983b).

Message/Argument Quality
The final procedure for assessing the extent of cognitive processing and the one we highlight in this monograph is based on the manipulation of message argument quality described earlier in this chapter. As we hinted above, our empirical method of defining argument quality allows us to assess the extent to which a variable affects argument processing and the extent to which this processing is relatively objective or relatively biased. We'll consider first the expected consequences of variables affecting relatively objective processing.

Relatively objective processing. Assume for the moment that we have created a control condition in which motivation or ability to process issue-relevant arguments is rather low. Subjects should show relatively little differentiation of strong from weak arguments in this condition. However, if a manipulation enhances argument processing in a relatively objective manner, then subjects should show greater differentiation of strong from weak arguments. More specifically, a message with strong arguments should tend to produce more agreement when it is scrutinized carefully than when scrutiny is low, but a message with weak arguments should tend to produce less overall agreement when scrutiny is high rather than low. The joint operation of these processes would result in people showing greater attitudinal differentiation of strong from weak arguments when processing is high than when it is low. This pattern of results is depicted in the left half of panel III in Figure 2-3. In a similar fashion we can assess the extent to which a variable disrupts processing in a relatively objective manner. Consider a situation in which subjects are processing the message arguments quite diligently. These subjects should show considerable differentiation of strong from weak arguments. However, if argument processing is disrupted, either because of reduced motivation or ability, argument quality should be a less important determinant of persuasion. More specifically, a strong message should tend to induce less agreement when processing is disrupted than when it is not, but a weak message should tend to produce more agreement when processing is disrupted than when it is not. The right half of panel 3 in Figure 2-3 depicts this pattern. In addition to subjects' attitudes being more differentiated to weak and strong messages when argument processing is high rather than low, as we noted earlier in this chapter, subjects' thoughts should also show greater differentiation of arguments when processing is high rather than low. Importantly, our predictions about discriminating arguments are *relative* rather than absolute. As processing increases, attitudes are more responsive to manipulations of argument quality, and as processing decreases, attitudes are less responsive to manipulations of argument quality.

Relatively biased processing. Panel IV in Figure 2-3 graphs the expected results for a variable that biases information-processing activity. In the left half of the panel, the effects of a variable that produces a positive cognitive bias (enhancing favorable thoughts and/or reducing negative thoughts) is depicted. It is instructive to compare this pattern of data with the patterns in the two panels above it. First, note that unlike a variable operating as a simple positive cue (left half of panel II), a variable producing a positive processing bias is not expected to affect all messages equally. Since the pure cue processor is not elaborating message arguments at all, the effectiveness of the cue is not constrained by the arguments presented. The biased processor, however, is attempting to elaborate the arguments and in this regard is similar to the objective processor. Nevertheless, an important difference between relatively objective and biased processing exists. The objective processor is motivated or is able to discover the "true (subjective) validity" of the message, and thus, strong arguments induce more persuasion and weak arguments induce less persuasion with more processing. In stark contrast, the biased processor is either particularly motivated or able to generate a particular kind of thought, often in defense of an initial attitude. However, even though the person is biased in processing a communication, the arguments in the message pose some limitation on this bias. For example, consider a person who is truly motivated to *counterargue* (and not simply discount) an advocacy. This person's task is simpler to the extent that the message provides weak rather than strong arguments in support of its position (see right half of panel IV in Figure 2-3).

As panel IV indicates, a treatment that biases thinking in a positive direction should generally have a greater impact on a strong than a weak message because it will be more difficult for a person to generate thoughts favorable to weak than to strong message arguments. On the other hand, a variable that biases thinking in a negative direction should generally have a greater impact on a weak than a strong message because it will be more difficult for a person to generate counterarguments to strong than weak arguments.

Importantly, these predictions (and the depictions in panel IV of Figure 2-3) assume that in the baseline (control) condition, relatively little issue-relevant thinking is occurring. However, consider a control (comparison) condition in which subjects are maximally processing strong and weak arguments. If the experimental treatment includes a variable that biases thinking in a positive direction, it will be difficult to observe more favorable attitudes to the strong arguments in the experimental than the control condition inasmuch as the arguments are already being processed maximally in the control cell (i.e., a ceiling effect is operating). However, the positive bias may result in more favorable attitudes toward the weak message than observed in the control condition (because no ceiling effect is operating). Thus, it may appear that the positive bias is working better for the weak than the strong message.

Similarly, if the experimental treatment includes a variable that biases thinking in a negative direction, it will be difficult to observe more negative attitudes toward the weak arguments than in the control condition if control subjects are highly motivated and able to process the message objectively (without bias). Thus, it may appear that the negative bias is working better for the strong than the weak message (because of a floor effect for the weak arguments). The caveat here is to include an appropriate control or baseline condition so that floor and ceiling effects do not cause problems. In general, when testing variables hypothesized to enhance processing it is better to include control conditions in which processing is minimal. When testing variables hypothesized to reduce processing, the opposite holds.

Self-reports of message quality. It is now clear that if a variable enhances objective or biased processing, subjects' attitudes should better discriminate strong from weak arguments when that variable is present. If the variable disrupts processing, subjects' attitudes should more poorly discriminate strong from weak arguments when that variable is present. A spin-off from the preceding technique that we have employed to assess the extent to which subjects carefully considered the cogency of the message arguments is to have subjects provide an overall evaluation of message quality. For instance, subjects might respond to the following questions: (a) "To what extent do you feel the communication made its point effectively?" (1 = not at all, 9 = completely), (b) "To what extent do you feel the communication was convincing?" (1 = not at all, 9 = completely). A subject's average response to these questions would serve as a measure of message evaluation.

As was the case when interpreting the effects of argument quality on postcommunication attitudes, the interesting outcome is not whether strong arguments are rated as being of higher quality than weak arguments, but rather how some variable combines with the manipulation of argument quality to affect subjects' overall evaluation of the cogency of the message.

For instance, if varying the level of some variable increases the extent to which recipients scrutinize the externally provided message arguments, then: (a) subjects' overall evaluations of strong versus weak versions of the message arguments should be more discriminable, and (b) because the postcommunication attitudes are more likely to reflect the thoughts and ideas evoked by the persuasive communication, the correlation between message evaluation and postcommunication attitudes should be higher.

Summary. Figure 2-3 summarizes the ways in which a treatment can affect attitude change according to the ELM, and it shows how these different processes can be tested by varying argument quality. First, a treatment can have no effect on persuasion for either strong or weak arguments (such as a peripheral cue under conditions of high elaboration likelihood; right side of panel I). Second, a treatment may produce only a main effect enhancing or reducing persuasion regardless of argument quality (panel II). If so, it suggests that the treatment is operating as a simple positive or negative cue. However, if a treatment interacts with message quality, it suggests that the treatment is affecting the elaboration likelihood. If the interaction follows the form depicted in panel III of Figure 2-3, it suggests that effect of the variable on information processing is relatively objective. If the interaction follows the form depicted in panel IV of Figure 2-3, on the other hand, it suggests that the effect of the variable on information processing is relatively biased.

Need for Cognition: Assessing Elaboration Likelihood via Individual Differences

In presenting the ELM in Chapter 1, we have emphasized that people have neither the resources to think about every persuasive appeal nor the luxury (or apparently the inclination) of being able to ignore them all. In the preceding sections of this chapter we have suggested various means of assessing the elaboration likelihood either during or following the presentation of a persuasive communication. However, the fact that the situational factors that have been employed to manipulate the extent to which attitudes are based on issue-relevant thinking sometimes account for only a small portion of variance is theoretically due in part to systematic individual differences among people in their desire to engage in issue-relevant thinking when dealing with their social environment generally and when formulating their attitudes specifically. This suggested to us that an individual differences strategy could be employed to measure chronic differences among people in elaboration likelihood prior to the presentation of a persuasive appeal (Cacioppo & Petty, 1982, 1984b; Cacioppo, Petty, & Morris, 1983). In particular, we reasoned that there were stable (though not invariant) individual differences in intrinsic motivation to engage in effortful cognitive endeavors generally, just as there are stable individual differences in intrinsic motivation to engage in effortful physical endeavors. Individual difference factors such as effectance, cognitive style, competency, and self-efficacy, although related when dealing with cognitive tasks to the theoretical distinction for which we were searching, failed to fully capture the specificity we sought. For instance, White (1959) described effectance motivation as follows:

> ... it is maintained that competence cannot be fully acquired simply through behavior instigated by (primary) drives. It receives substantial contributions from activities which, though playful and exploratory in character, at the same time show direction, selectivity, and persistence in interacting with the environment. Such activities in the ultimate service of competence must therefore be conceived to be motivated in their own right. It is proposed to designate this motivation by the term effectance, and to characterize the experience produced as a *feeling of efficacy*. (p. 329)

General differences across individuals in self-efficacy or effectance, therefore, should influence people's behavior on noncognitive (e.g., physical) as well as cognitive tasks.

The Construct of Need for Cognition

Our analysis of Cohen and his colleagues' work on *need for cognition* (1957; Cohen, Stotland, & Wolfe, 1955) suggested that it might be possible to scale individuals along their tendency to engage in and enjoy effortful cognitive endeavors. Cohen, Stotland, and Wolfe (1955) conceptualized need for cognition (NC) as "a need to experience an integrated and meaningful world." However, while one might avoid ambiguity and achieve an integrated and meaningful world through carefully scrutinizing incoming information, one might also achieve this goal by employing heuristics and by seeking the advice of experts. That this may be a feature of Cohen and his colleagues' conceptualization of NC is evident in the following description by Adams (1959):

> Given the existence of a measurable need for cognition, as defined (by Cohen and his colleagues), it may be hypothesized that a mother whose child presents a behavioral problem which she cannot handle or about which she is uncertain will experience tension and will try to reduce the tension if she has a need for cognition. One way of reducing the attendant tension under these circumstances is to seek information or advice about the problem from an appropriate source. An appropriate source is seen as one which, in the past, under similar circumstances has reduced tensions resulting from frustration of the need for cognition. (p. 17)

It is also clear from the early research that the emphasis in Cohen and his colleagues' conceptualization of NC was on tension reduction (Cohen, Stotland, & Wolfe, 1955, p. 291). In contrast, the emphasis in contemporary research on NC is on the statistical tendency of and intrinsic enjoyment individuals derive from engaging in effortful cognitive activities (Cacioppo & Petty, 1982). In this sense, our conceptualization of NC embraces White's (1959) central thesis that there are directed and persistent behaviors that have a motivational aspect which cannot be wholly derived from sources of energy conceptualized as drives or instincts. Individuals low in need for cognition (LNC) are conceived as being cognitive misers relative to individuals high in need for cognition (HNC), and this difference is conceived as attained slowly through repeated or prolonged episodes of effortful problem solving. When developing a method of measuring this individual difference construct (Cacioppo & Petty, 1982), we retained the term "need for cognition" despite our modifications to the original conceptualization in deference to Cohen's (1957) pioneering emphasis in persuasion research on individual differences in cognitive motivation (cf., Cohen, 1957).[3]

Scaling Individual Differences in Need for Cognition
Our initial efforts were aimed at constructing and validating an assessment instrument that tapped individual differences in people's intrinsic motivation to engage in and enjoy effortful cognitive endeavors (Cacioppo & Petty, 1982; Cacioppo, Petty, & Kao, 1984). In our initial study, we generated a pool of questions concerning a person's reactions to demands for effortful thinking in a variety of situations (Cacioppo & Petty, 1982, Experiment 1). When generating these, we specifically included items describing a variety of situations in which people could choose to garner information, analyze available evidence, abstract from past experiences, or synthesize ideas. We explictly excluded items dealing with inner broodings, reverie, mystical or religious experience, mind wandering, and artistic imaginings. Hence, the need for cognition scale (NCS) was designed to distinguish between individuals who are intrinsically motivated to engage in and enjoy effortful analytic activities and those who are not. Following pilot testing to identify ambiguous items in need of rewording or deletion, the set of items was

---

[3]The original objective tests used by Cohen and colleagues to gauge individual differences in need for cognition were never described in detail and are apparently no longer available. It might be noted, however, that Rosen and his colleagues (Rydell & Rosen, 1966; Rosen, 1963, 1964; Rosen, Siegelman, & Teeter, 1964) also scaled an individual difference they termed the need for cognition, but they conceived of NC as representing cognitive motivation, broadly defined. Accordingly, their scale tapped twelve separate factors (e.g., "cognitive bookworm," "religious anti-intellectualism"), whereas like Cohen and colleagues, we sought to identify and measure a more specific and limited individual difference in cognitive motivation. It might also be noted that Rosen and colleagues never marshalled strong evidence for the stability and validity of their various scales. For instance, Rosen (1964) reported that students from a college honors program scored higher than liberal arts and sciences students on subscales such as cognitive-bookworm and social and religious anti-intellectualism, but the liberal arts and sciences students did not differ from, or actually scored lower than, students in a two-year general program on these subscales.

administered to two groups of individuals presumed to differ substantially in their tendency to engage in and enjoy effortful cognitive endeavors (i.e., members of the University of Iowa faculty vs. assembly line workers in the neighboring communities). Criteria of ambiguity, irrelevance, and internal consistency were employed to select the items for the NCS, and a factor analysis of these items confirmed that one factor was dominant. A second study, in which the NCS was administered to a more homogeneous population (undergraduate students in introductory psychology classes at the University of Missouri) again revealed one factor was dominant (Cacioppo & Petty, 1982, Experiment 2). Moreover, despite the dramatically different subject populations and testing circumstances, the factor loadings obtained in Studies 1 and 2 were found to be highly correlated ($r = + 0.72$). Hence, the factor structure obtained in the first study was cross-validated. To simplify its administration, we subsequently developed a short-form of the NCS. This 18-item version of the NCS was found to possess the same factor structure as our original NCS and, indeed, correlated very highly ($r = +0.98$) with the original (Cacioppo, Petty, & Kao, 1984; see Table 2-1 for the specific items).

Additional evidence for the stability of the factor structure and internal consistency of the NCS was provided in three recent laboratory studies involving college undergraduates (Chaiken, in press) and in a field study involving a random sample of 233 residents from Gainesville, Florida (Furguson, Chung, & Weigold, 1985). In the former studies, factor analyses revealed one dominant factor best characterized as a tendency to engage in and enjoy effortful cognitive endeavors. Furguson et al. did not report a factor analysis, but rather they reported a Chronbach's alpha of 0.86 for the subset of 15 items they selected from the Cacioppo and Petty (1982) NCS.

Validation of the Need for Cognition Construct
It is important to know whether individuals high in need for cognition enjoy relatively effortful cognitive tasks even in the absence of feedback about performance. To examine this question, subjects were given either simple or complex instructions to use while performing a boring number-circling task (Cacioppo & Petty, 1982, Experiment 4). Subjects in the *simple* number-circling task condition were instructed to circle all 1s, 5s, and 7s. Subjects in the *complex* number-circling task condition were instructed to circle all the 3s, any 6 that preceded a 7, and every other 4. Subjects were given tables containing 3,500 random numbers, and all subjects performed the task for 10 minutes. Afterward, subjects expressed their attitude toward the task and completed the NCS, which was embedded among ancillary measures. Results revealed that subjects generally disliked the task, a not too surprising finding given its boring and tedious nature. More importantly, a significant interaction revealed that people high in need for cognition tended to prefer the complex to the simple task, whereas individuals low in need for cognition tended to prefer the simple to the complex task.

There is also evidence for the convergent and discriminant validity of our

Table 2-1. 18-Item Need for Cognition Scale

Item Number	Item Wording
1	I would prefer complex to simple problems.
2	I like to have the responsibility of handling a situation that requires a lot of thinking.
3	Thinking is not my idea of fun.*
4	I would rather do something that requires little thought than something that is sure to challenge my thinking abilities.*
5	I try to anticipate and avoid situations where there is likely chance I will have to think in depth about something.*
6	I find satisfaction in deliberating hard and for long hours.
7	I only think as hard as I have to.*
8	I prefer to think about small, daily projects to long-term ones.*
9	I like tasks that require little thought once I've learned them.*
10	The idea of relying on thought to make my way to the top appeals to me.
11	I really enjoy a task that involves coming up with new solutions to problems.
12	Learning new ways to think doesn't excite me very much.*
13	I prefer my life to be filled with puzzles that I must solve.
14	The notion of thinking abstractly is appealing to me.
15	I would prefer a task that is intellectual, difficult, and important to one that is somewhat important but does not require much thought.
16	I feel relief rather than satisfaction after completing a task that required a lot of mental effort.*
17	It's enough for me that something gets the job done; I don't care how or why it works.*
18	I usually end up deliberating about issues even when they do not affect me personally.

*Reverse scoring is used on this item.
Note: Subjects are asked to respond to the items on scales indicating their "agreement" or "disagreement," or to rate the extent to which the statements are "characteristic" or "uncharacteristic" of them (see Cacioppo & Petty, 1982).

conceptualization of need for cognition. In studies of personality variables we have found need for cognition to be: (a) positively and weakly related to field independence ($r = +0.19$, $N = 419$, $p < 0.05$), (b) negatively related to closed-mindedness ($r = -0.27$, $N = 104$, and $r = -0.23$, $N = 97$, $ps < 0.05$), (c) unrelated to Sarason's (1972) measure of test anxiety ($r = +0.02$, $N = 419$, n.s.), and (d) weakly if at all related to social desirability ($r = +0.08$, $N = 104$, n.s., and $r = +0.21$, N $= 97, p <0.05$). Olson, Camp, and Fuller (1984) found that the NCS correlated significantly with eight measures of curiosity (mean correlation $= +0.57$), but did not correlate significantly with social desirability, gender, or state or trait anger. Heppner, Reeder, and Larson (1983) found that subjects who scored high on a problem-solving inventory also had significantly higher NCS scores than subjects who scored low on the problem-solving inventory. Moreover, subjects high, in contrast to low, in need for cognition have been found to report possessing more prior knowledge about and confidence in their position on a broad range of attitude issues, and to express significantly more favorable attitudes toward positions that involved effortful thinking (e.g., instituting senior comprehensive exams, reading novels) but similar attitudes toward nonintellective issues (e.g., pets, sports, university tuition, money) (Sidera, 1983; Cacioppo, Petty, & Morris, 1983, pp. 810–811).

Cacioppo and Petty (1984b) found further evidence of the specificity of need for cognition. Subjects completed an inventory identifying situations that aroused fear and anxiety. Seven broad categories of stressors were examined. Analyses revealed that HNC people expressed significantly less fear and anxiety about matters involving academic challenges (e.g., "evaluation of performance," "tests and grades") than LNC individuals, but similar levels of fear and anxiety about being harmed physically, observing others being harmed physically, dating, establishing or maintaining relationships, and nonacademic aspects of college life. Similar levels of overall fear and anxiety were also found for individuals high versus low in need for cognition.

Importantly, evidence has also shown that individuals high in need for cognition are more intrinsically motivated to engage specifically in effortful cognitive analyses. Recent research has demonstrated that individuals put less effort into a task when they share responsibility for the outcome as part of a group than when they are individually responsible for the outcome (e.g., Ingham, Levinger, Graves, & Peckham, 1974). This effect, which has been dubbed "social loafing" (Latane, Williams, & Harkins, 1979), is equally evident in cognitive (Harkins & Petty, 1982), attitudinal (Petty, Harkins, & Williams, 1980), and physical tasks (Williams, Harkins, & Latane, 1981). We reasoned that if HNC individuals are more intrinsically motivated to engage in effortful cognitive endeavors, then they should be less likely to socially loaf on an interesting cognitive task than LNC individuals (Petty, Cacioppo, & Kasmer, 1985). To test this hypothesis, we asked subjects to perform a brainstorming task (generating uses for objects) after they were led to believe that they were individually responsible or part of a group that was responsible for performing the task. Results revealed a significant interaction showing that LNC subjects generated fewer ideas under group than individual conditions, whereas HNC subjects generated equally high numbers of ideas regardless of social condition. For comparison purposes, another group of subjects performed a cognitively unengaging physical task (screwing and unscrewing bolts and nuts) under individual or group instructions. Results revealed a main effect for social condition, showing greater loafing by subjects both low and high in need for cognition under the group conditions. These results are clearly consistent with the notion that individuals high in need for cognition are intrinsically motivated to engage in effortful cognitive endeavors in particular, and that this motivation has socially relevant behavioral consequences.

Although individuals high in need for cognition tend to engage in more effortful cognitive endeavors, this is not to suggest that their cognitive work is unfocused. In a study of person memory demonstrating this point, Srull, Lichtenstein, and Rothbart (1985) exposed subjects to congruent, incongruent, and irrelevant trait information. Results revealed that individuals high in need for cognition recalled more items than individuals low in need for cognition. This difference was most evident for incongruent items, moderate for congruent items, and nonsignificant for the items irrelevant to their forming a coherent impression. These data are consistent with the view that not only do individuals high in need for cognition think more about incoming information, but more specifically that they tend to elaborate upon previously unintegrated task-relevant information.

Finally, evidence for the notion that need for cognition can be used to assess chronic differences in elaboration likelihood via an individual differences approach has been obtained in field surveys as well as in the laboratory studies reviewed above. In a study conducted during the presidential election in the fall of 1984, Cacioppo, Petty, Kao, and Rodriguez (in press) matched subjects high and low in NC in terms of the attitudes they expressed toward the Democratic (Mondale/Ferraro) and Republican (Reagan/Bush) nominees 8 weeks prior to the election. Although this study is described in more detail in Chapter 7, for now we note that HNC subjects not only reported having thought more about and knowing more about the presidential candidates, but HNC individuals also listed significantly more facts about the presidential candidates than LNC individuals. Similarly, Ahlering and McClure (1985) found that significantly more HNC individuals reported intending to watch the presidential and vice-presidential debates and that HNC individuals actually produced significantly more thoughts regarding the consequences of electing a particular candidate than did LNC individuals. In another relevant study, Pieters (1986) surveyed residents of Columbia, Missouri to assess beliefs, attitudes, and intentions toward a city sponsored energy conservation program. The survey included an abbreviated version of the need for cognition scale. As expected, regression analyses revealed that the attitudes of high need for cognition subjects could be explained significantly by the perceived advantages and disadvantages of the energy program ($R = .62$), but this was not the case for those low in need for cognition ($R = .32$).

Summary
In sum, one of the major sources of variability in studies of attitude change is that attributable to individual differences. The ELM allows individual differences to be an integral part of theoretical thinking. Specifically, theory and research on need for cognition suggest that, unless overbearing situational constraints are operative, individuals high in need for cognition are characterized generally by higher levels of elaboration likelihood than individuals low in need for cognition. Hence, individuals high in need for cognition are consistently more likely to base their attitudes on a diligent analysis of relevant information, whereas individuals low in need for cognition should be more likely to utilize cognitively less taxing peripheral processes (see Cacioppo & Petty, 1984b; Heesacker, in press, for reviews). The role of need for cognition in persuasion is addressed explicity in Chapters 4 and 6.

Retrospective

In this chapter, we discussed methodological factors involved in testing the Elaboration Likelihood Model of persuasion. After discussing our typical procedures for assessing attitudes and persuasion, we operationalized the key constructs in the ELM. Specifically, procedures for assessing the constructs of argument quality, peripheral cues, and message elaboration were addressed. We ended the chapter with a discussion of individual differences in "need for cognition" and the role of this construct in testing the ELM. In the remaining chapters of this book we present the empirical research assessing the validity of the ELM. This research employs the methodological features outlined in this chapter.

Appendix: Examples of Strong and Weak Arguments Used to Create Strong and Weak Messages in Favor of Implementing Senior Comprehensive Exams[4]

Example Strong Arguments

S1. The National Scholarship Achievement Board recently revealed the results of a five-year study conducted on the effectiveness of comprehensive

---

[4]These arguments, typical of those used in our research employing the senior comprehensive exam topic (e.g., Cacioppo, Petty, & Morris, 1983; Petty & Cacioppo, 1979b, 1984a) are reprinted for illustrative purposes. It is important to note that our conceptualization of *strong* and *weak* messages is tied not to particular statements or arguments (such as those above), but to an empirical criterion. Specifically, strong messages should elicit a profile of predominately favorable thoughts (e.g., 65%

exams at Duke University. The results of the study showed that since the comprehensive exam has been introduced at Duke, the grade point average of undergraduates has increased by 31%. At comparable schools without the exams, grades increased by only 8% over the same period. The prospect of a comprehensive exam clearly seems to be effective in challenging students to work harder and faculty to teach more effectively. It is likely that the benefits observed at Duke University could also be observed at other universities that adopt the exam policy.

S2.   Graduate schools and law and medical schools are beginning to show clear and significant preferences for students who received their undergraduate degrees from institutions with comprehensive exams. As the Dean of the Harvard Business School said: "Although Harvard has not and will not discriminate on the basis of race or sex, we do show a strong preference for applicants who have demonstrated their expertise in an area of study by passing a comprehensive exam at the undergraduate level." Admissions officers of law, medical, and graduate schools have also endorsed the comprehensive exam policy and indicated that students at schools without the exams would be at a significant disadvantage in the very near future. Thus, the institution of comprehensive exams will be an aid to those who seek admission to graduate and professional schools after graduation.

S3.   A member of the Board of Curators has stated publicly that alumni nationwide have refused to increase their contributions to the University because of what they feel are lax educational standards. In fact, the prestigious National Accrediting Board of Higher Education (NAB) has recently rejected the University's application for membership citing lack of a comprehensive exam as a major reason. Accreditation by the NAB enhances a university's reputation to graduate schools, employers, and demonstrates to alumni that the school is worth supporting. A recent survey of influential alumni in corporations and the state legislature has revealed that contributions would improve significantly if the exams were instituted. With increased alumni support, continued increases in tuition might be avoided.

---

favorable, 35% unfavorable) when subjects are instructed to think about them, but weak messages should elicit a profile of predominately unfavorable thoughts (e.g., 65% unfavorable, 35% favorable) when subjects are instructed to scrutinize them. Since the thoughts elicited by particular arguments and messages might be expected to vary with different people, times, and contexts, pretesting is an essential aspect of message construction for any given experiment. For example, over the past 10 years we have found that students have generally become more knowledgeable about and accepting of the senior comprehensive exam idea. One consequence of this is that over the years we have had to develop arguments that are more specious in order to create empirically "weak" messages on this topic.

S4. A study conducted by the Educational Testing Service of Princeton, New Jersey, revealed that most of the Ivy League schools and several of the Big 10 universities have senior comprehensive exams to maintain their academic excellence. Professors at those schools who were interviewed recently said that senior comprehensive exams assured that only high quality and knowledgeable students would be associated with the university. This, of course, increases the prestige of current students, alumni of the school, and the university as a whole. The exams should be instituted to increase the academic reputation of the university. A national educator's publication recently predicted that within the next 10 years, the top universities would have the exam policy, and the weaker ones would not.

S5. An interesting and important feature of the comprehensive exam requirement is that it has led to a significant improvement in the quality of undergraduate teaching in the schools where it has been tried. Data from the Educational Testing Service confirm that teachers and courses at the schools with comprehensive exams were rated more positively by students after the exams than before. The improvement in teaching effectiveness appears to be due to departments placing more emphasis on high quality and stimulating teaching because departments look bad when their majors do poorly on the exam. For example, at the University of Florida, student ratings of courses increased significantly after comprehensive exams were instituted.

S6. One aspect of the comprehensive exam requirement that students at the schools where it has been tried seem to like is that all regular final examinations for seniors are typically eliminated. This elimination of final exams in all courses for seniors allows them to better integrate and think about the material in their major area just prior to graduation rather than "wasting" a lot of time cramming to pass tests in courses in which they are really not interested. Students presently have to take too many courses in subjects that are irrelevant to their career plans. The comprehensive exam places somewhat greater emphasis on the student's major and allows greater concentration on the material that the student feels is most relevant.

S7. Faculty members at universities with the comprehensive exams who were interviewed by researchers from the Carnegie Commission on Higher Education revealed that the comprehensive exams appeared to provide an incentive for students to study the material in their major area. A thorough study undertaken by the Department of Education at the University of Notre Dame showed that universities with comprehensive exams have resisted the national trend of declining scores on standardized achievement tests. Average scores on achievement tests for the universities with comprehensive exams have actually risen over the last five years.

S8. Data from the University of Virginia, where comprehensive exams were recently instituted, indicate that the average starting salary of graduates increased over $4000 over the two-year period in which the exams were begun. At comparable universities without comprehensive exams, salaries increased only $850 over the same period. As Saul Siegel, a vice-president of IBM put it in *Business Week* recently, "We are much quicker to offer the large salaries and executive positions to these kids because by passing their area exam, they have proven to us that they have expertise in their area rather than being people who may or may not be dependable and reliable." Another benefit is that universities with the exams attract larger and more well-known corporations to campus to recruit students for their open positions. The end result is that students at schools with comprehensive exams have a 55% greater chance of landing a good job than students at schools without the exams.

S9. A study by the U.S. Department of Education revealed that universities with the comprehensive exam requirement average about 32% more financial aid available to students than comparable universities without the exams. Richard Collings, Director of Financial Aid at the University of Southern California (USC) has written that since the comprehensive exam was instituted at USC five years ago, more individuals and corporations have been willing to donate money for student scholarships.

Example Weak Arguments

W1. The National Scholarship Achievement Board recently revealed the results of a study they conducted on the effectiveness of comprehensive exams at Duke University. One major finding was that student anxiety had increased by 31%. At comparable schools without the exam, anxiety increased by only 8%. The Board reasoned that anxiety over the exams, or fear of failure, would motivate students to study more in their courses while they were taking them. It is likely that this increase in anxiety observed at Duke University would also be observed and be of benefit at other universities that adopt the exam policy.

W2. Graduate students have always had to take a comprehensive exam in their major area before receiving their degrees, and it is only fair that undergraduates should have to take them also. As the Dean of the Harvard Business School said, "If a comprehensive exam is considered necessary to demonstrate competence for a masters or doctoral degree, by what logic is it excluded as a requirement for the bachelors degree? What administrators don't realize is that this is discrimination just like discrimination against Blacks or Jews. There would be a lot of trouble if universities required only whites to take comprehensive exams but not Blacks. Yet universities all over the country are getting away with the same thing by requiring graduate students but not undergraduates to take the exams." Thus, the institution of comprehensive exams could be as useful for undergraduates as they have been for graduate students.

W3. A member of the Board of Curators has stated publicly that his brother had to take a comprehensive exam while in college and now he is manager of a large restaurant. He indicated that he realized the value of the exams since their father was a migrant worker who didn't even finish high school. He also indicated that the university has received several letters from parents in support of the exam. In fact, 4 of the 6 parents who wrote in thought that the exams were an excellent idea. Also, the prestigious National Accrediting Board of Higher Education seeks input from parents as well as students, faculty, and administrators when evaluating a university. Since most parents contribute financially to their child's education and also favor the exams, the university should institute them. This would show that the university is willing to listen to and follow the parents' wishes over those of students and faculty who may simply fear the work involved in comprehensive exams.

W4. A study conducted by the Educational Testing Service of Princeton, New Jersey revealed that many universities are considering adopting comprehensive exams. Thus, any university that adopted the exams could be at the forefront of a national trend. Some professors at schools with the exams who were interviewed felt that high school students would be impressed by a university that kept pace with current trends. In fact, whether or not a school had a comprehensive exam might be a determining factor in their choice of a university. Therefore, the enrollments of universities with the exams should increase as the information about the exams spreads among high school students.

W5. An interesting and important feature of the comprehensive exam requirement is that if the exams were instituted nationwide, students across the country could use the exam to compare their achievements with those of students at other schools. Data from the Educational Testing Service confirm that students are eager to compare their grades in a particular course with those of other students. Just imagine how exciting it would be for students in the Midwest to be able to compare their scores with those of students at the University of Florida, for example. This possibility for comparison would provide an incentive for students to study and achieve as high a score as possible so they would not be embarassed when comparing scores with their friends.

W6. One feature of the comprehensive exam requirement that students at the schools where it has been tried seem to like is that passing the exams provides a very difficult challenge. For example, many students want jobs in business when they graduate and the corporate world is very tough. Yet, most students' lives are filled with few challenges whatsoever. Everything has been provided for them since the day they were born. It's not that students are not grateful, but knowing that they had to pass a difficult exam before they graduated would prepare them for the hard and cold realities of life. Students would be nervous about passing the exam and fear that if they did not pass and graduate, four years of time would be wasted. However, that is what life is all about—taking risks and overcoming them. Having to pass a comprehensive exam is a challenge most students would welcome.

W7.   Faculty members at universities with the comprehensive exams who were interviewed by researchers from the Carnegie Commission on Higher Education revealed that they liked the exams because it reduced the number of tests they felt they had to give in their classes knowing that students would still face one ultimate test of their knowledge in the comprehensive exam. A study at Norte Dame showed that this reduction in regular course tests saved enough paper to cover the cost of painting two classrooms.

W8.   Data from the University of Virginia show that some students favor the senior comprehensive exam policy. For example, one faculty member asked his son to survey his fellow students at the school since it recently instituted the exams. Over 55% of his son's friends agreed that in principle, the exams would be beneficial. Of course, they didn't all agree but the fact that most did proves that undergraduates want the exams. As Saul Siegel, a student whose father is a vice-president of IBM wrote in the school newspaper: "The history of the exams can be traced to the ancient Greeks. If comprehensive exams were to be instituted, we could feel pleasure at following traditions begun by Plato and Aristotle. Even if there were no other benefits of the exams, it would be worth it just to follow tradition."

W9.   A study by the U.S. Department of Education revealed that several national testing companies were developing comprehensive exams for use by universities in the U.S. The tests would be similar to the SAT and ACT tests which currently generate millions of dollars for the companies that make them. Richard Collings, a former Director of Financial Aid at the University of Southern California who now works for the Educational Testing Service, wrote recently in *Business Week:* "At ETS, we are not pushing comprehensive exams simply because of the huge amount of money involved. We are genuinely interested in marketing a good product. Just as our SAT and GRE tests are used to determine who is qualified for college and graduate work, so too should our comprehensive exams be used to determine who should graduate from college. We expect to have 32% of the market in 5 years."

Chapter 3
The Ability to Elaborate in a Relatively Objective Manner

Introduction

If a person is going to carefully scrutinize the arguments in a persuasive message and thereby follow the central route to persuasion, the person must have the *ability* to evaluate the arguments. Some people may have a greater ability to process a message than others, and some persuasion situations will provide a better opportunity for relatively objective elaboration than others. As we noted in Chapter 2, it is possible to tell whether a target variable enhances or reduces argument processing in a relatively objective manner by manipulating argument quality along with the target variable. If the variable enhances argument processing, subjects' thoughts and attitudes should be more polarized when the variable is present rather than absent, but if the variable reduces argument processing, subjects' thoughts and attitudes should be less polarized when the variable is present rather than absent. In this chapter, we first highlight three variables that appear to affect information processing in a relatively objective way—distraction, message repetition, and recipient posture. Then, we will briefly note some additional variables that may also affect relatively objective information processing.

Factors Affecting the Ability to Elaborate Objectively

Effects of Distraction on Message Elaboration and Persuasion

Research on the effects of distraction on persuasion can be traced to an intriguing experiment by Allyn & Festinger (1961) in which high school students were presented with a speech which argued that teenage drivers are dangerous. The students were either forewarned of the message topic and told that their attitudes would be assesed (attitude orientation) or were simply told that they were to assesss the personality of the speaker (personality orientation). Although these two conditions did not differ in the average attitude change they induced, when analyses were conducted on the most involved subjects (those with extreme attitudes or those who said the issue was important), a significant difference was found such that there was more persuasion in the personality than in the attitude orientation condition. Two possible explanations for this effect were offered. The initial explanation favored by Allyn and Festinger was that the forewarning in the attitude orientation condition stimulated the involved students to counterargue and/or derrogate the source (see also Freedman & Sears, 1965). A second explanation, proposed intitially by Festinger and Maccoby (1964) was that the involved subjects in the personality orientation condition were distracted from the counterarguing and/or source derrogating that normally would have occurred.

In the 25 years since the Allyn and Festinger experiment, a considerable number of studies have accumulated on both "forewarning" and "distraction," and it is now clear that both effects are viable. In this section we apply the ELM framework to "distraction" and discuss how this variable appears to work by affecting information processing in a relatively *objective* manner. In Chapter 5 we apply the ELM to "forewarning" and address how this variable appears to work by affecting information processing in a relatively *biased* manner.

In 1973, Baron, Baron, and Miller reviewed the accumulated research on "distraction" and concluded that although many individual studies were susceptible to a wide variety of mediational interpretations, there were just two theoretical explanations that could account for the existing data parsimoniously. One explanation was the disruption of counterarguing interpretation favored by Festinger and Maccoby. Another interpretation offered by Baren et al., however, was based, ironically, on Festigner's (1957) theory of cognitive dissonance. Baron et al. argued that distraction manipulations require subjects to exert more effort than usual in order to understand the message. Furthermore, "since choosing to hear a counterattitudinal message can be viewed as attitude-discrepant behavior, the effort required to comprehend a counterattitudinal message will directly determine the amount of dissonance created by the choice" (p. 317). One way for subjects to reduce this dissonance, of course, is for them to justify their effort by overvaluing the communication.

At the time of the review by Baron et al., the available experiments did not allow a distinction between the two alternative theories because evidence that appeared to support either the counterargument or the dissonance position could also be seen as consistent with the other position. For example, the early Festinger and Maccoby study indicated that distraction enhanced persuasion for counterattitudinal but not proattitudinal messages. Was this because only counterattitudinal messages elicited counterarguments, or because counterattitudinal messages induced more dissonance?

Similarly, the accumulated research suggested that distraction enhanced persuasion only when attention was focused on the message and not on the distraction (e.g., Insko, Turnbull, & Yandell, 1974; Zimbardo, Synder, Thomas, Gold, & Gurwitz, 1970). Was this because message attention enhanced counterarguing, or was it because message attention made the attitude-discrepant behavior of choosing to listen to the advocacy more salient? Importantly, even research using the thought-listing technique, which showed that with increasing distraction the number of counterarguments listed decreased (Keating & Brock, 1974; Osterhouse & Brock, 1970), was open to multiple interpretations. Was a reduction in negative thoughts obtained with distraction because distraction disrupted counterarguing, or was it because distraction induced attitude change via dissonance (or some other process), which was subsequently justified in the thought-listings (Miller & Baron, 1973)?

Testing the Disruption of Message Elaboration Hypothesis
Our initial use of the manipulation of strong and weak arguments (see Chapter 2) came in an experiment that attempted to distinguish the dissonance from the counterargument disruption interpretations of distraction (Petty, Wells, & Brock, 1976, Experiment 1). A second aim of our experiment was to test a more general distraction formulation than "counterargument disruption." Specifically, we reasoned that if the predominant thoughts to a message without distraction were unfavorable, then distraction should disrupt these unfavorable thoughts and lead to increased agreement. However, if the predominant thoughts to a message without distraction were favorable, then distraction should disrupt these favorable thoughts resulting in decreased agreement. Our manipulation of argument quality provides a means of assessing this general "elaboration disruption" hypothesis as well as testing it against the predicted results from dissonance theory.

The disruption of elaboration interpretation holds that distraction should enhance persuasion for a message containing weak arguments (because unfavorable thoughts should dominate under no distraction and would therefore be disrupted), but that distraction should *reduce* persuasion for a message containing strong arguments (because favorable thoughts should dominate under no distraction and would be disrupted). The predictions from dissonance theory are quite different, however. Research on selective exposure and attention indicates that people prefer to hear weak rather than strong arguments against their own position (Kleinhesselink & Edwards, 1975; Lowin, 1967), suggesting that exerting effort to hear strong counterattitudinal arguments induces more dissonance than exerting effort to hear weak ones. Because of this, dissonance theory predicts that for counterattitudinal messages, distraction should enhance persuasion more for strong arguments than for weak ones.

Method. A total of 132 students participated in a 4 (Distraction: no, low, medium, high) × 2 (Argument quality: weak, strong) × 2 (Order of attitude assessment: before or after thought-listing) between-subjects factorial design. Subjects were tested in groups while seated in cubicles constructed so that no subject could have visual or auditory contact with other subjects. During any one session, in which one level of distraction was run, some subjects heard strong message arguments while others heard weak message arguments.

Upon arrival at the lab, subjects were told that the experiment concerned the ability to do two things at once. The subjects were told that while they listened to the message, an X would flash periodically in one of the four quadrants of a screen before them. Their task was to record on monitor recording forms the quadrant in which the X appeared. Subjects were either told that "no Xs would flash for now," (no distraction), or the Xs appeared on the screen at 15- (low distraction), 5- (medium distraction), or 3- (high distraction) second intervals during the message. All subjects were instructed to try to pay close attention to the message as they monitored the Xs. It is important to note that the manipulation of distraction was also intended to be a manipulation of effort expenditure (i.e., no, low, medium, and high effort). This was crucial for allowing a test of the dissonance versus disruption of message elaboration interpretations.

Two discrepant messages were prepared for our study. Both messages argued that tuition at the students' university should be increased by 20%, but the messages differed in the presentation of five key arguments. As explained in Chapter 2, the strong arguments were selected so that they elicited primarily favorable thoughts when subjects were instructed to think about them (e.g., raising tuition would allow needed library improvements to be made), and the weak arguments were selected so that they elicited primarily negative thoughts (e.g., raising tuition would allow more trees to be planted on campus). Ratings in a pretest indicated that the messages did not differ in the extent to which they were "difficult to understand," "hard to follow," or possessed "complex structure." Each message was approximately 3 minutes long when recorded. After hearing one of the messages over headphones, subjects completed attitude measures, were given 2.5 minutes to list their thoughts (with the order of attitude and thought assessment counterbalanced), and responded to ancillary questions.

Results. Analyses of manipulation checks revealed that subjects reported feeling increasingly distracted from paying attention to the message and that the task was perceived as increasingly effortful as the number of Xs that flashed increased. Furthermore, analyses revealed that across all levels of distraction, 41% of the thoughts listed in the weak argument conditions were unfavorable, 35% were favorable, and 24% were neutral or irrelevant; whereas in the strong argument conditions 30% were unfavorable, 48% were favorable, and 22% were neutral or irrelevant.

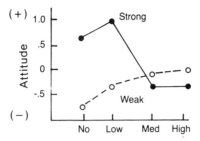

Figure 3-1. Postmessage attitudes as a function of distraction and argument quality (data from Petty, Wells, & Brock, 1976, Experiment 1).

Order of attitude/thought assessment did not affect the attitude or thought measures. The attitude results are presented in Figure 3-1. Consistent with the general elaboration disruption hypothesis, a significant Argument quality × Distraction interaction was obtained: increasing distraction was associated with more favorable attitudes when the message was weak, but increasing distraction was associated with less favorable attitudes when the message was strong. Importantly, this interaction supports the elaboration disruption hypothesis, but is inconsistent with the effort justification prediction, which expected message acceptance to increase with effort/distraction for both messages.[1]

Analyses of the postmessage thoughts listed indicated that overall the messages differed in the number of counterarguments they elicited. In addition, high distraction reduced the production of unfavorable thoughts for the weak, but not the strong message; high distraction tended to reduce the number of favorable thoughts elicited by the strong ($p < 0.10$), but not the weak message. Finally, subjects' recall of the message arguments was assessed. This measure indicated that the recall scores for the no, low, and medium groups did not differ from each other, but the high distraction group recalled fewer arguments than any of the other groups. It is important to note that the attitudinal effects of distraction were most evident between the low and medium distraction groups, consistent with the disruption of message elaboration hypothesis (i.e., the drop in recall did not mediate the effect of distraction on attitudes). Certainly at some high level of distraction, reception of the message could be so severely impaired that this would outweigh other processess (cf., Romer, 1979).

---

[1] In addition, a main effect for message quality was observed (strong arguments induced more agreement than weak arguments). Since this message main effect is also apparent in virtually all of the studies that we report, we will not note this repeatedly for the remaining studies. Instead, we will highlight the more theoretically interesting interaction effects. All ps for effects noted here and throughout the text are < 0.05 unless otherwise noted.

Extending the Generality of the Elaboration-Disruption Hypothesis
The elaboration-disruption hypothesis predicts that, given message reception is comparable across conditions, the dominant thoughts to the message are disrupted by distraction. This effect should hold whether the message topic is proattitudinal or counterattitudinal. Although the results of the previous experiment were consistent with the elaboration-disruption hypothesis, the reduction in favorable thoughts with distraction was only marginally significant. To provide a better test of favorable thought disruption, strong and weak *proattitudinal* messages were employed in a second study (Petty, Wells, & Brock, 1976, Experiment 2).

Method. In this study, 54 students participated in a 2 (Distraction: low or medium) × 2 (Argument quality: weak or strong) between-subjects factorial design. The procedure and cover story were the same as employed in the preceding experiment, as were the operationalizations of low and medium distraction. These middle levels of distraction were selected because although these levels affected perceptions of distraction and effort, they did not affect message recall. All subjects were exposed to a message arguing that the tuition at their university should be reduced by 50%. As in the first study, two messages were prepared supporting this position, one containing weak arguments and one containing strong arguments. After hearing one of the messages over headphones, all subjects responded to the attitude, thought-listing, and ancillary measures.

Results. Analyses of manipulation checks again revealed that subjects reported feeling increasingly distracted from attending to the message and that the task was increasingly effortful as distraction increased. Furthermore, analyses revealed that consistent with pilot testing, 60% of the thoughts listed in the weak argument conditions were unfavorable, 27% were favorable, and 13% were neutral or irrelevant. In the strong argument conditions 8% of the thoughts listed were unfavorable, 62% were favorable,

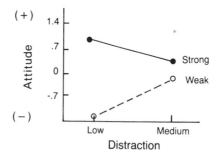

Figure 3-2. Postmessage attitudes as a function of distraction and argument quality (data from Petty, Wells, & Brock, 1976, Experiment 2).

and 30% were neutral or irrelevant. Finally, as anticipated, distraction had no effects on the number of arguments subjects could recall.

The attitude results are presented in Figure 3-2. As in the previous study, the crucial Argument quality × Distraction interaction was obtained: distraction was associated with increased agreement when the message was weak, but with decreased agreement when the message was strong. Analyses of the postmessage thoughts listed showed that increasing distraction decreased the number of unfavorable thoughts elicited by the weak message and decreased the number of favorable thoughts elicited by the strong message.[2] As was the case for the preceding study, these data support the elaboration-disruption hypothesis over explanations based on effort justification or message learning.

Additional Support for the Elaboration-Disruption Hypothesis

Two conceptual replications of our distraction studies have been reported. In one, Lammers and Becker (1980) had undergraduates listen to either a counterattitudinal message in favor of doubling tuition (which elicited predominantly unfavorable thoughts) or a proattitudinal message opposed to raising tuition (which elicited predominantly favorable thoughts). After hearing the message under one of the three levels of distraction (judging the pleasantness of irrelevant slides presented at varying rates), subjects rated the perceived extremity of the message's position. Under increasing distraction, subjects tended to see the proattitudinal message as being further from their own position (presumably indicating greater rejection of the message with increasing distraction), and the counterattitudinal message as being closer to their own position (presumably indicating greater acceptance of the message with increasing distraction).

In a closer conceptual replication, Tsal (1984) prepared strong and weak messages (print ads) for a variety of consumer products. As subjects were exposed to the ads via slides, they were either not distracted or were required to count the number of random "clicks" presented on tape. An analysis of subjects' attitudes toward the products revealed a Message quality × Distraction interaction (see Figure 3-3). Distraction was associated with more favorable attitudes toward the products when the ad arguments were weak, but with less favorable attitudes toward the products when the ad arguments were strong.

The accumulated literature is very consistent with the view that distraction is one variable that affects a person's ability to process a message in a relatively objective manner. Specifically, distraction disrupts the thoughts that would normally be elicited by a message. If the thoughts would normally have been mostly favorable, distraction reduces agreement. If the

---

[2]Since the thought data follow and support the attitude data in virtually all of the studies that we report in this volume, we will not detail the thought-listing results for most of the remaining studies. Readers should consult the original reports.

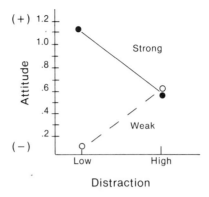

Figure 3-3. Postmessage attitudes as a function of distraction and argument quality (data from Tsal, 1984).

thoughts would normally have been mostly unfavorable, then distraction is associated with enhanced agreement. Distraction should be especially important as a disruptor of message elaboration when people would normally be highly motivated and able to process the message. If motivation and/or ability to process the message would normally be low, distraction should have little effect. The accumulated literature is consistent with this proposition (see Petty & Brock, 1981, for a review).

Effects of Moderate Message Repetition on Message Elaboration and Persuasion

Just as some variables, such as distraction, disrupt message processing, others, such as message repetition, may enhance message processing. Early thinking regarding the effects of message repetition on persuasion came from two sources. One source was from the message learning orientation of Hovland and his colleagues. For instance, Hovland, Janis, and Kelley (1953) stated that "exposure to a persuasive communication which successfully induces the individual to accept a new opinion constitutes a learning experience in which a new verbal habit is acquired" (p. 10). According to Hovland and his associates, then, changing an attitude involves changing a verbal habit. According to this logic, repetition of a persuasive communication, which enhances the likelihood and extent a person attends to, comprehends, and retains the advocacy, should generally increase the likelihood or amount of attitude change, as well (McGuire, 1969).

Evidence consistent with this analysis was provided by McCullough and Ostrom (1974), who presented several different pictorial advertisements to individuals. The presentations of these different advertisements led to more positive evaluations of the product than a single presentation of any one of the advertisements. This study, however, does not address whether the repeated exposures or the varied advertisements were instrumental in enhancing the regard for the product. Nevertheless, their findings are compatible with Hovland's notion of message learning and attitude change.

A second major framework for understanding repetition stems from the work by Zajonc and his colleagues on mere exposure (see reviews by Harrison, 1977; Sawyer, 1981). Zajonc (1968) reported that a person's attitude toward a stimulus was related positively to its exposure frequency, an effect he attributed to the pleasantness associated with exposure to an increasingly familiar stimulus. Reinterpreting Zajonc's findings, Stang (1975) suggested that these attitudinal effects were mediated by the individual's satisfaction in having learned the attributes of the stimulus (cf., Birnbaum & Mellers, 1979). Although subsequent research by Zajonc and his colleagues (e.g., Kunst-Wilson & Zajonc, 1980; Moreland & Zajonc, 1967) suggests that exposure frequency independently alters both the subjective familiarity and the recognizability of the stimulus, Zajonc (1968) has emphasized that his model applies to nonassociative stimuli (e.g., nonsense syllables, ideographs). More interestingly for theoretical analyses of message repetition is that Sawyer (1981) has argued that Zajonc's mere exposure model may apply to message repetition effects. Also, Stang's (1975) learning perspective on mere exposure, when applied to persuasive communications, is indistinguishable in its predictions from Hovland's message-learning formulation.

Contrary to the predictions of these formulations, however, repetition of meaningful verbal stimuli has not only been shown to increase liking (e.g., McCullough & Ostrom, 1974), but also to decrease liking (e.g., Cantor, 1968; Grush, 1976) and to have no effect on attitudes (e.g., Belch, 1982). Indeed, the most common finding in the persuasion literature is that repeating a persuasive communication tends to first increase and then decrease agreement (e.g., Cacioppo & Petty, 1979b; Calder, & Sternthal, 1980; Gorn & Goldberg, 1980; Miller, 1976).

Based on the ELM, all of these effects are to be expected under prescribable conditions. Specifically, we have proposed that message repetition guides a sequence of reactions to a persuasive communication best conceptualized as a two-stage attitude-modification process (Cacioppo & Petty, 1979b, 1985). In the first stage, repeated presentations of a persuasive communication provide recipients with a greater opportunity to consider the associations and implications of the advocacy in a relatively objective manner. In a persuasion context, subjects should be better able to discern the merits of an advocacy with moderate repetition. Thus, just as distraction can disrupt information processing, moderate message repetition can enhance a person's ability to process the message arguments. The benefit of repetiton should be most apparent when additional opportunities are needed to process a message, such as when ability to process the full implications of the message with only one exposure is low (e.g., the message is not very simple). Once a person has exhausted the associations and has fully considered the implications of the stimulus, the second processing stage becomes dominant. In this stage, attitudinal processes are driven by tedium and/or reactance. Both tedium and reactance will tend to result in decreased message acceptance either by serving as simple negative affective cues or by biasing the nature of message elaboration in a negative direction (see Chapter 5). In this section we explore the consequences of the first (objective) stage of information processing.

It is important to note that in considering the effects of repetition that the number of repetitions required to enhance argument processing but not induce tedium or reactance will depend on a numer of factors. For example, the more complex, the more lengthy, or the more rapidly the message is presented, the more repetitions that may be necessary for the full implications of the arguments to be realized. Conversely, the more familiar subjects are with the arguments or information in the message, the fewer the repetitions that may be required to induce tedium or reactance (Batra & Ray, 1986). Thus, what is "moderate" and what is "excessive" repetition will depend on a number of factors (see Cacioppo & Petty, 1985). In our own research, the levels of message repetition appropriate for our specific messages were determined in pilot research.

Testing the Enhancement of Message Elaboration Hypothesis
In order to provide a test of our view that moderate repetition affects persuasion by increasing the opportunity to scrutinize arguments in a relatively objective manner, we conducted a study in which students were exposed to a moderately complex message that was presented either once or three consecutive times (see Cacioppo & Petty, 1985). The message learning, mere exposure, and message elaboration hypotheses can all accommodate repetition increasing message recall. However, the theories differ in their predictions regarding postcommunication attitudes. The elaboration enhancement interpretation predicts the joint outcome that more favorable attitudes are fostered by moderate repetition of strong message arguments, whereas less favorable attitudes are fostered by moderate repetition of weak message arguments. In contrast, the simple message learning hypothesis holds that agreement should increase as learning increases (Stang, 1974); and the mere exposure hypothesis as applied to message repetition (cf., Sawyer, 1981) holds that more positive attitudes develop as the number of exposures increases whether the stimulus is initially evaluated positively or negatively (Zajonc, Shaver, Tavris, & Vankreveld, 1972).

Method. A total of 105 students participated in a 2 (Message repetition: 1 or 3 exposures) × 2 (Argument quality: strong or weak) between-subjects factorial design. Upon arrival at the lab, subjects were instructed that they were to listen carefully to a message prepared by a campus group using one of several different recording techniques and that their task was to answer questions about the sound quality of the tape following their exposure to the message. All subjects heard a message advocating that seniors at their university be required to pass a comprehensive exam in their major area as a requirement for graduation. As in our work on distraction, half of the subjects heard a message containing strong arguments and half heard a message containing weak arguments. In addition, half of the subjects heard the message once, and half heard the message three times in succession. Immediately following the presentation of the message, subjects were told that since their attitudes toward the recommendation might affect how they rated the sound quality of the audiotape, we wanted to know how they felt about the issue. Subjects responded to attitude, recall, and ancillary measures.

Results. As expected, subjects recalled more message arguments when the message was presented three times than when the message was presented once. An analysis of subjects' postcommunication attitudes toward the senior comprehensive exam issue revealed an Argument quality × Repetition interaction (see Figure 3-4) mirroring that found for distraction in the research described above. Specifically, the interaction was a result of the fact that moderate repetition led subjects to express more positive attitudes toward the recommendation when it was supported by a set of strong arguments, whereas moderate repetition caused subjects to express more negative attitudes toward the recommendation when it was supported by a set of weak arguments. This particular interaction pattern is inconsistent with the simple learning or mere exposure accounts of message repetition and supports the view that moderate repetition affects attitudes by enhancing message elaboration.

Extending the Generality of the Elaboration-Enhancement Hypothesis
The studies on distraction and repetition described thus far were characterized by the immediate measurement of attitudes in the same laboratory context in which the persuasive message was presented. Although this procedure allows strict control of irrelevant features and maximizes impact of the independent variables, the effects of elaboration on attitudes should

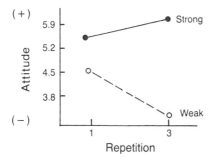

Figure 3-4. Postmessage attitudes as a function of repetition and argument quality (data from Cacioppo & Petty, 1985).

not be confined to this measurement context. In order to extend the generality of our analysis of ability to elaborate, we conducted a second study in which the crucial attitude measure was dissociated in time and setting from the message presentation (Cacioppo & Petty, 1980a, Experiment 2).

Method. A total of 89 students participated in a 3 (Message repetition: 1, 3, or 5 presentations) × 2 (Argument quality: strong, weak) between-subjects factorial design.[3] In this study, students were exposed to a strong or weak message in favor of raising the price of their local newspaper. The message was presented to subjects as an audiotape of a telephone interview with a local resident. The strong message emphasized the benefits subscribers would receive from the price increase, whereas the weak message emphasized the benefits to management. The message was played either 1, 3, or 5 times in succession, and as in the previous study, subjects were instructed to evaluate the sound quality of the tapes.

Immediately following exposure, subjects listed their thoughts about the tapes, rated the sound quality, and recalled all of the message arguments they could remember. From 8 to 14 days later, individuals were contacted by a phone interviewer who appeared unrelated to the initial experimeter. The second experimenter, who was blind to the respondents' initial experimental conditions, inquired about a number of community issues including attitudes toward increasing the price of the local paper.

Results. Consistent with the previous study on message repetition, recall of both strong and weak message arguments increased with repeated exposures. Analyses of the thought-listings indicated that the strong arguments elicited more favorable thoughts and nonsignificantly fewer unfavorable thoughts than the weak arguments. Importantly, analyses of the attitude data revealed an Argument quality × Repetition interaction (see Figure 3-5). Consistent with the elaboration-enhancement hypothesis, the interaction was a result of the fact that moderate repetition led subjects to express more positive attitudes toward the recommendation when it was supported by a set of strong arguments, whereas moderate repetition caused subjects to express more negative attitudes toward the recommendation when it was supported by a set of weak arguments.

Additional Support for the Elaboration-Enhancement Hypothesis
Corlett (1984) recently reported a conceptual replication of our repetition studies using mock television advertisements rather than audiotaped editorials. Corlett developed strong and weak versions of advertisements

---

[3]For exploratory purposes, a third group of subjects received a message containing novel arguments that were weak but "subtly contradictory." Subjects exposed to this message showed an inverted-U pattern of acceptance with repetition.

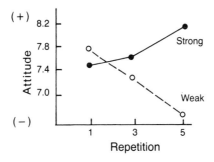

Figure 3-5. Delayed attitudes as a function of repetition and argument quality (data from Cacioppo & Petty, 1980b).

promoting a little-known beer. Half of the subjects were exposed to the strong version of the advertisement embedded among other commercials in a 60-min television show, and half of the subjects were exposed to the weak version of the advertisement. Results indicated that male undergraduates expressed more positive attitudes toward the beer as exposures increased from 1 to 3 when the ad-arguments were strong, but they expressed more negative attitudes as repetition increased when the ad-arguments were weak (see Figure 3-6).[4] Interestingly, repetition had no significant impact on the attitudes of female students. These results are interesting in light of the fact that males are the primary consumers of beer and, therefore are more likely to view advertisements regarding beer as personally relevant. As we have already noted and will document in the next chapter, both motivation (e.g., personal relevance) and ability (e.g., distraction, repetition) variables are important determinants of the extent of message elaboration.

Effects of Recipient Posture on Message Elaboration and Persuasion

Although evidence continues to accumulate regarding how nonverbal bodily cues emanating from a communicator can affect perceptions of the source (e.g., Argyle & Kendon, 1967; Zuckerman, DePaulo & Rosenthal, 1981; Mehrabian, 1981) and thereby persuasion (e.g., McGinley, LeFevre, & McGinley, 1975), little attention has been paid to how the bodily orientation of a message recipient affects message processing and persuasion. In an exploratory study we had undergraduates listen to a cogent message advocating a 20% increase in tuition at their university while they were positioned in one of several postures—standing, sitting, or reclining (Petty,

---

[4]When repetitions were increased to more extreme levels (5 and 7 exposures), subjects hearing the strong arguments showed a slight (nonsignificant) decline in attitudes, and subjects exposed to the weak arguments showed a more substantial decline. See Chapter 5 for discussion of excessive repetition.

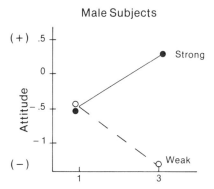

Figure 3-6. Postmessage attitudes for male subjects as a function of moderate repetition and argument quality (data from Corlett, 1984).

Wells, Heesacker, Brock, & Cacioppo, 1983, Experiment 1). The results of this study indicated that subjects who were reclining on a cushioned table while listening to the message expressed more agreement with a tuition increase than subjects who were standing during message exposure. Interestingly, although subjects who were seated during message exposure indicated that they were the most "comfortable," they were no more persuaded than standing or supine subjects. Additionally, the insignificant correlation between rated comfort and message agreement ($r = 0.07$) provided evidence against the view that posture influenced attitudes simply by inducing a pleasant affect or mood that became associated with the advocacy. It was possible, however, that the supine posture was associated with greater message elaboration. Since the arguments in the message were strong, the results of greater scrutiny would be enhanced agreement.

Testing the Message Processing Hypothesis
In order to provide a specific test of the elaboration interpretation, we conducted a second study in which recipient posture was manipulated along with the quality of the issue-relevant arguments contained in the message (Petty, Wells, Heesacker, Brock, & Cacioppo, 1983, Experiment 2).

Method. In this study, 65 female students participated in a 2 (Body posture: standing or reclining) × 2 (Argument quality: strong or weak) between-subjects factorial design. Subjects were told that they were participating in a cooperative investigation between the psychology department and Tech-Headphones, Inc. It was explained that the headphone company was funding a study that would provide information about basic auditory processes and about how to design headphones to provide maximum listening pleasure in a wide variety of naturalistic settings. Following these instructions, subjects were led to individual cubicles where they were instructed either to stand or to lie down on a cot while listening through their headphones. The subjects were told that they would hear a brief excerpt from a recent campus radio broadcast. After they had assumed the appropriate posture, they heard several minutes of instrumental music followed by an editorial message arguing that seniors should be required to pass a comprehensive exam in their major area as a requirement for graduation. After hearing either the strong or the weak arguments version of this editorial, subjects expressed their attitudes on the issue, listed their thoughts, rated the headphones, and responded to ancillary measures.

Results. Subjects reported that they were more comfortable in the reclining than in the standing posture, and that they were less "distracted" from thinking about the editorial in the supine position. The attitude results are presented in Figure 3-7. Of greatest interest was the appearance of a significant Argument quality × Posture interaction that provided support for the view that a reclining posture facilitates (or a standing posture disrupts) careful processing of a message. A decomposition of the interaction revealed that subjects did not attitudinally distinguish the strong from the weak arguments when they were processed in the standing position, but that the arguments did differ significantly in their persuasibility when processed in the reclining posture.

Unanswered Questions about Posture
Although it appears clear that posture is capable of influencing message elaboration and thereby persuasion, at least two important questions about recipient posture remain unanswered. One concerns *why* a reclining posture facilitates and/or a standing posture inhibits message-relevant thinking. One possibility is that reclining leads to a reduced degree of self-focus compared with standing (Wegner & Guiliano, 1980), and the less attention allocated to the self, the more that is available for processing information from the external environment (Scheier, Carver, & Matthews, 1983).

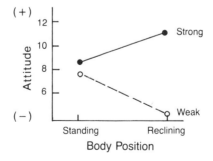

Figure 3-7. Postmessage attitudes as a function of recipient posture and argument quality (data from Petty, Wells, Heesacker, Brock, & Cacioppo, 1983, Experiment 2).

Another possibility is that subjects are more willing to undertake cognitive work when their mood is positive (reclining) rather than negative (standing). A second important question concerns the limitations on the posture effect. In our research, the message recipients were in the reclining posture for only a brief period of time. If they had remained in the supine position for a relatively long period of time, perhaps relaxation would have become so great that processing would have been inhibited. Although a wide variety of interesting questions remain to be addressed concerning recipient posture and persuasion, it does appear that under some circumstances at least, body posture can affect the extent of message processing and thereby persuasion. We briefly consider the posture effect again in Chapter 8.

Other Variables Affecting Ability to Process Objectively

The variables of distraction, repetition, and body posture were considered to affect information processing in a relatively objective manner because they tended to disrupt or facilitate whatever the dominant cognitive response to the message was. When the arguments were strong, favorable thoughts were disrupted or facilitated, but when the arguments were weak, unfavorable thoughts were disrupted or facilitated. Other variables studied by persuasion researchers may also be important because of their effects on a person's ability to elaborate a message. We note a few of these below.

Message Complexity/Comprehensibility
Researchers have studied the complexity or comprehensibility of message arguments (e.g., Eagly, 1974; Regan & Cheng, 1973) mostly in the context of McGuire's (1968, 1969) information-processing model. The ELM holds that the strengths of cogent arguments and the flaws in specious ones should become more apparent as complexity is reduced and comprehensibility is increased. Thus, these variables, like repetition, distraction, and posture should be able to enhance or reduce agreement depending upon whether the message arguments are strong or weak. Importantly, our analysis assumes that subjects are also motivated to process the persuasive message (see Chapter 4). If motivation was low, then message factors such as complexity and comprehensibility might affect agreement by serving as simple validity cues via the peripheral route. For example, consider a person who is unmotivated to process a message that employs difficult vocabulary. To the extent that the message recipient takes the complex vocabulary as a sign of the author's intelligence and credibility, agreement might be increased as a result of this complexity cue.

Message Modality
In addition to message factors that are capable of affecting the ability to process such as complexity, the modality of message presentation may also be important. For example, research indicates that messages presented on audio or videotape may be more difficult to process than the same message

presented in print (e.g., Chaiken & Eagly, 1976; see Wright, 1981). In print, the recipient may process the message at an optimal pace, stopping to consider difficult points and elaborating at will. On radio or television, however, the pace of the message is externally controlled. Unless the message is very simple, complete elaboration may not be permitted with one exposure. Based on this analysis, the ELM would predict that given sufficient motivation to process an advocacy, print should generally enhance agreement to strong but reduce agreement to weak messages compared with the same message presented on tape.

Heart Rate

Cacioppo, Sandman, and Walker (1978) proposed that transient and specific accelerations in a message recipient's heart rate could facilitate the processing of a communication. This analysis was based on the accumulated evidence that phasic heart rate deceleration is associated with increased sensory sensitivity, and phasic heart rate acceleration is associated with greater cognitive work (e.g., Lacey & Lacey, 1974; Lacey, Kagan, Lacey, & Moss, 1963). In an initial test of this idea, Cacioppo, Sandman, and Walker (1978) operantly conditioned subjects to momentarily accelerate and decelerate their heart rates without altering respiratory or somatic activity. After successful training, subjects were presented with brief counterarguable messages during periods of acceleration, deceleration, and basal heart rate. The major result of this study was that cardiac acceleration was associated with the increased production of counterarguments and reduced agreement with the advocacy.

   In a more definitive test of the hypothesis that transient and specific heart rate could affect message processing, Cacioppo (1979) conducted an additional persuasion study in a cardiology clinic using fully informed outpatients who had implanted cardiac pacemakers. The patients' pacemakers were "demand type," so called because they paced the heart at a constant rate (72 bpm) when natural pacing produced a rate below the set level. However, the pacemaker level could be accelerated to 88 bpm when an uncapped magnet was placed appropriately over the pacemaker. In this study, senior citizens read counterarguable communications on two involving issues under basal and accelerated heart rate conditions although subjects were unaware of when this manipulation occurred. The major result of this study was that subjects generated significantly more counterarguments when the message was read under accelerated than under basal heart rate conditions. In both studies of cardiac activity, then, the persuasive messages employed elicited primarily unfavorable thoughts, and accelerated heart rate was associated with enhanced negative thinking. The ELM predicts that if transient and specific heart rate acceleration enhances relatively objective processing, then enhanced heart rate should be associated with the production of more unfavorable thoughts if the message arguments are counterarguable and weak, but more favorable thoughts if the message arguments are strong. The latter possibility has not yet been examined.

Recipient Intelligence/Education

Two potentially important individual difference variables that have received attention over the years are the general intelligence and educational levels of a message recipient (e.g., Eagly & Warren, 1976; Hovland, Lumsdaine, & Sheffield, 1949; Janis & Rife, 1959; see review by McGuire, 1969). Based on the ELM, one might be tempted to propose that the greater a person's general intelligence or education, the greater the person's ability to process a message. However, would this processing be relatively objective or relatively biased? If a message contained strong or weak arguments that could be judged on the basis of logic alone, then intelligence or training in logic or reasoning would be expected to show the pattern indicative of objective processing—especially if the chain of reasoning required to evaluate the message was relatively complex (i.e., intelligence or education would be associated with more agreement to strong and less agreement to weak arguments). However, as we noted in the previous chapters, perceptions of argument strength are often quite subjective and idiosyncratic. The same argument may be seen as strong or weak depending upon the store of prior information available in memory. To the extent that intelligence or education is associated with more extensive attitude-congruent knowledge, this could give people greater ability to process arguments in an attitude-consistent fashion (see Chapter 5). Intelligent or highly educated people may also be more motivated to defend their beliefs because perceived correctness may be an integral part of their self-esteem (cf., McGuire, 1968).

Finally, it is interesting to note that intelligent or well-educated people may be more susceptible to particular peripheral cues than people of less intelligence or education in certain situations. For example, intelligent or educated people (because of their inherent reasoning powers, knowledge, or training) may be more likely to believe that there are two reasonable sides to most issues. Because of this, when an issue arises for which motivation or ability (e.g., prior knowledge) are low, intelligence or education may be associated with greater reliance on the cue value of a two-sided message. Specifically, these subjects may be more likely to reason that a source that is aware of both sides is more credible (intelligent or knowledgeable) than a source that presents only one side. On the other hand, people of less intelligence or education may be more likely to reason that the source is confused. Because of the sparse literature on intelligence and educational level, we will not discuss these variables further (except to distinguish intelligence from need for cognition in Chapter 4). However, in Chapter 5 we discuss the impact of a variable that is closely related—the extent of prior knowledge on an issue.

Retrospective

In this chapter we reviewed evidence consistent with the proposition that some variables affect persuasion by modifying a person's ability to elaborate issue-relevant arguments in a relatively objective manner. Thus, when external distraction accompanies a communication and this distraction engages cognitive capacity, people become less able to elaborate the merits of the arguments presented. The net result is that strong arguments are not accepted as much as they would be without distraction, but weak arguments are not rejected as much as they would be without distraction. Likewise, strong arguments are accepted more when they are repeated a moderate number of times, but weak arguments are rejected more when repetition allows full elaboration of their flaws. Among the other variables that may affect a person's ability to process a message in a relatively objective manner are message complexity/comprehensibility, the modality of message presentation, and recipient factors such as body posture and phasic heart rate accelerations. In the next chapter we discuss variables that modify a person's *motivation* to process a message in a relatively objective manner.

Chapter 4

The Motivation to Elaborate in a Relatively Objective Manner

Introduction

We have now discussed some of the major variables that can affect a person's *ability* to scrutinize issue-relevant arguments in a relatively objective manner. Motivational variables are also important in affecting the elaboration likelihood. If a person is highly able to process a message but lacks the requisite motivation, little processing will occur. In this chapter we first discuss three situational variables that exert an important effect on motivation to process—the personal relevance of an issue, personal responsibility for message evaluation, and the number of message sources. Then, we discuss an individual difference variable we have developed that assesses motivation to think—the need for cognition.

Factors Affecting the Motivation to Elaborate Objectively

Effects of Personal Relevance on Message Elaboration and Persuasion

Perhaps the most important variable affecting the motivation to process a persuasive message is the personal relevance of the advocacy. Previous social psychological analyses of personal relevance have labeled this construct (or variations of it) "ego-involvement" (Rhine & Severance, 1970; Sherif, Sherif, & Nebergall, 1965), "issue involvement" (Kiesler, Collins, & Miller, 1969), "personal involvement" (e.g., Apsler & Sears, 1968; Sherif, Kelly, Rodgers, Sarup, & Tittler, 1973), "vested interest" (Sivacek & Crano, 1982), and others. In brief, we regard personal relevance as the extent to which an advocacy has "intrinsic importance" (Sherif & Hovland, 1961) or "personal meaning" (Sherif et al., 1973). Personal relevance occurs when people expect the issue "to have significant consequences for their own lives" (Apsler & Sears, 1968). Of course, relevance can be judged in terms of a variety of dimensions such as the number of personal consequences of an issue, the magnitude of the consequences, and their duration. For example, some advocacies may remain high in personal relevance for many people over a long period of time (e.g., changing the U.S. income tax structure), other advocacies may have personal relevance for a more circumscribed period and/or audience (e.g., raising college tuition), and still other advocacies may have personal relevance only under certain very transient conditions (e.g., refrigerator ads have higher relevance when a person is in the market for this appliance).

Most of the early research on the personal relevance of an issue indicated that increasing personal involvement was associated with resistance to persuasion (Miller, 1965; Sherif & Hovland, 1961), and the most prominently mentioned explanation for this finding was derived from social judgment theory (Sherif, Sherif, & Nebergall, 1965). Involvement was believed to be associated with a greater probability of message rejection because people were postulated to hold expanded "latitudes of rejection" as personal involvement increased, and incoming messages would therefore be more likely to fall within the unacceptable range of a person's implicit attitude continuum (Eagly & Manis, 1966). To account for the fact that increasing relevance was associated with increased resistance mostly for counterattitudinal and not proattitudinal issues (e.g., Eagly, 1967), Pallak, Mueller, Dollar, and Pallak (1972) proposed that increasing involvement (or commitment) increased the probability of rejecting counterattitudinal messages because these messages were *contrasted* (seen as further away from one's own position than they really were and therefore more objectionable), but proattitudinal messages were assimilated (seen as closer to one's own position and therefore more acceptable).

Importantly, explanations of involvement based on social judgment theory did not consider the nature of the issue-relevant arguments presented in the communication. Instead, as involvement increased, some messages were thought to induce increased assimilation (and acceptance) or increased contrast (and rejection) based on the particular positions they were judged to espouse. We suggested an alternative analysis of the effects of personal involvement (Petty & Cacioppo, 1979b). Specifically, we proposed that as personal relevance increases, people become more motivated to process the issue-relevant arguments presented. As the personal consequences of an advocacy increase, it becomes more important for people to form a veridical opinion because the consequences of being incorrect are greater. Because of these greater personal consequences, people should be more motivated to engage in the cognitive work necessary to evaluate the true merits of the proposal.

Much of the early work on issue involvement was conducted by finding existing groups of people who differed in the extent to which an issue was important, and thus was correlational in nature (e.g., Hovland, Harvey, & Sherif, 1957). More recent investigators have chosen to study issue relevance by varying the issue and message between subjects (e.g., Lastovicka & Gardner, 1979; Rhine & Severance, 1970). In other words, some undergraduate students might receive a message on a highly involving issue (e.g., instituting a new exam policy), whereas others would receive an issue of low relevance (e.g., raising import duties on raw silk). Although this research is interesting in that these involvement classifications probably capture the relevance concept as it occurs in the "real world," several interpretive problems are introduced. Specifically, distinctions based on different kinds of people or different issues may confound personal relevance with other factors (see discussion by Kiesler, Collins, & Miller, 1969). One particularly likely confound is that people in the high relevance groups or who receive the high relevance issues may be more familiar with the issue and may have more topic-relevant knowledge (e.g., Lutz, MacKenzie, & Belch, 1983; Wood, 1982). Thus, in addition to possessing greater motivation to process the messages, it is likely that these subjects also have greater ability to do so. Thus, when a message contains information that is inconsistent with subjects' initial opinions, high relevance subjects should be more motivated and generally more able to generate counterarguments to the arguments presented. However, when a message contains information that is consistent with the subjects' initial attitudes, high relevance subjects should be more motivated and generally more able to elaborate the strengths of the arguments. In sum, it is possible that differences in message-relevant elaboration between high and low relevance subjects may account for the different effects obtained for pro and counterattitudinal issues in previous research on personal involvement.

Personal Relevance Can Enhance Message Elaboration
In order to test our formulation, we first sought to replicate previous research using a manipulation of personal relevance that did not include differences in familiarity with the issue and arguments as a component (Petty & Cacioppo, 1979b, Experiment 1). Employing a procedure introduced by Apsler and Sears (1968), we had subjects in both high and low relevance groups receive the same message on the same topic, but high involvement subjects were led to believe that the advocacy would affect them personally, whereas low involvement subjects were led to believe that the advocacy would have no personally relevant implications. The message arguments were pretested so that the counterattitudinal message arguments were weak and elicited predominantly unfavorable thoughts and the proattitudinal message arguments were strong and elicited predominantly favorable thoughts when subjects were instructed to think about them. According to the enhancement of elaboration hypothesis, increased personal relevance should increase the motivation to process the message content. As a result of this, increased involvement should increase agreement with the proattitudinal (strong) advocacy and decrease agreement with the counterattitudinal (weak) advocacy.

Method. A total of 24 students participated in a 2 (Personal relevance: high or low) × 2 (Message type: strong proattitudinal or weak counterattitudinal) between-subjects factorial design. Upon arrival at the lab, subjects were told that students in a sound engineering course had prepared the communications that were to be employed in the investigation and that in return for the use of the tapes in other research, the investigators had agreed to obtain evaluations of the sound quality of the audiotapes. The subjects were asked to aid in this endeavor.

Subjects listened to either a strong proattitudinal message extolling the virtues of more lenient coed visitation hours on college campuses, or a weak counterattitudinal message contending that colleges should be more strict in their coed visitation policies. To manipulate personal relevance, half of the subjects were told that the speaker was advocating that the change in visitation hours be implemented at their own university, whereas the other half were told that the speaker advocated the change for a distant college. After the presentation of the message, subjects read: "Because your own opinion about the position advocated on the tape may influence the way you rate the quality of the tape, we would like to obtain a measure of how you feel about the views proposed by the speaker on each scale below." Subjects responded to attitude, thought-listing, and ancillary measures.

Results. Subjects rated the extent to which they found the communication "involving" on an 11-point scale where 11 indicated "extremely involving." Subjects in the high involvement conditions rated the message as significantly more involving than subjects in the low involvement condition. In addition, analyses of the listed thoughts indicated that subjects generated predominantly favorable thoughts to the proattitudinal communication, whereas they generated predominantly unfavorable thoughts to the counterattitudinal communication. These data provide support for the effectiveness of the experimental manipulations.

As depicted in Figure 4-1, a Message type × Personal relevance

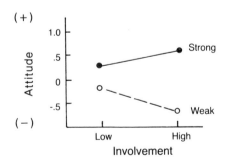

Figure 4-1. Postmessage attitudes as a function of the personal relevance of the issue and type of message (Proattitudinal/Strong or Counterattitudinal/Weak) (data from Petty & Cacioppo, 1979b, Experiment 1).

interaction was obtained on the measure of subjects' attitudes toward the change in visitation policy. When the message was counterattitudinal (and weak), increased relevance was associated with decreased acceptance, but when the message was proattitudinal (and strong), increased relevance was associated with greater acceptance. Similar Message type × Relevance interactions on the thought-listing data provided further support for the elaboration-enhancement explanation of involvement effects: under high involvement, subjects generated more favorable thoughts and fewer unfavorable thoughts to the proattitudinal than counterattitudinal advocacy; under low involvement, however, neither the number of favorable thoughts nor unfavorable thoughts was affected by message type.

A More Stringent Test of the Motivation to Elaborate Hypothesis
Although our initial study on personal relevance provided evidence consistent with the view that increasing personal relevance enhances motivation to scrutinize message content, it is still possible that attitude change was mediated by assimilation/contrast effects (cf., Pallak, Mueller, Dollar, & Pallak, 1972), inasmuch as the strong arguments advocated a proattitudinal position and the weak arguments advocated a counterattitudinal one. To provide a stricter test of the view that personal relevance enhances message scrutiny, we conducted a second experiment (Petty & Cacioppo, 1979b, Experiment 2) in which all subjects were exposed to a counterattitudinal message advocating that college seniors should be required to pass a comprehensive exam in their major area as a requirement for graduation. For half of the subjects, the arguments in the message were strong and compelling, and for the other half, the arguments were weak and specious. Given that the messages advocated an identical counterattitudinal position, but differed in the quality of the arguments used to support that position, it becomes possible to evaluate various explanations of issue involvement. We expected that increased personal involvement would motivate subjects to process the information contained in the communication more carefully. Thus, even though high involvement may initially increase a subject's motivation to reject a counterattitudinal advocacy (or accept a proattitudinal one), subjects should ultimately show greater appreciation for the flaws in the weak communication and the virtues in the strong one as relevance increases.[1] The modified social judgment formulation, as outlined by Pallak et al. (1972), predicts that increased personal involvement will produce decreased persuasion for both messages, because each message adopts an identical position in opposition to the subjects.

---

[1]In short, we are suggesting that message position (pro or counterattitudinal) may bias message processing, whereas personal relevance per se affects information processing in a relatively objective manner. Of course, in any one persuasion context, unless a neutral advocacy is presented, both factors will determine the direction and intensity of message elaboration.

Method. In this study, 72 students participated in a 2 (Personal relevance: high or low) × 2 (Argument quality: strong or weak) between-subjects factorial design. Upon arrival at the lab, subjects were told that each year the psychology department assists the school of journalism in evaluating radio editorials that are sent in by colleges and universities throughout the country; their task would be to provide ratings of the quality of the editorials. Following these instructions, subjects heard the strong or weak 4-minute taped communication on senior comprehensive exams over head-phones. For high relevance subjects, the editorial advocated that the exams be instituted at their own university, whereas for low relevance subjects, the editorial advocated that the exams be instituted at a distant university. After message exposure, subjects responded to attitude, thought-listing, recall, and ancillary measures.

Results. In order to determine whether our manipulation of involvement affected the amount of message processing in which subjects engaged, subjects were asked to rate on an 11-point scale how much thought they put into evaluating what the speaker had to say. Analyses revealed that subjects in the high involvement conditions reported doing more thinking about the messages than subjects in the low involvement conditions. These data support the view that increasing personal involvement affects the hy-pothesized mediating variable of message processing. The results on the attitude measure were similar to those in the preceding study (see Figure 4-2). An Argument quality × Relevance interaction indicated that as relevance increased, subjects' attitudes showed greater discrimination of strong from weak arguments. More specifically, when the message was strong, increasing relevance produced a significant increase in attitudes, but when the message was weak, increasing relevance produced a significant

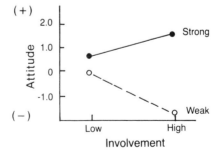

Figure 4-2. Postmessage attitudes as a function of the personal relevance of the issue and argument quality (data from Petty & Cacioppo, 1979b, Experiment 2).

decrease in attitudes. Similar Argument quality × Relevance interactions on the thought-listing data also replicated the results of the preceding experiment: subjects generated more favorable thoughts and fewer unfavorable thoughts to the strong than weak arguments under high involvement, whereas neither the number of favorable thoughts nor unfavorable thoughts was affected by argument quality under low involvement.

Finally, there was no significant difference in argument recall between involvement conditions, although consistent with the message elaboration notion (cf., Craik & Lockhart, 1972), there was a slight tendency for subjects in the high involvement conditions to recall more arguments than subjects in the low involvement conditions ($p < 0.08$, one-tailed). Since message recall is an imperfect index of differences in message encoding (see Chapter 2), correlations were calculated separately for high and low involvement subjects between the measures of attitudes and issue-relevant thinking. The obtained pattern of correlations revealed that issue-relevant thinking was a better predictor of subjects' postcommunication attitudes under high than low relevance conditions. This has been found to be a replicable result in conceptually similar studies (Chaiken, 1980; Petty & Cacioppo, 1979a). Further analyses showed that the ability to recall message arguments did not allow any reliable prediction of postcommunication attitudes. Together, these data provide support for the view that increasing the personal relevance of a communication increases the importance of message *elaboration* in producing persuasion.

Reconsideration of Personal Relevance

In the context of examining the effects of other variables, we have replicated the interaction of personal relevance and argument quality several times (e.g., Petty, Cacioppo, & Heesacker, 1981; Petty, Cacioppo, & Schumann, 1983; Petty & Cacioppo, 1984a). These interactions provide support for the view that as the personal relevance of a message increases, people become more likely to undertake the cognitive work of evaluating the issue-relevant arguments presented. We have been able to show that this increased processing can result in people showing greater appreciation for the strengths of cogent arguments and the flaws in specious ones. Several cautions are in order, however, concerning the possible limitations of this effect. First, we suspect that there are some circumstances where personal interests are so intense, as when as issue is intimately asociated with central values (e.g., Ostrom & Brock, 1968), that processing will either terminate in the interest of self-protection or will become biased in the service of one's own ego (e.g., Greenwald, 1980, 1981). Second, although we believe that personal relevance per se motivates people to seek correct attitudes, the direction of a message (pro or counterattitudinal) may more particularly motivate acceptance or rejection. All else equal, people would presumably prefer to accept messages that agree with their initial attitudes and reject messages that disagree with them. In our study, subjects were exposed to a message advocating a change in university policy that, if implemented, might have prevented some students from obtaining their degrees. Although this advocacy was clearly counterattitudinal, it was not so threatening that the biased processing induced by the discrepancy overpowered the relatively objective processing of the strong arguments motivated by the high relevance of the communication. The joint consideration of personal relevance and message discrepancy suggests that as a message becomes more counterattitudinal, the message arguments may have to be stronger to produce the same degree of acceptance. Likewise, as a message becomes more proattitudinal, the message arguments may have to be weaker to produce the same degree of message rejection.

A third factor to consider about personal relevance is that in the "real world," there is likely to be a natural confounding between the personal relevance of an issue and the amount of prior thinking a person has done about the pool of issue-relevant arguments. There are at least two potentially important consequences of this prior thinking. First, because of the prior consideration, people may have a greater ability or may be more practiced in defending their beliefs. This would reduce susceptibility to influence. Second, if a person has considered an issue many times in the past, it may be more difficult to motivate the person to think about another message on the same topic because the person may feel that all arguments have been evaluated (and rejected) already. This would make it less likely that new compelling arguments would be accepted.

A final factor to consider is the empirically derived nature of the strong and weak arguments used in our research. This empirical derivation is an important methodological tool in that it allows us to test the extent of argument processing induced by different variables (see Chapter 2). However, in the "real world," where persuaders are often confined to posing arguments that are veridical (rather than plausible), it may generally be difficult to generate arguments on some issues that elicit primarily favorable thoughts when people scrutinize them. Importantly, even if all of these factors combine to make it generally more difficult to obtain increased persuasion on counterattitudinal issues with increased personal relevance in the real world, the ELM accounts for this resistance by tracking the extent to which enhancing relevance affects the elaboration of the issue-relevant arguments presented.

Issue Involvement vs. Response Involvement
The variable of "issue involvement" or personal relevance with with we have been concerned can be contrasted with another kind of self-relevance referred to as "response involvement" (Zimbardo, 1960) or "task involvement" (Sherif & Hovland, 1961). In this second kind of involvement, the attitudinal issue per se is not particularly important or relevant to the person, but adopting a position that will maximize the immediate situational rewards is. For example, the issue of raising taxes in the U.S. has

personal implications for most U.S. taxpayers (high issue-involvement), whereas the issue of raising taxes in England does not. However, one's expressed attitude on the latter topic may become important while entertaining one's British boss for dinner (high response involvement; cf., Schlenker, 1980). In some cases, response involvement should lead to increased influence (e.g., Zimbardo, 1960) and in other cases to decreased influence (e.g., Freedman, 1964), depending upon which position the rewards favor.

Chaiken (1980) has argued and provided some evidence for the view that just as issue involvement can lead to enhanced message processing, so too can response involvement, such as whether or not a person expects to be interviewed on an issue. We suspect that to the extent that this is true, it would occur mostly when issue involvement is moderate. If issue relevance was very low, but response involvement was very high, impression management concerns (rather than concerns about adopting a veridical position based on examination of issue-relevant arguments) may determine the attitude expressed (see Cialdini, Levy, Herman, Kozlowski, & Petty, 1976, for evidence). Although it is possible for impression management concerns to lead to extensive issue-relevant cognitive activity in some situations (e.g., a student assigned to argue in a public debate may carefully research the position in order to make a favorable impression), more typically impression management concerns will not produce a systematic evaluation of issue-relevant arguments (Cialdini & Petty, 1981).

If high response involvement was introduced into a situation in which issue involvement was also very high, it would be difficult to enhance information processing further. In fact, Leippe and Elkin (in press) have provided evidence for the view that response involvement may actually *reduce* argument processing in these situations. In their experiment, subjects heard a message containing strong or weak arguments advocating either the institution of senior comprehensive exams (messages adapted from Petty, Harkins, & Williams, 1980) or the imposition of a campus parking fee (messages designed specifically for this study). Since the same effects were observed for both topics, this variation will not be discussed further. Both issue and response involvement were manipulated in the study. In the high issue involvement conditions, subjects were told that the exams or parking fees were being considered for institution the following year, whereas in the low relevance conditions, subjects were told that the policy change was being considered for six years in the future (cf., Apsler & Sears, 1968; Petty & Cacioppo, 1979b). In the high response involvement conditions, subjects were told that following the message they would discuss their attitudes with another student and would be interviewed about the discussion by a psychology professor, whereas in the low response involvement conditions they were told nothing about the discussion or interview (cf., Chaiken, 1980, Experiment 1; Cialdini, Levy, Herman, Kozlowski, & Petty 1976).

The attitude results from the Leippe and Elkin (in press) study are depicted in Figure 4-3. In addition to a main effect for argument quality, two two-way interactions and a three-way interaction were obtained. An Issue involvement × Argument quality interaction replicated the results for issue relevance that we reported previously (i.e., Petty & Cacioppo, 1979b, see Figure 4-2). Increased issue relevance enhanced message processing such that high relevance subjects were more responsive to message quality than low relevance subjects. Interestingly, the Response involvement × Argument quality interaction indicated that increased response involvement *reduced* message processing such that high response involvement subjects were less attentive to argument quality than low response involvement subjects. Finally a three-way interaction (see Figure 4-3) indicated that response involvement disrupted processing mostly when issue relevance was high.

In sum, it is now clear that increased issue relevance enhances processing of the arguments in a persuasive communication (see also Burnkrant & Sawyer, 1983). However, this effect appears most likely when people are free of impression management concerns. When response involvement is high, people may be distracted from processing the message arguments owing to anxiety about self-presentation. Alternatively, people may still engage in message processing under high response involvement conditions (if issue involvement is also high), but may simply *report* less polarized attitudes because these more cautious attitudes may be easier to defend in public (cf., Cialdini & Petty, 1981; Leippe & Elkin, in press). Future research that includes both public and private measures of opinion may untangle these possibilities.

Effects of Personal Responsibility on Message Elaboration and Persuasion

We have argued and provided evidence for the view that personal relevance (issue involvement) enhances motivation to process issue relevant arguments. There is also reason to believe that personal responsibility produces similar effects. Ever since Ringelmann found that group productivity on a rope-pulling task failed to reach the levels predicted based on individual performance (see Steiner, 1972), several contemporary social psychologists have replicated this effect and pursued its underlying cause. Recent research has documented that at least paret of the reduced performance in groups (called "social loafing" by Latane, Williams, & Harkins, 1979) results from loss of motivation rather than ability (Ingham, Levinger, Graves, & Peckham, 1974; Latane et al., 1979). In addition to rope pulling, the reticence to exert physical effort in groups has been shown on a wide variety of tasks including helping another person in distress (Latane & Darley, 1970), picking up coins in an elevator (Latane & Dabbs, 1975), clapping one's hands (Harkins, Latane, & Williams, 1980), using a hand pump (Kerr &

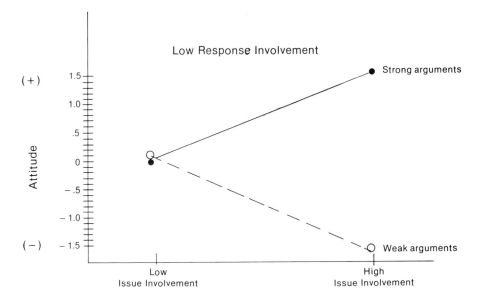

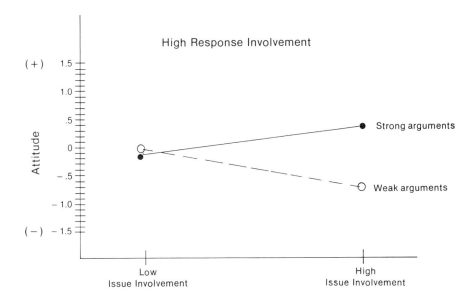

Figure 4-3. Postmessage attitudes as a function of the personal relevance of the issue, response involvement, and argument quality (data from Leippe & Elkin, in press).

Bruun, 1981), shouting out loud (Williams, Harkins, & Latane, 1981), fastening nuts and bolts (Petty, Cacioppo, & Kasmer, 1985), and others.

Personal Responsibility Enhances Cognitive Work
Although most of the research following Ringlemann has focused on tasks requiring physical exertion (e.g., Harkins, Latane, & Williams, 1980; Kerr & Bruun, 1981), in an exploratory study we examined the possibility that people who shared responsibility for a *cognitive* task would exert less *mental* effort than people who were individually responsible (Petty, Harkins, Williams, & Latane, 1977). Students were led to believe that they would either be the only person evaluating a communication, one of four, or one of 16 evaluators. We predicted that to the extent that cognitive effort is seen as costly and others are available to share the load, individual members of a group may be tempted to reduce their own efforts.

The college student subjects in this study were told that the journalism school at their university was evaluating its programs and needed feedback on the writing abilities of its students. The subjects were given booklets containing an editorial and a poem, rating scales, and written instructions informing them that, "Your task is to critically evaluate the poem (editorial). You are the only (one of four) (one of 16) person(s) who will be reading this particular poem (editorial). Thus, you alone (the four of you) (the 16 of you) have (share) the full responsibility for the critical evaluation." In addition, group evaluators were instructed that, "Your reactions will be combined with those of the other three (15) persons to form one overall rating for the poem (editorial) all of you read."

All subjects actually read and rated the same two communications; a short poem on life's unanswered questions and a two-page editorial containing a number of arguments favoring a reduction in tuition. After exposure to each stimulus, subjects were asked three questions designed to measure their perceived cognitive involvement in the task (e.g., to what extent were you trying hard to evaluate the communication?), and three evaluative questions about the material (e.g., to what extent do you feel the communication made its point effectively?). Consistent with the view that shared responsibility reduces cognitive work, subjects who were individually responsible for evaluating the communications reported putting more effort into their evaluations than those who worked in groups. In this initial investigation, the communications were not pilot tested; however, subjects were found to rate both the editorial and the poem favorably. Moreover, students who were solely responsible for the evaluation rated the communications more positively than those who shared responsibility.

Additional Evidence for the Link between Responsibility and Cognitive Work
Although only self-report measures of congitive work were obtained in our initial study of group responsibility and cognitive effort, subsequent research has obtained convergent evidence. For example, Harkins and Petty (1982) employed a brainstorming task in which students were asked to

generate uses for objects. The students were either told that "you alone are responsible for listing uses" or that "you share the responsibility for listing uses for this object with nine other persons whose uses will be combined with yours." When confronted with objects for which it was relatively easy to generate uses (i.e., knife, box), solely responsible subjects generated significantly more uses than subjects who shared the responsibility.

In three studies, Brickner, Harkins, & Ostrom (in press) explored social loafing on an attitudinal task. Student subjects were asked to list their thoughts about the implementation of senior comprehensive exams (no messages were presented). Subjects were either told that they were the only person listing thoughts or that they shared the responsibility with a partner. In addition, the personal relevance of the exam proposal was varied by telling subjects either that the exam proposal was being considered for next year at their own university or that it was being considered either for a future date or for another university. When the issue was low in personal relevance, subjects who shared responsibility generated significantly fewer thoughts than those who were individually responsible. As might be expected if personal relevance motivates issue-relevant thinking (Petty & Cacioppo, 1979b), less loafing occurred in groups when the issue had high personal relevance.

Finally, Weldon and Gargano (1985) asked students to give an overall evaluation of various part-time jobs that were described on five different dimensions. The subjects were told either that they were the only person responsible for evaluating the jobs or one of 16 (whose ratings would be averaged). In their first experiment, subjects were told to evaluate as many jobs as possible in the time allotted. Subjects who were solely responsible evaluated significantly more jobs than those who shared responsibility. In their second experiment, all subjects were required to evaluate the same number of jobs. Interestingly, however, regression analyses indicated that subjects who were solely responsible used more of the available dimensions in forming their job ratings than subjects who shared responsibility. In sum, increasing personal responsibility for a task appears to affect both the quantity and quality of the cognitive effort expended.

Personal Responsibility Enhances Message Elaboration
The implications of the research on cognitive effort and responsibility for persuasion are straightforward: The greater the personal responsibility for evaluating an issue, the more people should be willing to exert the cognitive effort necessary to evaluate the issue-relevant arguments presented. Hence, individual evaluators are expected to regard a strong version of a message more favorably and a weak version of a message less favorably than group evaluators. To test this hypothesis, we asked undergraduates to provide peer feedback on strong or weak versions of editorial messages ostensibly written by journalism students (Petty, Harkins, & Williams, 1980, Experiment 2). It should be noted that at least three other social psychological models—

cognitive dissonance theory (Festinger, 1957), commodity theory (Brock, 1968), and deindividuation theory (Zimbardo, 1970), make a constrasting prediction in this study: individuals should provide more favorable evaluations than group evaluators, regardless of argument quality (see Petty, Cacioppo, & Harkins, 1983, for further discussion).

Method. A total of 180 students participated in a 2 (Group size: 1 or 10) × 3 (Argument quality: strong, mixed, or weak) between-subjects factorial design. Subjects were led to believe that they were either the only person responsible for evaluating an editorial or one of ten people who shared the responsibility. Subjects received one of three versions of a message arguing that seniors should be required to pass a comprehensive exam in their major as a requirement for graduation. Pilot testing indicated that one message contained strong arguments, another contained weak arguments, and a third contained a mixture of arguments (and elicited a mixture of favorable and unfavorable thoughts). After reading the appropriate message, subjects provided an evaluation of the message, and listed their thoughts.

Results. Conceptually replicating the results of the Petty, Harkins, Williams, and Latane (1977) study, subjects who believed they were the only evaluator of the editorial reported expending more cognitive effort than did subjects who believed they were one of ten evaluators. The attitude results, graphed in Figure 4-4, revealed an Argument quality × Responsibility interaction. As personal responsibility for evaluation decreased, the quality of the arguments in the message became a less important determinant of the evaluations. More specifically, group evaluators were significantly more favorable toward the weak message, but were significantly less favorable toward the strong message than individual evaluators. As expected, evaluations of the mixed message were unaffected by the extent of responsibility. Analyses of the listed thoughts provided further support for the hypothesis. Increasing the number of evaluators reduced the number of unfavorable thoughts elicited by the weak message and reduced the number of favorable thoughts elicited by the strong message. The group size manipulation had no effect on the profile of thoughts elicited by the mixed message.

In sum, subjects who were part of a group that was responsible for an evaluation generated fewer favorable thoughts about the strong version of the editorial than did subjects who were solely responsible for the evaluation and fewer unfavorable thoughts about the weak version. Thus, in addition to replicating the results of our initial study on the effects of personal responsibility on perceived cognitive effort (Petty, Harkins, Williams, & Latane, 1977), this experiment demonstrated that group evaluators actually generated fewer thoughts consistent with the quality of

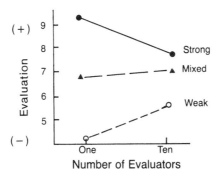

Figure 4-4. Postmessage evaluations as a function of the perceived number of message evaluators and argument quality (data from Petty, Harkins, & Williams, 1980, Experiment 2).

the message arguments than did individual evaluators. In addition, group evaluators rated the weak version more favorably, and the strong version less favorably, than did individual evaluators. When the stimulus to be evaluated was neither very strong nor very weak, group size did not produce significant effects on thoughts or evaluations. Finally, within-cell correlations revealed that the more perceived effort expended, the more favorable the evaluation of the strong version of the editorial, but the more negative the evaluation of the weak version of the editorial. The extra message elaboration characterizing individual evaluators apparently renders them better able to discover and appreciate the virtues of a strong appeal and the flaws of a weak one.

One important area of potential applicability of the research on group cognitive resposibility is to jury decision making. The work on group responsibility and effort suggests that as jury size increases people may be less motivated to participate in the group. Kessler (1973) examined the participation rates of mock jurors in 6 and 12 member groups and found evidence consistent with this speculation. Her results revealed that although only 4% of jurors in 6-member juries were completely silent, 25% of jurors in 12-member juries said nothing. One direct implication of the reduced motivation to process issue-relevant arguments in groups is that small juries should be more sympathetic to defendants than large juries when the evidence against the defendant is weak, because small (more responsible) juries will better realize how flawed the testimony is. On the other hand, when the evidence against the defendant is strong, a large (less individually responsible) jury should be preferred by the defendant (though not society) since it will be less likely to realize the cogency of the damaging testimony. Results consistent with this hypothesis were obtained in a study of mock juries by Valenti and Downing (1975). When the evidence against a defendant was weak, 80% of 6-member juries and 60% of 12-member juries voted for acquital; when the evidence against the defendant was strong, however, 90% of 6-member juries voted for conviction, whereas only 20% of 12-member juries did so.

Effects of Number of Message Sources on Message Elaboration and Persuasion

In the previous section we provided evidence for the view that increasing the number of message recipients responsible for message evaluation could reduce motivation to process an advocacy. In this section we provide evidence for the view that increasing the number of message sources presenting an advocacy can enhance motivation to process a message. There are number of everyday situations in which persuasive information is provided by several sources rather than just one. For example, at political rallies, a number of speakers argue in favor of or against a candidate or some issue position. In advertising, multiple spokespersons provided testimonials for a product. In trials, several witnesses provide character evidence about a defendant. Despite the frequency of occurrence of persuasion by multiple sources, relatively little is known about the underlying processes mediating the effectiveness of this strategy (Harkins & Petty, 1983).

Traditional analyses of the number of message sources have assumed that the more people who are perceived to advocate a position (up to some limit), the more conformity pressure that is induced, and the more agreement that results (e.g., Asch, 1951; Latane & Wolf, 1981; White, 1975). One popular explanation for this conformity effect is that people shift toward the majority view out of a desire to hold a correct opinion (Festinger, 1954). The more people who endorse a position, the more correct it presumably is. However, Burnstein and Vinokur and their colleagues (e.g., Burnstein & Sentis, 1981; Burnstein & Vinokur, 1977) have suggested that an alternative process underlies the effects of multiple sources. Specifically, they have argued that when people are confronted by the opinions of others, they are motivated to figure out *why* the others have advocated these views. According to this analysis, the more other people who advocate a position, the greater is the motivation to consider possible reasons behind the proposal. This curiosity can result in people self-generating arguments in favor of the position advocated. Both the "conformity" and the "persuasive arguments" explanations are relevant to situations in which no arguments are presented by the sources, and both theories predict that multiple sources should be associated with enhanced agreement. The conformity explanation postulates attitude change via the peripheral route (a simple inference about correctness is sufficient to induce change), whereas the persuasive arguments explanation postulates attitude change via the central route (change is a result of effortful issue-relevant argument generation). Harkins and Petty (1981a) proposed a variation of the "persuasive arguments" hypothesis to account for situations in which a varying number of other people actually presented arguments to message recipients. Specifically, it was argued that the more people who presented the arguments, the more scrutiny each argument would receive.

Initial Evidence for the Multiple Source Effect

In an initial study designed to explore the information processing effects of multiple sources, Harkins and Petty (1981a, Experiment 1) exposed students to one or three arguments presented by one or three sources. Subjects were told that a faculty committee had videotaped three fellow students giving their views on a recent proposal to implement senior comprehensive exams. The subjects were further told that each of the students favored the comprehensive exam idea and that all were instructed to provide three agruments in favor of their positions. Subjects were led to believe that they would be exposed to a randomly selected segment of the tapes made so far. Subjects in fact saw either: (a) one source giving one argument in favor of the exams, (b) one source giving three arguments, (c) three sources giving the same basic argument, or (d) three sources each giving three different arguments. Two control groups were also incorporated into the design. A "background-only" control group was exposed only to the background information that three sources had each given three arguments in favor of the exams, but they were not actually exposed to any sources or arguments. An "attitude-only" control group completed the attitude measures without exposure to the background information, sources, or arguments. These control groups allowed a determination of whether actual exposure to multiple sources and arguments had persuasive impact on message recipients over and above that achieved by the mere knowledge of the number of sources and arguments to which they might be exposed.

Analysis of attitudes toward senior comprehensive exams revealed that "background-only" control subjects expressed more favorable attitudes than those held by the "attitude-only" subjects. Thus, simple knowledge of the number of sources and arguments in favor of a position was sufficient to produce attitude change. It was not clear, of course, whether this change was due to the simple "conformity" (peripheral route) or "persuasive arguments" (central route) explanation because subjects may have changed as a result of simple inferences based on the background information, or may have actively attempted to generate arguments in favor of senior comprehensive exams as a result of exposure to the background information (Burnstein & Sentis, 1981). Importantly, however, subjects exposed to multiple sources presenting multiple arguments showed significantly more agreement with the exam proposal than subjects in both control groups.

The fact that subjects exposed to multiple sources presenting multiple arguments showed more agreement than subjects in any other condition is consistent with two plausible explanations. The first is an *attributional* hypothesis. Participants seeing three different sources each generate a different argument might reasonably conclude that a large pool of good arguments in favor of the advocated position must exist, and change as a result of this simple inference (peripheral route). Subjects in the other cells would be less likely to make this inference. A second explanation is based on *message elaboration.* This account suggests that participants seeing multiple sources present multiple arguments engage in more argument-relevant processing than participants in the other conditions. That is, each time a novel person appears, the particpant is motivated to hear what this new source has to say. If the arguments are new, this enhanced processing may result in the generation of additional thoughts favorable to the advocacy. If the arguments are old, however, the enhanced processing might result in no *new* favorable thoughts, especially if the repeated argument was sufficiently simple as to have been processed completely during the initial exposure (see Chapter 3 discussion of message repetition; Cacioppo & Petty, 1985). If the same source appears again, even though with new arguments, less effort may be put into processing because the recipient feels that this source has been heard from already. Consistent with this reasoning, we found that subjects receiving multiple arguments from multiple sources generated more favorable thoughts about senior comprehensive exams than subjects in any other cell.

The attributional and elaboration interpretations were compared in a second study (Harkins & Petty, 1981a, Experiment 2). In a key condition of this study, subjects receiving multiple arguments from multiple sources were told that the arguments that were presented exhausted the pool of good arguments favoring the position. In this condition, the attributional interpretation would predict no persuasive advantage resulting from multiple sources presenting multiple arguments, since the argument pool was limited to the number of arguments presented. Although manipulation checks revealed that the argument pool induction was successful, limiting the pool of arguments did not reduce persuasion. Multiple sources pre-senting multiple strong arguments were still more persuasive than when the same strong arguments were presented by one source.

Testing the Elaboration-Enhancement Hypothesis
In order to provide more definitive evidence for the view that multiple sources enhance message processing, and following the logic presented in Chapter 2, a third study was conducted in which the number of message sources was manipulated along with the quality of the issue-relevant arguments supporting the advocacy (Harkins & Petty, 1981a, Experiment 3). If multiple sources enhance argument processing, then strong arguments should become more persuasive when presented by multiple sources, but weak arguments should become less persuasive when presented by multiple sources.

Method. A total of 100 students was randomly assigned to the cells of a 2 (Number of sources: one or three) × 2 (Argument quality: strong or weak) between-subjects factorial design. Subjects were told that the Faculty Committee on Academic Affairs had solicited students' written opinions on the issue of instituting senior comprehensive exams. All subjects were told that the opinions of three students had been obtained, and so far all the students favored the exam proposal. Subjects were told that each student had written three arguments in favor of the proposal, and that they would examine a random selection from the materials collected. The subjects were given an envelope containing the written materials. Each argument appeared on a separate page and before each argument a statement attributed the message to one of three male students: "Here is an argument generated by (one of three male names), who is a Junior." If the subject was in the one-source condition, the statement preceding the remaining arguments said: "Here is another argument generated by (same name as before), who is a Junior." In the multiple source conditions, the statement preceding the remaining arguments said: "Here is an argument generated by another student, (different name), who is a Junior." Which of the three names was used, with what arguments the names were paired, and in what order they were presented was randomly determined for each subject. In sum, the subjects were exposed to either three strong or three weak arguments presented by one or three sources. Following examination of the written materials, subjects responded to attitude, thought-listing, and ancillary measures.

Results. Subjects exposed to three writers who generated weak arguments felt that fewer of their classmates would support the proposal than one-source subjects, but there were no differences for the subjects exposed to high quality arguments. Also, there were no differences among conditions in the number of good arguments that subjects believed existed in support of the proposal.

Importantly, an analysis of the measure of attitudes toward senior comprehensive exams revealed a Number of sources × Argument quality interaction (see Figure 4-5): subjects exposed to three persons presenting strong arguments were more persuaded and subjects exposed to three persons presenting weak arguments were less persuaded than subjects exposed to exactly the same information presented by just one person. The results for the thought generation measure followed the same pattern. Three-source subjects exposed to the strong arguments generated more favorable thoughts and tended to generate fewer unfavorable thoughts than one-source subjects exposed to the same arguments. On the other hand, three-source subjects exposed to the weak arguments generated more unfavorable thoughts and fewer favorable thoughts than one-source subjects exposed to the same information.

Consistent with the elaboration-enhancement hypothesis, then, increasing the number of message sources intensified information-processing activity. Further support for the view that multiple sources affect persuasion

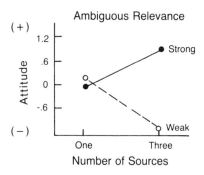

Figure 4-5. Postmessage attitudes as a function of the perceived number of message sources and argument quality (data from Harkins, & Petty, 1981a, Experiment 3).

by increasing issue-relevant elaboration comes from an additional study (Harkins & Petty, 1981b) in which it was found that having subjects perform a secondary distraction task eliminated the multiple source effect without affecting recall, the number of good arguments thought to exist in favor of the advocacy, or the percentage of classmates thought to support the proposal. When no distraction was present, the multiple source effect was replicated. In short, this study suggests that distraction appears to disrupt the additional processing elicited by multiple sources (see discussion of distraction in Chapter 3).

Why Do Multiple Sources Enhance Elaboration?
The evidence we have just reviewed is very consistent with the view that people think more about information that comes from multiple sources than the same information presented by a single individual. However, it is not clear what it is about multiple sources that leads to the additional processing. One possibility is that subjects may reason that it is more worthwhile to think about information from multiple sources because this information, compared with that generated by one source, is more likely to be based on different perspectives and independent pools of knowledge. If arguments from multiple sources are perceived as representing independent perspectives on an issue, then this information may be more worthy of diligent consideration than information from only one perspective.

Harkins and Petty (in press) report three studies that are consistent with this analysis. In one experiment, students were exposed to three strong arguments in favor of senior comprehensive exams that were presented by either one source, three independent sources, or three sources that were made nonindependent by telling subjects that the sources belonged to a committee that had worked together in generating their arguments (cf., Wilder, 1977). Multiple independent sources produced more agreement than when the same information was presented by a single source (replicating the research described above), but multiple sources described as belonging to a committee did not.

In a second study, subjects were informed either before or after argument exposure that the multiple sources had formed a committee. When the committee information preceded argument exposure, the persuasive advantage of multiple sources was lost. However, when this information came after message exposure, the multiple source effect remained. When subjects learn of the nonindependence of the sources after message exposure, it is too late to affect argument processing.

Finally, in a third study, subjects were led to believe that the multiple sources who had formed a four-member committee were either very similar or very different from each other. In the similar perspectives condition, subjects were told that the committee members had been selected to be as similar as possible. Also, in introducing the committee members, each was described as having the same major (either English, Education, Marketing, or Physics). In the divergent perspectives condition, subjects were told that the committee members had been selected to be as different as possible. In addition, all of the committee members were introduced as having different majors. When the different perspectives of the committee members were made salient, multiple sources presenting strong arguments were more persuasive than a single source presenting the same information. However, multiple similar sources who had formed a committee were no more persuasive than a single source. These studies are consistent with the view that the power of multiple sources to enhance elaboration lies in their perceived informational independence and in the divergent perspectives they are presumed to represent.[2]

Effects of Need for Cognition on Message Elaboration and Persuasion

Need for Cognition Enhances Cognitive Work and Message Evaluation
In Chapter 3 and in the preceding sections of this chapter, we have suggested that situational factors can play an important role in enabling and motivating individuals to think extensively versus superficially about the merits of an appeal. We reasoned that just as there are situational factors such as distraction, issue relevance, personal responsibility, and number of message sources that influence the likelihood that individuals will think about and elaborate upon the externally provided message arguments, so too must there be dispositional factors governing message processing and, indirectly, persuasion. As noted in Chapter 2, we proposed a functional relationship between an individual's level of need for cognition and his or her tendency to extract and cognitively elaborate on information from a persuasive communication. Our first experimental test of this hypothesis was designed to be a conceptual replication of the Petty, Harkins, and Williams (1980) study on group responsibility, with the major difference

---

[2]In Chapter 8 we address the issue of when multiple sources could serve as peripheral cues according to the ELM.

being that we examined the role of a dispositional (need for cognition) rather than a situational (group size) factor on cognitive effort and message evaluation (Cacioppo, Petty, & Morris, 1983, Experiment 1).

Method. A group of 527 undergraduate students in introductory psychology classes participated in a preliminary testing session during which they completed a battery of tests. Included in the battery was the need for cognition scale (NCS: Cacioppo & Petty, 1982) and an attitude survey regarding campus issues. Students were classified as being low, moderate, or high in need for cognition based on their responses to the NCS. Pairs of students who fell in the bottom or the top tripartite of scores and who reported approximately the same attitude toward instituting senior comprehensive exams were recruited for participation in the experiment. Students did not know what facet of the preliminary testing was responsible for their eligibility, and the experimenter did not know the subjects' levels of need for cognition when they participated in the experiment. Ultimately, 114 undergraduates participated in a 2 (Need for cognition: high, low) × 2 (Argument quality: strong, weak) between-subjects factorial design.[3]

At the beginning of the session, subjects were instructed that their university branch of the (fictitious) National Society of Journalism Teachers was undergoing an evaluation of its program and that the psychology department was assisting by studying the subjective impact of various journalistic styles. The subjects were further told that that would be reading an editorial prepared by a journalism student for possible broadcast and publication. Subjects then read either a strong or weak set of arguments favoring the recommendation that senior comprehensive exams be instituted as a prerequisite for graduation at their university. Afterward, subjects indicated their evaluation of the communication, rated how much cognitive effort they exerted in evaluating the message, tried to recall the message

---

[3]As noted in Chapter 2, argument quality has been defined operationally such that "strong" arguments elicit more favorable than unfavorable thoughts about the recommendation, whereas "weak" arguments elicit more unfavorable than favorable thoughts about the recommendation. In pretests for this study, we observed that a "strong" message that we had used previously again tended to elicit more favorable than unfavorable thoughts when need for cognition was ignored. However, when the profile of thought-listings was examined within each NC group, we found that people high in NC were actually generating slightly more unfavorable thoughts (e.g., counterarguments) than favorable thoughts to the "strong" message. Perhaps because of their greater tendency to think about incoming information, individuals high in NC access more prior knowledge and/or a more developed attitude schema. If so, it should be more difficult to generate what individuals high, in contrast to low, in NC respond to as strong arguments on a counterattitudinal issue. In any case, modifying the strong arguments proved sufficient to elicit primarily favorable thoughts from both individuals high and low in NC, but these observations underscore the importance of equating conditions for such factors when using the individual differences approach for theory testing.

arguments, expressed their impressions of the communicator, and completed several ancillary measures.

Results. Cell means for message evaluation are depicted in Figure 4-6. As expected, the crucial Need for cognition × Argument quality interaction appeared. Pairwise comparisons revealed that individuals high in need for cognition provided more discriminating judgments of the externally provided message arguments than did individuals low in need for cognition. The analysis of the recall data revealed that individuals high in need for cognition recalled substantially more message arguments (M = 3.98) than their counterparts (M = 2.91). Moreover, analysis of the measure of cognitive effort revealed that subjects high in need for cognition reported expending more effort thinking about the editorial (M = 5.93) than did subjects low in need for cognition (M = 4.98). A main effect for argument quality signified that subjects reported thinking more about the weak than the strong message arguments, but a Need for cognition × Argument quality interaction indicated that this effect primarily characterized subjects high in need for cognition.

Additional Evidence for the Link between Need for Cognition, Message
Elaboration, and Persuasion
The data from the first experiment support the notion that individuals high in need for cognition are inclined to extract more from and think more about the message arguments than individuals low in need for cognition. A second experiment was conducted, however, to replicate and extend these findings (Cacioppo, Petty & Morris, 1983, Experiment 2). Pretesting replicated previous surveys showing that students high and those low in NC did not differ in their attitudes toward raising student tuition at their university, so this topic was selected to avoid concerns about using

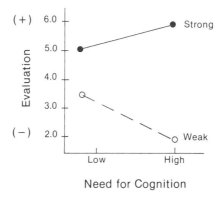

Figure 4-6. Postmessage evaluations as a function of need for cognition and argument quality (data from Cacioppo, Petty, & Morris, 1983 Experiment 1).

unrepresentative samples from the population of students high versus low in NC. Furthermore, postcommunication measures of attitudes were collected in addition to measures of message evaluation to determine whether the attitudes of individuals high, in contrast to low, in NC were more likely to be formed through effortful deliberations regarding the merits of the recommendation.

Method. A group of 110 female undergraduates participated in a 2 (Need for cognition: high or low) × 2 (Argument quality: strong or weak) between-subjects factorial. Subjects were informed that the Office of Student Academic Affairs at their university was reevaluating its policies and was seeking recommendations about possible changes. Subjects were told that policy statements had been prepared for possible broadcast and publication in the local media to inform and to obtain the reactions of people in the university community. Subjects were asked to read one of the policy statements, rate it for readability, and respond to the questions about the policy statement that followed it in their booklet.

Following this background material, subjects read an approximately 300-word message justifying the proposal that student tuition be increased at their university; half of the subjects read a set of strong message arguments, and half read a set of weak message arguments. Next, subjects completed scales to assess their attitudes, message evaluation, level of need for cognition, and other ancillary measures.

Results. Analysis of the measure of message evaluation yielded main effects for Argument quality and for Need for cognition that were qualified by the expected Need for cognition × Argument quality interaction. Pairwise comparisons revealed that, as in the previous experiment, argument quality had a greater impact on the evaluations of subjects high than of those low in NC. This result again suggests that the former individuals scrutinized more the message arguments that were provided.

The analysis of the attitude index yielded a main effect for Argument quality and the expected Need for cognition × Argument quality interaction (see Figure 4-7). Importantly, the pattern of means on the attitude measure was similar, but not identical, to that found for message evaluation ($r = 0.52$). We reasoned that if subjects high in need for cognition were more likely to derive their attitude through a considered evaluation of the arguments central to the recommendation, then there should be a stronger association between message evaluations and attitudes in subjects high than in those low in NC. To test this reasoning, a separate correlation was calculated between these measures in the high and the low NC groups. As expected, this correlation was significantly larger in the HNC group ($r = 0.70$) than in the LNC group ($r = 0.22$).

To further test the notion that it was the deliberation about the merits of the message arguments that led to the observed attitudes rather than vice

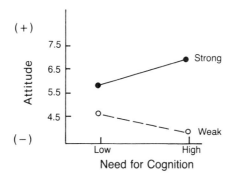

Figure 4-7. Postmessage attitudes as a function of need for cognition and argument quality (data from Cacioppo, Petty, & Morris, 1983, Experiment 2).

versa, we conducted two analyses of covariance (ANCOVAs). In the first, postcommunication attitude served as the criterion measure, and message evaluation served as the covariate; in the second, message evaluation served as the criterion, and postcommunication attitude served as the covariate. The results revealed that the Need for cognition × Argument quality interaction for message evaluation remained significant when attitudes served as the covariate, whereas any hint of a significant Need for cognition × Argument quality interaction on the attitude measure was eliminated when the measure of message evaluation served as the covariate. These results, too, are consistent with the view that need for cognition affects message processing and thereby affects people's susceptibility or resistance to persuasion.

Individuals Low in Need for Cognition: Verbal Dolts or Cognitive Misers?
Throughout this research, we have conceived need for cognition as acting primarily as a motivational factor—or more specifically, that need for cognition represents a person's level of intrinsic motivation to engage in and enjoy effortful cognitive endeavors. Although it is certainly reasonable that intelligent individuals are more likely to experience success and attain aspired goals in difficult cognitive tasks, positive reinforcement per se is not sufficient for the development of intrinsic motivation (e.g., Deci, 1975; Deci & Ryan, 1980). Hence, a strong correlation between need for cognition and intelligence would be expected only when dealing with very heterogeneous populations (e.g., assembly line workers vs. university faculty); and the tendency for individuals high in need for cognition to deliberate more about the merits of the arguments in a persuasive appeal should be obtained even when controlling for individual differences in intelligence.

Previous research is consistent with this reasoning. Cacioppo, Petty, and Morris (1983) administered the NCS and the Shipley-Hartford (1940) scale to 104 undergraduates drawn from introductory psychology courses and found that the need for cognition was unrelated to abstract reasoning ($r =$

−0.03) and weakly and nonsignificantly related to verbal reasoning (r = 0.15). In a subsequent replication, Morris, Bachman, Bromwell, and Sterling (1982) found need for cognition to be unrelated to abstract reasoning (r = 0.12) and weakly related to verbal reasoning (r = 0.21). Yet these results are not definitive. Hence, an experiment was conducted in which both need for cognition and intelligence were gauged to examine more rigorously whether the effect of need for cognition on message processing is best explained by the view that individuals low in need for cognition act as cognitive misers (motivational difference) or that they are verbal dolts (ability) (Cacioppo, Petty, Kao, & Rodriguez, in press, Experiment 1).

Method. A group of 185 undergraduates completed participation in a 2 (Need for cognition: high or low) × 2 (Argument quality: strong or weak) between-subjects factorial. When subjects arrived at the laboratory, they were told that the study bore on extrasensory communication. They were informed that their role in this study was to listen to an audiotaped message and to try to transmit their thoughts during the message to a "receiver" located in another room. To lend credence to the cover story, the experimenter recruited a volunteer to act as the receiver. After placing the receiver in a separate room, subjects read background information stating that the recommendation about which they would be hearing had been advanced recently by a University Committee on Academic Affairs and Policy Formation. They read that the committee was considering policies for the university in the 1990s. Subjects then listened to an audiotaped message in which the speaker was introduced and which consisted of either eight strong or eight weak arguments favoring the proposal that tuition be substantially increased in 1990—a proposal that presumably would not affect any of the subjects. Afterward, subjects completed scales designed to assess their attitudes, evaluation of the message, and cognitive effort expended. In addition, subjects completed the NCS and the Shipley-Hartford Vocabulary Test (Shipley, 1940), and they were given 5 min to recall message arguments. It might be noted that a number of studies have found that correlations between the Shipley-Hartford scale and other assessments of intellectual functioning are quite high (e.g., Watson & Klett, 1968; Wiens & Banaka, 1960). Watson and Klett (1968), for example, reported a correlation of +0.78 between this scale and the Wechsler Adult Intelligence Scale (WAIS).

Results. Analyses of the indices of attitude and message evaluation replicated the Need for cognition × Argument quality interactions observed in previous studies (see Table 4-1), and individuals high in need for cognition were again found to recall significantly more message arguments (M = 4.44) than those low in need for cognition (M = 3.72). The correlation between the measures of need for cognition and verbal intelligence, on the

Table 4-1. Message Evaluation and Postcommunication Attitude as a Function of
          Need for Cognition and Argument Quality

Measure	Low Need for Cognition		High Need for Cognition	
	Weak	Strong	Weak	Strong
	Arguments		Arguments	
Message Evaluation	5.37[b]	6.29[c]	4.38[a]	6.20[c]
Attitude	5.01[b]	6.30[c]	4.04[a]	6.62[c]

Note: Means in a given row with the same superscript are not significantly different at $p < 0.05$
by the Newman-Keuls test. Data from Cacioppo, Petty, Kao, & Rodriguez, in press).

other hand, was stronger than observed previously ($r = 0.32$), providing a
rich context in which to examine our conceptualization.

To reiterate, the notion underlying this research is that individuals low in
need for cognition are avoiding effortful analyses of the persuasive
communication (cognitive misers) rather than scrutinizing but failing to
differentiate cogent from specious message arguments (verbal dolts). Our
examination proceeded along three fronts. First, the effects of need for
cognition and argument quality on reported cognitive effort were determined. If individuals low, in contrast to high, in NC are trying unsuccess-
fully to evaluate the strong and weak message arguments, then the cognitive
effort they report having expended in evaluating the message should be
comparable. Results revealed instead that individuals high in need for
cognition reported expending more cognitive effort than individuals low in
need for cognition—replicating our initial study in this area.

Second, subjects were divided into high and low intelligence groups on
the basis of a median split on their verbal intelligence distribution. Separate
2 (Verbal intelligence) × 2 (Argument quality) ANOVAs were performed to
determine whether the effects of intelligence mirrored those of need for
cognition. Results revealed that individuals high in verbal intelligence
recalled more message arguments ($M = 4.37$) than did individuals low in
verbal intelligence ($M = 3.75$), apparently mirroring the need for cognition
analysis. However, we have not argued that intelligence and other ability
factors have *no* effects on message processing, but rather that the effects of
need for cognition are separable. To test this reasoning, a stepwise
regression analysis was performed using the number of arguments recalled
as the criterion, and the verbal intelligence and need for cognition scores as
the predictors. Consistent with the conceptualization of need for cognition
as reflecting intrinsic motivation to engage generally in effortful cognitive
endeavors, both verbal intelligence *and* need for cognition were found to
account for significant and distinct sources of variance in the number of
arguments recalled by subjects.

Further evidence for the conceptualization of need for cognition and intelligence as separable factors was provided by the remaining analyses. Recall that subjects high in NC reported expending more cognitive effort than subjects low in NC, yet there was no significant difference between people high versus low in verbal intelligence on this measure. Moreover, the Dispositional factor × Argument quality interactions on the indices of attitude and message evaluation, which were significant when subjects were blocked in terms of their need for cognition scores, were *not* significant when subjects were blocked in terms of their verbal intelligence scores. Instead, a significant main effect for verbal intelligence on the measure of message evaluation indicated that intelligent subjects rated the message more negatively overall than did their less intelligent counterparts.

Third, to yet further explore the effects on message processing of the subjects' need for cognition without variations in verbal intelligence, ANCOVAs were conducted with need for cognition serving as the blocking variable and verbal intelligence serving as the covariate (cf., Insko, Turnbull, & Yandell, 1974, for a discussion of this procedure). Results revealed that the interaction between need for cognition and argument quality on the indicies of attitude and message evaluation remained significant even when variations in subjects' verbal intelligence were statistically controlled. The main effect for need for cognition on recall and on reported cognitive effort also remained significant.

Together, these data indicate that need for cognition and verbal intelligence are accounting for at least partially independent components of message processing. Verbal intelligence was found to be superior to need for cognition in predicting message recall, suggesting both that people's comprehension of externally provided message arguments is strongly influenced by their level of verbal intelligence (Eagly & Warren, 1976) and that verbal intelligence was assessed validly in the present research. But consistent with previous research, the retention of the externally provided message arguments neither predicted overall postcommunication attitude scores ($r = -0.09$, n.s.) nor the postcommunication attitudes observed within the strong arguments condition ($r = 0.01$, n.s.) or the weak arguments condition ($r = -0.18$, n.s.) (cf., Cacioppo & Petty, 1979a; Greenwald, 1968; Insko, Lind, & LaTour, 1976; Petty, Cacioppo, & Goldman, 1981).

Moreover, none of the significant effects of need for cognition on message processing and attitudes were obtained when intelligence served as the blocking variable, and all of the former effects remained significant when variations in people's verbal intelligence were controlled statistically. Thus, the present research provides evidence for the view that individuals low in need for cognition think less about persuasive communications than individuals high in need for cognition, and that this difference is due to the relative likelihood that individuals low in need for cognition will try to avoid effortful cognitive analyses of the incoming information.

Retrospective

In this chapter, we have reviewed evidence consistent with the proposition that some variables affect persuasion by modifying a person's motivation to elaborate issue-relevant arguments in a relatively objective manner. Thus, when the personal relevance of a message is increased, or people have more personal responsibility for evaluating the message, or the information is provided by multiple independent sources, people become more motivated to process the issue-relevant arguments presented. The net result is that strong arguments are accepted more when motivation to process is high but weak arguments are rejected more. In addition, the individual difference variable, need for cognition, was shown to be an important determinant of elaboration likelihood. People who dispositionally tend to enjoy thinking show greater differentiation of strong and weak arguments than people who do not characteristically enjoy thinking. These results held even when differences in intelligence were controlled. Now that we have addressed both ability (Chapter 3) and motivational (Chapter 4) varibles that affect information processing in a relatively objective manner, we turn in the next chapter to ability and motivational variables that tend to bias issue-relevant elaboration.

Chapter 5

Biased Elaboration

Introduction

We have now seen that a wide variety of variables can moderate the route to persuasion by increasing or decreasing the extent to which a person is motivated or able to process the issue-relevant arguments in a relatively objective manner. As we noted in the preceding chapters, however, variables can also affect persuasion by affecting motivation and/or ability to process message arguments in a more biased fashion. There are a number of ways to induce biased processing. In this chapter we focus first on a variable that typically *enables* biased elaboration—the extent to which a person has a preexisting attitude schema or structure. Then, we highlight research on forewarnings that *motivate* more biased information processing. Finally, we briefly address some other variables that appear to lead to biased elaboration of persuasive communications.

Ability Variables that Bias Elaboration: Focus on Prior Knowledge

Our first focus in this chapter is on one of the most important variables that affects information processing activity—the extent to which a person has an organized structure of knowledge (schema) concerning an issue (cf., Britton & Tesser, 1982; Higgins, Herman, & Zanna, 1981; Wyer & Srull, 1984). Although it is possible for prior knowledge to enable more objective information processing in some instances (Bobrow & Norman, 1975), because stored knowledge tends to be biased in favor of an initial opinion, more often than not this prior knowledge will enable biased scrutiny of externally provided communications (Craik, 1979; Fiske & Taylor, 1984). Specifically, schema-driven processing tends to be baised such that external information is processed in a manner that contributes to the perseverance of the guiding schema (e.g., Ross, Lepper, & Hubbard, 1975). Thus, the more issue-relevant knowledge people have, the more they tend to be able to counterargue communications opposing their initial positions and to cognitively bolster (proargue) congruent messages.

The impact of knowledge structures on attitude-relevant processing is shown clearly in Tesser's program of research on the effects of "mere thought" (e.g., Sadler & Tesser, 1973; Tesser & Conlee, 1975; Tesser, 1976). In a series of studies, Tesser has shown that when people are instructed to think about an issue or object, their attitudes tend to become more polarized in the direction of their initial tendency (i.e., they become more schema-consistent; see Tesser, 1978, for a review). Importantly, this polarization effect requires that subjects have an organized store of interrelated issue-relevant information to guide processing, and that subjects are motivated to employ this issue-relevant knowledge (Chaiken & Yates, 1985; Tesser & Leone, 1977). In the absence of these conditions, such as when motivation to think is low or when the issue-relevant information in memory represents independent dimensions of knowledge rather than a well integrated system of beliefs, mere thought may not be related to attitude extremity (Judd & Lusk, 1984; Linville, 1982; Millar & Tesser, 1984).

Effects of Schemata on Processing One-Sided Messages

Although the work of Tesser and his colleagues has focused on situations in which no messages are provided to subjects, similar schema-driven processing can be observed when people evaluate persuasive messages. In this section we examine the effects of issue-relevant schemata on processing pro and counterattitudinal communications.

Effects of Schemata on Processing Proattitudinal Messages
In one study we explored the consequences of self-schemata for processing proattitudinal messages (Cacioppo, Petty, & Sidera, 1982). Our hypothesis was that schema-relevant messages would be more likely to invoke schematic processing than schema-irrelevant messages (e.g., Cantor & Mischel, 1979), and that schema activation would enhance a person's ability to cognitively bolster a congruent message.

Method. A total of 39 undergraduates at a major Catholic university participated in a 2 (Self schema: religious or legalistic) × 2 (Message perspective: religious or legalistic arguments) × 2 (Message topic: abortion or capital punishment) between-subjects factorial design. Employing a procedure adapted from Markus (1977), we identified one group of students that could be categorized as possessing a "religious" schema and another that could be categorized as possessing a "legalistic" schema. This was done by employing subjects' reaction times to making self-descriptiveness judgments of traits rated by pilot subjects as characterizing legalistic (e.g., "shrewd") versus religious (e.g., "honest") people.

The persuasive messages were presented to subjects approximately one month following the session in which they responded to the legalistic and religious trait adjectives. Testing at the initial session indicated that both legalistic and religious subjects were equivalently opposed to governmental support of abortion and capital punishment, so proattitudinal messages on these topics were prepared. The legalistic messages consisted of five arguments employing a legalistic perspective on the issue (e.g., "the right to life is one that is constitutionally safeguarded") and three aschematic arguments, whereas the religious messages contained five arguments employing a religious perspective on the issue (e.g., "there is a sacramental quality to the nature of life that demands that we show the utmost reverance for it") along with the same three aschematic arguments. These arguments were selected based on their ratings in a pretest in which pilot subjects rated the extent to which they employed a religious or a legalistic perspective on the issue. Aschematic arguments were those that were rated as neither legalistic nor religious in orientation. Importantly, the religious and legalistic arguments selected for the study were rated by pilot subjects as relatively weak and equally unpersuasive.

Subjects were led to believe that the message was based on a statement issued by a Congressional subcommittee. Their task was to examine the message to provide feedback on a possible course being developed for their university. Following exposure to the message, which subjects heard over headphones in a language laboratory, they were asked to rate how "persuasive" the message was. Subjects also retrospectively listed the thoughts that occured to them during message exposure.

Results. An analysis of subjects' ratings of message persuasiveness revealed a Self-schema type × Message perspective interaction: the legalistic message was seen as more persuasive by the legalistic than the religious subjects, and the religious message was seen as more persuasive by the religious than the legalistic subjects (see top panel of Figure 5-1). In addition, recipients generated more topic-relevant thoughts when the message was congruent than when it was incongruent with their self-schema. Further analyses revealed that this effect was accounted for mostly by the increased generation of favorable thoughts to schema-congruent messages ($p < 0.10$; see bottom panel of Figure 5-1). Finally, the number of favorable thoughts generated by subjects was a better predictor of per-suasiveness ratings than the number of unfavorable thoughts generated. These results are consistent with the view that people are motivated to cognitively bolster and accept proattitudinal messages that are schema-congruent.

Effects of Schemata on Processing Counterattitudinal Messages
In the previous study, we saw that an issue-relevant schema was associated with the acceptance of a proattitudinal message. If a message is *inconsistent* with a person's initial opinion, however, it would be expected that prior

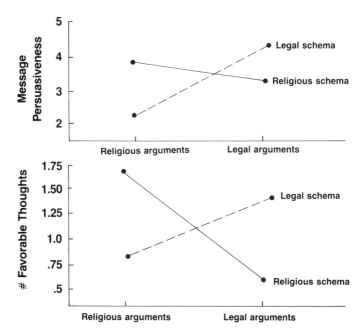

Figure 5-1. *Top panel*—postmessage ratings of message persuasiveness as a function of self-schema and argument type. *Bottom panel*—number of favorable issue-relevant thoughts listed after the message as a function of self-schema and argument type (data from Cacioppo, Petty, & Sidera, 1982).

knowledge would enhance the person's ability to counterargue the message. In a test of this hypothesis, Wood (1982; Experiment 1) assessed the prior knowledge and experience people had on the issue of environmental preservation by asking them to list their beliefs and previous behaviors concerning environmental preservation. Subjects were divided into high and low belief and behavior retrieval groups based on a median split of the number of beliefs and behaviors listed. Consistent with the view that this assessment technique taps prior knowledge, subjects who generated more behaviors indicated that they had thought more about preservation, knew more about the topic, and were more involved than subjects who generated fewer behaviors (no effects were found for belief retrieval, however). One to two weeks later subjects returned and read a counterattitudinal message providing four arguments against environmental preservation. After message exposure, subjects reported their attitudes and listed their thoughts. Subjects who had high prior knowledge changed less in the direction of the message than subjects with low prior knowledge. In addition, subjects with high prior knowledge (as assessed by behavior retrieval) generated more counterarguments and fewer favorable thoughts in response to the message. These results are consistent with the view that people are motivated to reject couterattitudinal appeals and they are better able to counterargue them the more issue-relevant knowledge they have.

Effects of Schemata on Processing Two-Sided Messages

If prior knowledge generally enables people to bolster attitudinally consistent appeals (Cacioppo, Petty, & Sidera, 1982) and to counterargue
inconsistent ones (Wood, 1982), then it follows that people who are exposed
to a communication presenting both sides of an issue should see the
message as mostly favoring the side that their prior attitudes and knowledge
support. Lord, Ross, and Lepper (1979) investigated the extent to which an
attitude schema can bias the processing of a two-sided message. In their
research, subjects who either supported capital punishment (pro-schema) or
opposed capital punishment (anti-schema) were presented in a counterbalanced design with two supposedly authentic research reports. One study
supported capital punishment and the other did not. Thus, subjects were
confronted with one communication that was consistent with their initial
opinions and knowledge and another that was inconsistent. Subjects were
asked to rate the quality of each of the studies and to rate their own attitudes
on capital punishment after reading the reports. As would be expected if
message processing was biased by subjects' initial opinions and knowledge,
subjects consistently rated the research that supported their initial positions
as "more convincing" and "better conducted." Importantly, the net effect of
reading both studies was to polarize subjects' beliefs: initially anti-
punishment subjects became even more opposed to capital punishment and
initially pro-punishment subjects became even more favorable toward
capital punishment.

Motivational Variables that Bias Elaboration: Focus
on Forewarning

Just as some variables generally enhance a person's ability to engage in
biased processing of a persuasive message, such as prior knowledge, so too
can variables enhance a person's *motivation* to process a message in a biased
fashion even if ability is held constant. For example, McGuire (1964) has
argued that inoculation treatments enhance resistance to persuasion mostly
by increasing people's motivation to defend their beliefs. The persuasion
literature has identified other variables that increase motivation to defend
beliefs, and the most researched category of variables is "forewarning" (see
Cialdini & Petty, 1981; Smith, 1982).

Papageorgis (1968) noted that two conceptually distinct kinds of warnings
have been studied by persuasion researchers. One kind of treatment
forewarns message recipients of the upcoming topic and/or position of the
persuasive message (warning of message content). A second kind of
treatment suggests to subjects that they are the targets of an influence
attempt (forewarning of persuasive intent). In our earlier discussion of
distraction in Chapter 3, we briefly noted Allyn and Festinger's (1961) initial
study of forewaring in which subjects who received both kinds of warnings

showed more unfavorable attitudes toward the advocacy than subjects who were unwarned.

Forewarning of Message Content

Although other studies have also explored the effects of combining the two kinds of forewarnings (e.g., Brock, 1967), it is possible to study their effects separately. Previous experiments on the effects of warning recipients of the content of impending discrepant communications have not produced uniform results, however. Some experiments have shown that the person becomes more resistant to the persuasive attempt (e.g., Allyn & Festinger, 1961; Freedman & Sears, 1965; Hass & Grady, 1975), while others have shown that the person becomes more susceptible (e.g., Cooper & Jones, 1970; Dinner, Lewkowicz, & Cooper, 1972; Mills & Aronson, 1965).

According to the ELM, when motivation (e.g., personal relevance) and/or ability (e.g., prior knowledge) to think about an issue are low, forewarnings should enhance the salience of various cues (e.g., attractive sources, others' opinions; e.g., Cialdini, Levy, Herman, & Evenbeck, 1973; Mills & Aronson, 1965) in the situation that are capable of inducing attitude change without issue-relevant thinking. When motivation and ability are high, however, forewarnings should modify attitudes by biasing issue-relevant thinking. Consistent with this reasoning, resistance or susceptibility can be predicted on the basis of how (a) ego involving or personally relevant (Apsler & Sears, 1968; Cialdini, Levy, Herman, Koslowski, & Petty, 1976) the topic of the communication is to the person, or (b) how committed the person is to a topic position (Freedman, Sears, & O'Connor, 1964; Kiesler, 1971). When a person is warned of an impending discrepant communication on a topic that is important or involving, resistance is typically found, but when the impending communication is on a topic of low importance, commitment, or personal relevance, susceptibility is more characterisitic.

Testing the Anticipatory Counterarguing (Biased Elaboration) Hypothesis

A forewarning of message content gives message recipients advance indication of what the message is about. McGuire and Papageorgis (1962) hypothesized that the advance warning would motivate recipients to begin considering information that would support their beliefs and counterargue opposing arguments (i.e., biased processing). Festinger and Maccoby (1964) considered this explanation for the Allyn and Festinger study (described in Chapter 3), but felt that the two-minute delay between warning and message would be insufficient time for such a process to occur. Subsequent research, however, strongly suggests that this brief time may be sufficient.

For example, in one early follow-up to the Allyn and Festinger study, Freedman and Sears (1965) told high school students to expect a talk opposing teenage driving. The message followed either 0, 2, or 10 minutes later. Just as would be expected if forewarnings work by motivating and giving people time to generate defenses, subjects who experienced no delay were least resistant, and subjects who experienced the 10-minute delay were most resistant to the advocacy. Hass and Grady (1975) similarly reported that a forewarning of the content of an impending communication produced resistance to persuasion only when a delay was present between warning and message. This suggests that a counterargumentation period was necessary for resistance. Neither of these studies, however, provided direct support for the counterargumentation hypothesis. The primary aims of our first experiment, therefore, were (a) to assess whether or not persons actually engage in counterargumentation in the postwarning-premessage interval by obtaining a listing of subjects' thoughts for that interval, and (b) to test whether the thought-listing procedure would modify the attitudinal results (Petty & Cacioppo, 1977, Experiment 1).

Method. A total of 120 introductory psychology students volunteered for an experiment entitled "Student Polling." The design was a 2 (warning or no warning) X 2 (list thoughts or do not list thoughts) factorial, with two control groups. Subjects were run in ten group sessions in a language laboratory constructed so that no subject could have visual or auditory contact with any other subject. When subjects arrived at the laboratory, they were seated in individual cubicles. After all subjects had arrived, the experimenter instructed them to turn over the booklets that were face down on the desks. Before subjects began to read the first page of the booklet (which contained the warning manipulation), the experimenter explained that he would have to leave for a few minutes to go upstairs and retrieve an "instructions sheet." The front page of the booklet stated that the psychology department was cooperating with the "Faculty Committee on Academic Affairs" in an attempt to measure students' opinions on various campus issues.

Subjects in the *unwarned* conditions read that they would be hearing a tape recording prepared by the faculty committee, which presented one of their recommendations. Subjects in the *warned* conditions read that they would be hearing the faculty committee's tape recommending that beginning next year all seniors should be required to take and pass a comprehensive exam covering all aspects of their major area before being permitted to graduate.

For half of the sessions, the experimenter returned with his instructions sheet in 2.5 min, told subjects to turn to the next page in their booklets and instructed them to take 2.5 min to list "only those ideas that you were thinking during the last few minutes." Shortly after the 2.5 min for writing thoughts had elasped, the subjects listened to the tape prepared by the "faculty committee" over headphones. Conditions in which subjects listed their thoughts are referred to as *actual-thoughts* conditions. In the remaining sessions, the experimenter returned with his instructions sheet in 5 min, and told subjects to turn to the next page in their booklets. Subjects in these conditions merely read a brief reminder that they would be hearing a tape prepared by the faculty committee and then listened to the tape. Conditions in which subjects did not list their thoughts are referred to as *attitude-only* conditions.

If *warned attitude-only* subjects were more resistant to persuasion than *unwarned attitude-only* subjects, this might be attributed to the warning per se. It was thus desirable to include a group that was warned, but did not have time to think about the topic before hearing the message. The *attitude-only control* served this purpose. Moreover, if *warned actual-thoughts* subjects wrote counterarguments on the topic while *unwarned actual-thoughts* subjects did not, this might be attributed to the fact that unwarned subjects did not know what the topic was before being asked to list their thoughts. It was thus desirable to include a group that did not have time to think about the topic before listing thoughts, but did at least have knowledge of the impending topic when listing their thoughts. The *actual-thoughts control* group served as a check on the validity of the actual-thoughts measure, and hence only the thought-listing data were of interest. The top panel of Table 5-1 summarizes the design of this experiment.

At the appropriate time, subjects heard over headphones a message that lasted about 3 min and contained seven major arguments in support of the contention that senior comprehensive exams be instituted. After hearing the message, subjects completed attitude measures and responded to ancillary questions.

Results. A 2 (warning or no warning) × 2 (write thoughts or do not write thoughts) ANOVA on the attitude measure in the experimental groups yielded a significant main effect for the warning factor, whereas neither the thought-listing factor nor the interaction approached significance (see bottom panel of Table 5-1). Pairwise comparisons revealed that unwarned subjects were more persuaded by the message than warned subjects within both the actual-thoughts groups and within the attitude-only groups. Thus, it is clear that the thought-listing procedure did not modify the attitude results in this study. Moreover, the attitude-only control group, which received a warning immediately prior to the communication, was significantly more persuaded by the message than the attitude-only group that received a 5.25-min warning, but it did not differ from the unwarned attitude-only group. These results indicate that resistance is not induced by a forewarning per se, but rather as predicted by the anticipatory counter-argumentation hypothesis, a delay between forewarning and message is required for resistance to occur.

The thought-listing data recorded for the actual-thoughts groups are also presented in the bottom panel of Table 5-1. The conditions were compared using nonparametric procedures, since some comparisons involved cells with zero variance. The actual-thoughts control group did not differ from the experimental unwarned group on any of the thought-listing measures. However, more subjects in the 5-min warning condition (65%) wrote

Table 5-1. Design and Results of Experiment on Warning and Persuasion

Design of Experiment

Condition	Warning Induction	Postwarning, Premessage Interval	Post-manipulations
Experimental groups			
Warned actual-thoughts	Warned of topic & position	Write thoughts (2.5 min) → Sit quietly (15 s)	Hear message and complete dependent variables
Warned attitude-only	Warned of topic & position	Sit quietly (5.25 min) → Sit quietly (15 s)	
Unwarned actual-thoughts	Told of an impending speech	Write thoughts (2.5 min) → Warned of topic & position (15 s)	
Unwarned attitude-only	Told of an impending speech	Sit quietly (5.25 min) → Warned of topic & position (15 s) Write thoughts (2.5 min)	
Control groups			
Attitude-only	Told of an impending speech	Sit quietly (5 min)	
Actual-thoughts	Told of an impending speech	Sit quietly (2.5 min) → Warned of topic & position (15 s) Write thoughts (2.5 min)	

Results of Experiment

Measure	Attitude-Only Groups			Actual-Thoughts Groups		
	5-min Warning	Unwarned	Immed. Warning Control	5-min Warning	Unwarned	Immed. Warning Control
Attitude	7.30	9.25	9.15	6.55	8.80	X
Unfavorable thoughts	X	X	X	1.70	0	0.10
Favorable thoughts	X	X	X	0.85	0	0

Note: Higher numbers on the attitude measure indicate more agreement with the position advocated in the message. For thought measures, numbers refer to the average number of thoughts listed. Data are from Petty & Cacioppo (1977; Experiment 1).

counterarguments than in either the unwarned (0%) or actual-thoughts control condition (5%). In addition, more subjects in the 5-min warning condition (45%) wrote favorable thoughts than in either the unwarned (0%) or actual-thoughts control condition (0%). Thus, evidence was obtained that the 5-min warning group engaged in issue-relevant thinking (primarily counterargumentation) in the premessage interval. The fact that an immediate warning did not lead to the recording of issue-relevant thoughts indicates that subjects complied with the instructions to record only those thoughts that occurred to them during the preceding 2.5-min wait.

A Psychophysiological Procedure for Examining the Anticipatory Counterargumentation Hypothesis
The thought-listing procedure has been criticized for placing post-hoc demands on people to report rational(izing) thoughts for their susceptibility or resistance to persuasion. Miller and Baron (1973), for instance, contend that requesting people to list their thoughts may produce listings of thoughts that do not occur prior to the instruction. Thus, although the results of the preceding study demonstrated that the thought-listing task did not affect the attitudinal results, it is not clear that the opposite was not the case. More cogent evidence that people covertly and spontaneously think about the advocacy and its implications during the premessage period requires a direct, concomitant measure of the extent and affectivity of information processing. Psychophysiological principles and techniques were employed to help resolve this theoretical impasse (cf., Cacioppo & Petty, 1981a). Specifically, the localized electromyographic (EMG) responses over the perioral musculature held promise in this regard, since their magnitude had been linked to silent language processing (McGuigan, 1978; Sokolov, 1972). If people are covertly thinking about the issues following the forewarning of an involving counterattitudinal appeal, then as documented in Chapter 2, greater EMG responses should be discernible over the perioral musculature. Our initial experiment was conducted to validate the assumption that EMG responses over the perioral musculature can be used to index the intensity of issue-relevant thinking in a persuasion context (Cacioppo & Petty, 1979a, Experiment 1).

Method. In this study, 24 undergraduates participated in a 3 (Replication) × 3 (Communication discrepancy: low, moderate, or high) × 2 (topic/ discrepancy) mixed-model factorial design, with the first serving as a between-subjects factor. A separate audiotape was prepared for each of the three replications. Each contained the experimental instructions and six announcements regarding the source of, topic of, and position to be advanced in an upcoming message. Each level of discrepancy appeared for each topic in one replication. The tapes (i.e., replications) differed in the order of the topics, which was determined randomly for each replication.

Subjects were told that in about 40 min they would hear several different messages having direct consequences for undergraduates, and that before the presentation of the messages, researchers would like to obtain their comments on and evaluations of the position to be advanced in the message. The subjects were asked to sit quietly and collect their thoughts for the minute following each announcement; then, at the experimenter's signal, subjects were asked to list everything about which they had been thinking and to rate their agreement with the upcoming advocacy. Thus, subjects were told the topic and position of an upcoming editorial and were *instructed* to think about the issue. In this way, subjects were obligated to engage in issue-relevant thinking when anticipating an involving counterattitudinal appeal. The size of the threat posed by the impending advocacy was also manipulated by varying how discrepant it was from subjects' initial attitudes. This provided a test of the sensitivity of perioral EMG responses to the emotional tone of the issue-relevant thinking. Psychophysiological assessments included EMG activity over perioral (e.g., orbicularis oris—lip, digastricus—chin) and nonoral (e.g., trapezius—back) muscle regions during the prewarning (baseline) and postwarning ("collect thoughts") intervals.

Results. Analyses of the thought-listing data revealed that as discrepancy increased, anticipatory counterargumentation increased and the generation of favorable thoughts and agreement decreased. However, total thought production during the collect-thoughts interval, as measured by the number of thoughts listed, was the same for the various levels of discrepancy. More interestingly, analyses of somatic activity during the collect-thoughts versus prewarning interval revealed that perioral EMG activity increased while nonoral EMG activity remained constant and quiescent. This pattern of somatic activity was the same regardless of the emotional tone (discrepancy) of the stimulus, which, by reckoning of the thought-listings and attitude measures, was manipulated as planned. This result suggests that the level of efference to the muscles of speech reflects the extent rather than the emotional tone of associative (linguistic) processing (see reviews by Cacioppo & Petty, in press; Cacioppo, Losch, Tassinary, & Petty, in press).

Psychophysiological Evidence for the Anticipatory Counterargumentation Hypothesis
The results of the previous study supported the notion that people's silent language processing in a persuasion context can be measured concurrently and without the subjects doing anything overt in particular. A second experiment was conducted to determine whether concentrated issue-relevant thinking would occur spontaneously when people anticipated hearing a communication attacking an important attitude (Cacioppo & Petty, 1979a, Experiment 2). Rather than asking the subjects to collect their thoughts on an issue, we simply monitored the level of perioral EMG activity displayed during the anticipation and presentation of a single advocacy.

In addition, we recorded EMG responses over three muscle groups in the face—the corrugator supercilii (brow), zygomatic major (cheek), and depressor anguli oris (below and to the side of the mouth, see Figure 2-5). Our purpose was to gauge the affective tone of issue-relevant thinking by monitoring the subtle and transient efferent discharges traveling to the muscles of emotional expression as subjects awaited and monitored a persuasive communication. As noted in Chapter 2, the selection of these sites for monitoring patterns of affect followed directly from the early observations of Darwin (1965/1872), the contemporary theory and research of Tomkins (1962, 1963), Izard (1971, 1977), and Ekman and Friesen (1975, 1978), and the early electromyographic work of Schwartz and his colleagues (cf., Schwartz, 1975). Schwartz and his colleagues, for instance, asked people to imagine positive or negative events in their lives. Results revealed that people generally showed more EMG activity over the zygomatic and depressor regions and less EMG activity over the corrugator muscle region when imagining happy as compared to sad events. We reasoned that measures of EMG activity over these muscle regions might yield a pattern of facial efference that would distinguish positive from negative reactions to a persuasive communication.

Method. A total of 60 male undergraduates participated in the study. Of these, 48 were forewarned about and heard either a proattitudinal or a counterattitudinal advocacy on one of two topics (alcoholic beverages or visitation hours). The additional 12 subjects, who served in an external control condition, were forewarned only that they would hear a taped communication, and they heard a news story about an obscure archeo-logical expedition.

When subjects arrived the laboratory, they were told that their task was to evaluate the sound quality of a taped radio editorial, that electrodes would be attached, and that during the study we would be recording the involuntary bodily responses that accompany listening to a communication. After sensors were attached and subjects adapted to the laboratory, they were told that the study would begin in a few minutes. Shortly thereafter, a computer-controlled procedure—which involved (a) a 60-s prewarning (baseline) interval, (b) a 15-s forewarning, (c) a 60-s postwarning-premessage interval, and (d) a 120-s message presentation—was initiated. After listening to the tape, subjects completed attitude scales, thought-listings, and ancillary measures.

Results. Analyses of the attitudinal and thought-listing data revealed that the counterattitudinal communications differed from the proattitudinal and news communication, but that the latter were evaluated and thought about similarly. Evidently the subjects enjoyed hearing the "neutral" news story about an archeological expedition. Analyses of the facial EMG data revealed several interesting findings. First, subjects who were expecting a proattitudinal (nonthreatening) or unidentified (neutral) message failed to display reliable increases in perioral EMG activity during the postwarning-premessage interval; subjects who were expecting a counterattitudinal message, on the other hand, displayed significant increases in perioral EMG activity during this interval, just as people in the previous experiment did when they were told to collect their thoughts on the issue. Second, and consistent with previous research linking perioral EMG activity to silent language processing (cf., McGuigan, 1970, 1978), *all* subjects, regardless of the type of advocacy, exhibited heightened perioral EMG activity during the message presentation. These data suggest that perioral EMG activity reflected the extent of ongoing silent language processing equally well for the various groups and, more importantly, that people spontaneously produced more concentrated or extensive silent language processing (e.g., issue-relevant thinking) following a forewarning when they expected the communication to attack their position on a personally important issue.

We next sought to determine if the affective nature of subjects' reactions was distinguishable by the pattern of facial EMG activity. Results revealed that anticipating and hearing proattitudinal, counterattitudinal, and "neutral" communications led to distinctive and predictable patterns of facial EMG activity during the stimulus sequence (see Figure 5-2). Specifically, recall that the EMG activity over the perioral region indicated that silent language processing became more concentrated during the postwarning-premessage interval when people anticipated hearing a counterattitudinal message. EMG activity over the corrugator region, which is responsive to unpleasant emotional imagery (Schwartz, Fair, Salt, Mandel, & Klerman,

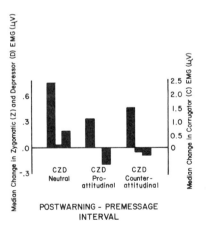
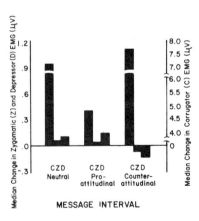

Figure 5-2. Median change from prewarning baseline for corrugator (C), zygomatic (Z), and depressor (D) electromyographic activity during the postwarning-premessage (*left panel*) and message (*right panel*) intervals for subject in the neutral, proattitudinal and counterattitudinal message conditions (data from Cacioppo & Petty, 1979a).

1976; Fridlund, Schwartz, & Fowler, in press), transient unpleasant affective reactions (Cacioppo, Petty, Losch, & Kim, 1986), and negative attitudinal sets (Cacioppo, Petty, & Marshall-Goodell, 1984) was larger during this interval when people anticipated hearing the counterattitudinal than the proattitudinal message. Second, the profiles of facial EMG activity evinced during the postwarning-premessage and message intervals were similar in form, though as might be expected, the pattern of EMG activity was magnified when the message was actually presented. That is, the counterattitudinal message presentation evoked higher corrugator and less zygomatic activity than was observed in response to the proattitudinal advocacy and liked news story, whereas the pattern of facial EMG activity—like the attitudinal and thought-listing data, was generally similar for the latter communications. Finally, EMG activity over the depressor anguli oris muscle region was generally unaffected by the affectivity or interval of the communication sequence (cf., Fridlund & Izard, 1983).

In sum, studies employing the thought-listing procedure and psychophysiological assessments have supported the view that when confronted with an impending counterattitudinal message on an involving issue, people use the period between the forewarning and the message to bolster their initial opinions. This "biased scanning" of arguments on the issue (cf., Janis & Gilmore, 1965) is hypothesized to produce resistance to the subsequent message.

Forewarning Produces Resistance Because of Biased Issue-Relevant Thinking
If accessing one's issue-relevant information prior to a persuasive attack assists in resisting the subsequent message, then a forewarning of the impending message topic is not really necessary for resistance, but rather it is necessary for people to access their issue-relevant knowledge in preparation for the message. In a final study on forewarning of message content, we tested this hypothesis (Petty & Cacioppo, 1977, Experiment 2).

Method. A total of 60 students in an introductory psychology class were randomly assigned to the cells of a 2 (warning or no warning) × 2 (instructed to write topic thoughts or actual thoughts) factorial design. An additional 15 introductory psychology students served in a control condition and merely responded to the attitude dependent measure.

When students arrived for their class, the instructor announced that since they were discussing psychotherapy techniques, he had invited a psychologist from the counseling center to speak. Half of the subjects were warned several minutes in advance of the lecture that the speaker would advocate that all freshmen and sophomores be required to live in campus dorms (an involving counterattitudinal issue). The remaining subjects were unaware of the topic of the speech. After 3 min of sitting quietly, the students were given either an additional 3 min to list the thoughts that occurred to them during the preceding minutes (actual-thoughts conditions) or they were instructed to list their thoughts on the topic of requiring freshmen and sophomores to live in dorms (topic-relevant thoughts conditions). Following this procedure, the guest speaker presented a 5-min advocacy on the topic, and the students' attitudes were measured. The control group of subjects responded to the attitude measure prior to the warning and advocacy.

Results. The results of the study are presented in Table 5-2. Analyses of the thought-listing data indicated that warned subjects generated significantly more counterarguments than unwarned subjects, and unwarned subjects generated significantly more neutral/irrelevant thoughts than did warned subjects. Thus, as in the preceding experiments, there is evidence that warned subjects engaged in anticipatory issue-relevant thinking in general and anticipatory counterargumentation in particular.

Subjects who were instructed to write thoughts on the topic wrote more counterarguments than subjects who were asked to write their actual thoughts, wrote more favorable thoughts than the actual-thoughts group, and wrote fewer neutral/irrelevant thoughts than those in the actual-thoughts group. Thus, the topic-thoughts instructions were effective in getting subjects to think about the topic.

Of primary interest on the thought-listing measures is that warned subjects who were asked to write their actual thoughts showed evidence of anticipatory counterargumentation. The number of counterarguments generated by subjects in the warned actual-thoughts cell did not differ from the number generated by subjects in the topic-thoughts cells. And while 60% of the subjects in the warned actual-thoughts conditions generated counter-arguments, no subjects in the unwarned actual-thoughts cell did (of course, these subjects did not know the impending message topic).

Analyses of the attitude data for subjects in the "actual-thoughts" groups

Table 5-2. Effects of Warning and Thought-Listing Instructions on Attitude and Cognitive-Response Measures

	Unwarned		Warned		
Measure	Actual Thoughts	Topic Thoughts	Actual Thoughts	Topic Thoughts	Control
Attitude	6.27	4.60	3.47	4.20	3.23
Counterarguments	0.00	2.67	2.20	3.46	
Favorable thoughts	0.00	1.73	0.27	2.20	
Neutral thoughts	4.93	0.60	2.87	0.27	

Note: Higher means on the attitude measure indicate more agreement with the speaker's position. Each cell contained 15 subjects. The within-cell correlation between attitude and number of counterarguments generated was -0.46; between attitude and number of favorable thoughts, 0.43; and between counterarguments and favorable thoughts, -0.37. Data from Petty and Cacioppo (1977, Experiment 2).

were in accord with previous research employing involving counterattitudinal issues (e.g., Freedman & Sears, 1965). Specifically, the unwarned subjects were influenced by the message, but the warned subjects did not differ from controls. Of greater interest is that when subjects listed their thoughts about the message topic prior to receiving it, the warning had no effect. Subjects resisted the message whether they were warned or not. The resistance of the unwarned group that accessed issue-relevant cognitions prior to message exposure indicates that it is not the forewarning per se that induces resistance. Rather, the accessing of attitude-supportive beliefs prior to message exposure (which can be triggered by a warning) facilitates resistance (cf., Miller, 1965).

Summary

In sum, a forewarning of message content, if delivered a sufficient time prior to message exposure, provides the *opportunity* for subjects to engage in issue-relevant bolstering of their initial attitudes and anticipatory counterarguing of opposing positions. Subjects will not engage in this cognitive activity spontaneously, however, unless they are also *motivated* to do so (e.g., when the issue is of high personal relevance). When this anticipatory biased processing (bolstering/counterarguing) takes place, it likely introduces a bias to the subsequent message processing. Unwarned subjects are less biased initially because their store of attitude-consistent knowledge has not yet been primed or accessed. Interestingly, a warning that triggers the accessing of a person's topic-relevant knowledge prior to message exposure should produce more resistance to a counterattitudinal message even if processing of the message is not allowed (e.g., because of distraction) because the attitude consistent cognitions would still be more salient for a warned than an unwarned group.

Forewarning of Persuasive Intent

A forewarning of persuasive intent must work differently than a warning of message content because a warning of intent does not indicate the topic of the message. Thus, this kind of warning does not enable a potential recipient to access the relevant store of issue-relevant cognitions prior to message exposure. As might be expected, then, unlike a warning of message content, a warning of persuasive intent is equally effective in inducing resistance whether it immediately precedes or comes several minutes before message exposure (Hass & Grady, 1975). What then is the psychological process responsible for the resistance conveyed by making the persuasive intent of a message salient? Brehm (1966, 1972) has argued that restricting a person's perceived freedom to think or act in a particular way arouses a psychological state of "reactance" that motivates people to restore their freedom. When a speaker announces an intention to persuade a recipient, this may be perceived as a direct threat to the person's freedom to hold a particular attitude (Hass & Grady, 1975). One way to demonstrate or reassert freedom, of course, is to resist the persuasive message.

Effects of Forewarning of Persuasive Intent and Involvement on Message Processing

According to the ELM, a warning of persuasive intent may induce resistance in one of three ways. First, the warning may serve as a simple rejection cue leading the person to discount the message without considering it (cue effect). Second, the warning may lead the person to more carefully scrutinize the message arguments leading to resistance when the arguments are weak but not when they are strong (objective processing). Finally, the warning may motivate the recipient to actively counterargue the message drawing upon previous knowledge in order to attack the message to the best of one's ability (biased processing). The results of several studies suggest that the latter process is responsible for the resistance conveyed by a warning of persuasive intent.

For example, in one study Kiesler and Kiesler (1964) varied whether the information about persuasive intent preceded or came after the message. Persuasive intent only reduced persuasion when it came before the message. If the statement of intent served as a simple rejection cue, it should have produced resistance regardless of its position. The fact that it reduced persuasion only when it came before the message is consistent with the view that the warning affected message processing. In another study (Watts & Holt, 1979), a warning of persuasive intent given before the message reduced persuasion only when the message was not accompanied by distraction. The fact that distraction during the message eliminated the effect of the forewarning is consistent with the view that a warning works by affecting ongoing message processing. When this processing is disrupted by distraction, the warning is ineffective. Finally, in an experiment in which low involving cultural truisms were employed as messages, McGuire and Papageorgis (1962) found that a forewarning of persuasive intent inhibited persuasion only if subjects had been given belief bolstering material prior to message exposure. When no belief bolstering material preceded the attack, the forewarning did not reduce persuasion, since presumably the forewarning could not elicit counterarguments that were unavailable.

Thus, although the existing evidence can be interpreted as supporting the view that a forewarning of persuasive intent reduces persuasion by eliciting counterarguments during message presentation, it does not indicate whether the processing is relatively objective or biased. To examine this issue, we employed a persuasive message that contained only strong arguments (Petty & Cacioppo, 1979a). If a forewarning of persuasive intent biases message processing by stimulating counterargumentation, then warned subjects should be more resistant to persuasion than unwarned subjects; if, however, a forewarning of persuasive intent enhances objective message processing, then warned subjects should show more susceptibility rather than resistance to the strong message arguments. Second, according to the ELM, both motivation and ability to engage in extensive issue-relevant thinking must be present; hence, the effects of a forewarning of persuasive intent should be more evident when the advocacy is personally relevant than when it is personally irrelevant.

Method. A total of 116 introductory psychology students participated in a 2 (Warned of persuasive intent or not) × 3 (Personal relevance: high relevance, low relevance-date, low relevance-place) between-subjects factorial design. Subjects were run in groups in a language laboratory constructed so that no subject could have visual or verbal contact with any other subject. After all subjects for any one session had arrived, they were instructed to read the front page of a booklet that had been placed on their desks (and contained the warning manipulation). The booklet stated that the psychology department was "cooperating with the School of Journalism in an attempt to evaluate various radio editorials." Subjects in the *warned* conditions read further that "the tape was designed specifically to try to persuade you and other college students of the desirability of changing certain college regulations." Subjects in the *unwarned* conditions read instead: "The tape was prepared as part of a journalism class project on radio recordings."

After the warning induction, all subjects heard a 3-min communication over headphones. The message presented five cogent arguments in support of the contention that university seniors should be required to pass a comprehensive exam in their major prior to graduation. Personal relevance was manipulated by changing the introductory paragraph to the communication. In the *high relevance* conditions, the message stated that the Faculty Committe on Academic Affairs at the students' institution had recommended that the plan for senior comprehensive exams be instituted in the coming year. Thus, the proposal was likely to affect all of the subjects personally. Two low relevance conditions were also created. In the *low relevance-date* condition subjects heard that the plan at their university would not be instituted for more than a decade. In the *low relevance-place* condition, subjects heard that the plan would be initiated at another institution beginning the following year. In neither case would the subjets be affected personally by the proposal. Following the message, subjects expressed their attitudes, responded to a thought-listing measure, and completed ancillary questions.

Results. Analyses revealed a main effect for warning and a Warning × Relevance interaction on the post message attitude measure (see Table 5-3). Although the warning decreased agreement overall, the effect was only significant under the high relevance conditions. The fact that the warning worked better under high than low relevance again suggests that the warning is not operating as a simple rejection cue. As we noted in Chapter 1

Table 5-3. Effects of Warning of Persuasive Intent and Involvement on Attitudes and Cognitive Responses

	High Involvement		Low Involvement-Date		Low Involvement-Place	
	Warned	Unwarned	Warned	Unwarned	Warned	Unwarned
Attitude	5.60	8.09	6.45	6.75	6.70	7.17
Counterarguments	2.05	0.95	1.35	1.80	1.35	1.44
Favorable thoughts	1.00	2.05	1.50	1.00	1.18	1.39
N	(20)	(21)	(20)	(20)	(17)	(18)

Note: Attitudes are scaled on an 11 point scale where 1 = do not agree at all, and 11 = agree completely. Data from Petty and Cacioppo (1979a).

and will document in Chapter 6, cues tend to work better when people are generally unmotivated to process a message, such as when personal relevance is low. Also, since the warning reduced persuasion even though the arguments were strong, this suggests that the warning induced biased rather than objective processing. When subjects were not warned, increasing involvement enhanced persuasion as would be expected if the arguments were strong and relevance increased subjects' motivation to process the arguments in a relatively objective manner (Petty & Cacioppo, 1979b; see Chapter 4). It appears that when a forewarning of persuasive intent was introduced under high involvement, the nature of the information processing changed as subjects became less objective and more intent on finding fault with the message arguments in order to reassert their attitudinal freedom. Consistent with this reasoning, under high involvement, subjects who were warned generated significantly more counterarguments and fewer favorable thoughts than unwarned subjects in a postmessage thought-listing.

Discussion. In a recent study, Fukada (1986) attempted to obtain further support for the view that a forewarning of persuasive intent induces reactance which then motivates counterarguing during the message. Two experimental groups were included in the study. In the "warned" condition, subjects were told that the intent of the communicator was to arouse fear and to change their opinions. Subjects in the "unwarned" condition did not receive this forewarning. Prior to message exposure, subjects were asked to rate their "degree of reactance against having one's opinion manipulated." Subjects in the warned group indicated significantly more reactance. Next, subjects were exposed to an involving messge recommending that they have a blood test for syphillis. A questionnaire administered after the message indicated that (a) the warned group was more resistant to the recommendation than the unwarned group, and (b) warned subjects rated themselves as having engaged in more counterargumentation during the message than unwarned subjects. In short, the avaliable evidence supports the view that a forewarning of persuasive intent biases message processing in the negative direction.

Other Variables that Bias Message Elaboration

Although we have focused on two highly researched variables that appear to bias information processing, prior knowledge and forewarning, other treatments may also bias the nature of message processing. We have already noted that McGuire's (1964) discussion of inoculation treatments provides one cogent example. Below we discuss some others.

Bogus Personality Feedback

In our own research we have suggested several procedures for biasing the processing of a persuasive message. For example, in one study we attempted to bias message processing by experimentally manipulating recipients' self-conceptions (Petty & Brock, 1979). Upon arrival at the experiment, college undergraduates completed a bogus personality test on a computer answer sheet The experimenter collected the sheets and presumably took them to the university computer center for processing. When he returned, subjects were instructed to look over their results, but not to discuss them with the others present. Each personality profile began with four general Barnum statements (Forer, 1949; e.g., "You are aware that some of your aspirations tend to be pretty unrealistic"). Following these statements, some subjects were led to believe that they had "open-minded" personalities (e.g., "It is clear that you are an open-minded person. You have the ability to see both sides of an issue . . . "). Other subjects were led to believe that they were closed-minded (e.g., "It is clear that you are not a wishy-washy person. You have the ability to know your positions and be confident that your position is the right one . . . "). In pilot testing, both versions were rated as equally and highly accurate.

Following this "personality study," the experimenter "debriefed" all subjects and signed their experiment credit cards. After this, a second experimenter entered the room and solicited subjects' participation in a presumably unrelated study. A booklet entitled "University Survey," which contained descriptions of two campus issues, was distributed. Subjects were instructed to respond "freely and honestly" to the issues. The survey booklet contained descriptions of two proposals (e.g., the university community should be incorporated as a separate city), along with two pro and two con arguments on each proposal. Subjects were given 3 min. to list their own thoughts on each issue.

Analyses of the thoughts listed indicated that the bogus personality feedback produced no significant differences on the total number of thoughts listed. However, subjects receiving the open-minded personality feedback were significantly more balanced in their thoughts as assessed by the absolute value of the difference between the number of positive and negative thoughts generated on each issue. These subjects were also significantly more balanced in their thoughts when this differnce score was turned into a ratio index by dividing by the total number of thoughts listed. This experiment, like the previously described study on religious versus legalistic schemata (Cacioppo, Petty, & Sidera, 1982), suggests that subjects' self-conceptions can have important effects on message processing and thereby persuasion. Interestingly, it appears that just as long as the self-conceptions are accepted by subjects, they may not have to be very long standing.

High Levels of Message Repetition

One important aspect of the ELM is that it holds that it is possible for any one factor, such as message repetition, to have multiple effects on message elaboration (Cacioppo & Petty, 1979b; see also, Chapter 8). As reviewed in Chapter 3, we have argued that moderate levels of repetition increase relatively objective message processing by providing recipients with additional opportunities to scrutinize the message arguments. In our own research, we have shown that with moderate repetition, strong arguments become more persuasive, but weak arguments become less persuasive (Cacioppo & Petty, 1985; see Figures 3-4 and 3-5). However, as we also noted in Chapter 3, the most common finding in research on message repetition is an inverted-U pattern (e.g., Miller, 1976). This suggests that high levels of repetition may induce tedium or reactance and bias recipients' message processing—in particular, to cause them to counterargue even strong arguments of proattitudinal positions. In short, based on the available data, we proposed that message repetition guides a sequence of attitudinal reactions to a persuasive communication best conceptualized as a two-stage attitude modification process. In the first stage (moderate repetition), repeated exposures provide people with a greater opportunity to consider the merits of the arguments in a relatively objective manner. In the second stage (excessive repetition), repeated exposures motivate message rejection.

In an explicit test of this two-stage process (Cacioppo & Petty, 1979b; Experiment 2), we led undergraduates to believe that they were assisting researchers by providing subjective reactions to the sound quality of audiotapes. Subjects were told that the tapes were made during a public meeting of a university faculty committee, and that they would have several occasions to examine the tape recording. In fact, we presented a tape recorded set of strong arguments supporting a recommendation to increase university expenditures. In half of the conditions it was noted in the opening comments of the taped message that the increase in expenditures would be financed by instituting a visitor's luxury tax. In the remaining messages it was noted that an increase in student tuition would fund the increased expenditures. This procedure allows the same cogent arguments in favor of the recommendation (increasing expenditures) to be used in both a pro (financed by luxury tax) and counterattitudinal (financed by raising tuition) context. Finally, subjects were exposed to either the pro or counterattitudinal versions of the advocacy either one, three, or five times in succession. Afterwards, subjects listed their thoughts, rated their attitudes toward the topic of increasing university expenditures, and attempted to recall the message arguments.

The results of this study are graphed in Figure 5-3. Analysis of the attitude measure revealed a significant main effect for message type (i.e., more agreement with the pro than counterattitudinal message), and a significant quadratic trend for message repetition. Moderate message repetition enhanced agreement with the strong message arguments regardless of whether the advocacy was pro or counterattitudinal. However, when exposures were increased to five, attitudes became less favorable. This pattern is consistent with our hypothesis that repetition would first provide an opportunity for sujbects to elaborate in a relatively objective manner the cogent message arguments. However, as repetition begins to arouse feelings of tedium or reactance, the message processing becomes more biased.

Analyses of subjects' listed thoughts (depicted in Figure 5-3) were also consistent with the view that high repetition changes the nature of information processing. Specifically, the measure of unfavorable thoughts showed a significant quadratic trend. At moderate repetition, negative thoughts declined (as the strong arguments were processed), but at high repetition negative thoughts increased (as tedium or reactance set in). Subjects' favorable thoughts showed the reverse quadratic trend, though not significantly. The pattern observed for issue-irrelevant thinking (e.g., complaints of boredom) showed increases with repetition, as would be expected if the repeated presentations of the same message arguments aroused feelings of tedium.

Finally, subjects were able to recall more message arguments with repeated exposures, suggesting that subjects were continuing to process some aspect of the arguments across levels of repetition. Also, they recalled more of the arguments when they were used to support the counter, rather than the proattitudinal position. This suggest that the former message received more scrutiny (see also, Cacioppo & Petty , 1979a). Importantly, the within-cell correlations between recall and agreement in the experiment were close to zero, whereas correlations of agreement with favorable and unfavorable thoughts were significant. As noted in Chapter 3, the simple act of learning the message arguments is not sufficient for achieving agreement.

It is noteworthy that this pattern of results is not limited to the laboratory.

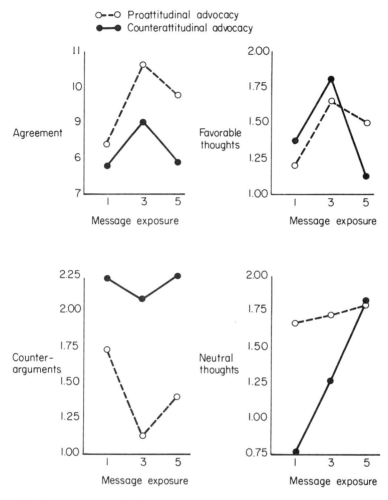

Figure 5-3. Postmessage attitudes and thoughts as a function of repetition and type of message (data from Cacioppo & Petty, 1979b, Experiment 2).

Gorn and Goldberg (1980), for example, reported that children who viewed commercials in the context of a Flintstone television program preferred a product (Danish Hill ice cream) more when they saw a commerical a moderate (three) than a low (one) or high (five) number of times during the program. Gorn and Goldberg also recorded the spontaneous verbalizations produced during the commercials. Like us, they found that high exposure frequency was accompanied by clear expressions of displeasure and annoyance (e.g., "Oh, not again!"). In short, as repetition goes beyond moderate levels, the nature of the information processing appears to shift from relatively objective to more biased.

Hemispheric Asymmetry

Bodily responses as well as message and contextual factors are relevant for understanding biased message elaboration. For instance, as noted in Chapter 2, biased message processing may be both affected by and reflected in a specific pattern of EEG activity (Cacioppo, Petty, & Quintanar, 1982). Recent research has indicated that the two hemispheres of the brain differ in their specialized functions. EEG measures from the frontal lobes, for instance, suggest that the hemispheres might differ in their affective tone (Davidson, Schwartz, Saron, Bennett, & Goleman, 1979; Tucker, Stenslie, Roth & Shearer, 1981). EEG measures from other brain areas do not demonstrate this pattern as clearly, however. In the research by Davidson et al. (1979), for instance, EEG measures taken from the right and left parietal areas indicated that the right hemisphere was relatively more active during both positive and negative emotion. This finding is consistent with the views of some that while the left hemisphere is relatively logical and analytical, the right is more emotional (e.g., see Tucker, 1981). If true, then people who display relative right-hemispheric activation during the presentation of a communication might also generate issue-relevant thoughts that are more affectively polarized than subjects who display relative left activation.

Another view of the two hemispheres is provided by Corballis (1980), who argues that the left hemisphere is more specialized for abstract representation, whereas the right tends to maintain "representations that are isomorphic with reality" (p. 288). This formulation also suggests that the relative activation of the right hemisphere might be associated with more polarized issue-relevant thinking. If a message was clearly proattitudinal then with relative right hemispheric involvement, a person's thoughts should polarize toward favorability (since this would best represent the subjective "reality" of the message), but if the message was clearly counterattitudinal, thoughts should polarize toward unfavorability. We sought to investigate the link between polarized thinking and hemispheric asymmetry in a series of exploratory studies.

In our initial study (Cacioppo, Petty, & Quintanar, 1982, Experiment 1), 40-right-handed men anticipated and received either a pro or counter-attitudinal message while EEG (alpha) activity was monitored over the left and right parietal areas. The specific sequence of events included a 60-s initial baseline period and then a 195-s communication period. The message subjects heard contained a mixture of strong and weak arguments—which was done to increase the likelihood that an analytical style of processing would result in a balanced profile of thoughts, and that subjective reality would be defined more by a person's own attitude than by argument quality. Following exposure to the message, subjects were given 2.5 min. to list the thoughts and ideas that occured to them during the communication period. Subjects then rated their thoughts as being favorable, unfavorable, or neutral/irrelevant toward the advocacy. A measure of the polarization of the issue-relevant thinking was calculated by subtracting the number of favorable from unfavorable thoughts for the counterattitudinal issue, and the reverse for the proattitudinal one. A second measure was employed to assess the simple total of evaluative thoughts about the issue and was calculated by summing the number of favorable and unfavorable thoughts listed.

Prior to analysis of the thought-listing data, a median split was calculated on the basis of the differential hemispheric alpha abundance evinced during the pretreatment baseline, and another was performed on the basis of the EEG data collected during the communication period. A blocking factor for relative hemispheric activation was then used in the analyses of the thought-listing data. The analyses revealed that the individual differences in hemispheric activation during the baseline period did not account for a significant portion of variance in either the polarization (one-sided thinking) index or the measure of total evaluative thinking. However, individual differences in hemispheric activation during the communication period showed the expected relationship to the polarization index. Subjects who showed relative activation of the right hemisphere during the communication period produced a more polarized profile of thoughts than did the subjects who showed relative activation of the left hemisphere. Differences in relative hemispheric activation during the communication period did not show a significant relationship to the total number of favorable and unfavorable thoughts listed.

In a second experiment (Caciopp, Petty, & Quintanar, Experiment 2), a conceptual replication of the first study was undertaken to assess the reliability of the effect. Three major changes in procedure were made: (a) communications on new topics were prepared; (b) the EEG sampling epochs were partitioned into four distinct periods—announcement of topic and position (15 s), postwarning-premessage period of silence (45 s); persuasive message (60 s), and postmessage period of silence (15 s); and (c) each subject was exposed to both pro and counterattitudinal communications (with order determined randomly for each subject). Separate median splits and analyses were performed on the basis of the relative hemispheric alpha abundance over the parietal areas obtained during each distinct period. As in the first study, subjects characterized by relative right-hemispheric activation generated more polarized (one-sided) thoughts regarding the attitude issue compared with subjects characterized by left-hemispheric activation. This effect emerged regardless of the communication period used to calculate the alpha ratio. Again, for none of the sampling periods did the EEG ratios relate to the total number of evaluative thoughts listed.

In a third study (Cacioppo, Petty, & Quintanar, 1982, Experiment 3), we examined the role of increasingly polarized thinking on differential hemispheric activation by employing a modification of Tesser's (1978) time-to-think paradigm. As noted earlier in this chapter, Tesser varies the time subjects have to simply think about attitude issues and finds that attitudes and thoughts polarize in the direction of their initial tendency with increased thinking. In our study, subjects were given either 20 or 90 s to think about attitude issues. Results revealed that as subjects thought longer about an issue, a shifting of relative hemispheric activation away from the typical dominance of the left hemisphere occurred. Interestingly, Krugman (1980) reported a conceptually similar finding in his reanalysis of data collected by Appel, Weinstein, and Weinstein (1979): As repetitions of an advertisement increased (allowing more thought; see Chapter 3), subjects showed a shifting of relative activation from the left to the right hemisphere.

In sum, the data from these studies suggest one quite reliable effect: individuals producing a relatively one-sided profile of issue-relevant thoughts also demonstrate relative right-hemispheric EEG activation as assessed by the absence of alpha activity over the parietal areas. Given past research demonstrating that hemispheric involvement affects the manner in which information about an incoming stimulus or task is processed (cf., Tucker, 1981), it seems highly plausible that hemispheric involvement can influence as well as reflect biased message elaboration.

Audience Expressions of Approval or Disapproval

Audience Hecklers

As a final example of biased processing, we mention briefly studies in which we have varied the responses audience members have made to a persuasive communication. In one experiment, we studied the impact of audience hecklers on persuasion. Previous research had strongly indicated that heckling was mostly detrimental to the effectiveness of a speaker (e.g., Sloan, Love, & Ostrom, 1974; Ware & Tucker, 1974), but in these studies, unlike the real world, the speaker was unable to respond to the audience comments. We attempted to study a more naturalistic heckling environment.

In our study (Petty & Brock, 1976), students in a introductory speech course were invited to attend a "Speakers' Workshop" in their student union. The subjects were told that as part of the workshop, speakers prepared and presented speeches on timely topics, and were then evaluated by the audience. All subjects heard a female speaker present a message advocating an increase in university expenditures. In the proattitudinal version of the speech, the speaker advocated that the expenditures be financed by a tax on visitor services. In the counterattitudinal version, the speaker advocated financing the expenditures by raising student tuition.

Five different versions of each speech were delivered. In one version, two audience members interrupted the speaker five times with derogatory comments (e.g., "this all sounds crazy") and counterarguments (e.g., "but we already have a campus bus service"), and the speaker ignored these comments. In a second version, the speaker calmly provided a relevant response to each heckle (e.g., "I've really studied this, and the present system just isn't adequate"). In a third version, the speaker appeared upset and responded with an irrelevant response (e.g., "OK, OK, let me finish, would you"). In a fourth, interruption control condition, a time keeper interrupted the speaker five times to indicate how much time was left (this was to assess mere distraction effects). Finally, in a message-only control condition, the speaker delivered the speech without any interruptions.

Analysis of subjects' attitudes toward increasing university expenditures revealed the following: (a) subjects agreed more with the proattitudinal than the counterattitudinal appeal, (b) speeches with audience heckles induced less agreement than speeches without these comments, and (c) if heckling did occur, the speaker's relevant response induced more agreement than the irrelevant response. One interpretation of these results is that negative comments from the similar audience members induced subjects to process the message in a biased manner (i.e., encouraging counterarguments rather than favorable thoughts). However, when the speaker responded to the heckles in a relevant manner (counterarguing the heckler's comments), this stifled the biased processing.

Audience Head Movements
In another (unrelated) study, we explored the possibility that responses made by the message recipients themselves durng the message exposure could influence the manner in which the message was processed and thereby determine the extent of influence. Recipient head movements were chosen for study because of their strong association with agreeing and disagreeing reactions in a wide variety of cultures (Eibl-Eibesfeldt, 1972). Darwin (1965/1872), in fact, suggested that head shaking has a universal negative meaning that originated from food refusal. The interesting question was whether or not vertical (agreeing) and horizontal (disagreeing) head movements on the part of message recipients could bias responses to a persuasive communication.

In our study (Wells & Petty, 1980), subjects were led to believe that they were participating in consumer research on the sound quality of stereo headphones. They were told that the manufacturer was interested in how headphones tested (as to sound quality, comfort, etc.) when listeners were engaged in movement (e.g., dancing, jogging). Three experimental conditions were created. Some subjects were told that they should move their heads up and down (vertical) about once per second to test the headphones, whereas others were told to move their heads from side to side (horizontal). A final group of subjects was told that they were controls and heard no specific statements about head movements. After subjects were given their instructions, a tape from a purported campus radio program was played. The tape began with music and then the disc jockey introduced a station editorial. Subjects either heard an editorial in favor of raising tuition at their university (counterattitudinal) or one in favor of reducing tuition (proattitudinal). Following the radio broadcast, subjects rated the headphones on a variety of dimensions and gave their opinions about the music and editorial.

The key attitude measure asked subjects what they thought the appropriate tuition should be. These data are graphed in Figure 5-4. Two significant effects emerged. A message main effect indicated that subjects advocated greater tuition after the raise than after the lower tuition message. More interestingly, however, was a Message × Head movement interaction. This interaction indicated that the vertical head movement subjects advocated more tuition than horizontal head movement subjects in response to the raise tuition message, but vertical movement subjects advocated less tuition than did horizontal movement subjects in response to the lower tuition message. In short, consistent with the view that head movements biased processing, vertical head movements led to greater agreement with both messages than horizontal head movements. The no movement control group showed intermediate agreement to both messages. Importantly, the head movements had not significant impact on ratings of the headphones or music. These results are consistent with the view that vertical head movements are compatible with and facilitate the production of favorable thoughts, but are incompatible with and inhibit the production of unfavorable thoughts. On the other hand, horizontal head movements are compatible with and facilitate the production of unfavorable thoughts, but inhibit the production of favorable thoughts. Interestingly, analyses of the number of head movements that subjects actually accomplished during

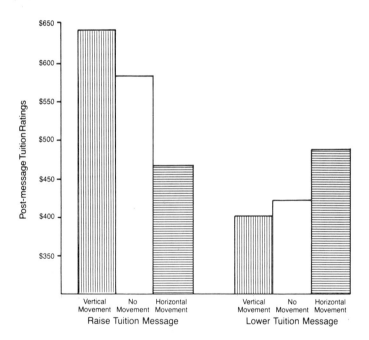

Figure 5-4. Postmessage attitudes as a function of vertical or horizontal head-movements and position of message (data from Wells & Petty, 1980).

the presentation of each message are consistent with this reasoning. Specifically, a Message × Head movement interaction revealed that subjects had a more difficult time making vertical than horizontal head movements to the counterattitudinal advocacy, but had a more difficult time making horizontal than vertical head movements to the proattitudinal advocacy.

Biased Processing or Peripheral Cues?

The research on the various independent variables discussed in this section (ie., open/closed minded personality feedback; excessive message repetition; hemispheric asymmetry; heckling; vertical/horizontal head movements) clearly indicates that these treatments do not simply enhance objective information processing. For example, excessive message repetition led to less agreement with an advocacy than moderate repetition, even though the arguments presented were strong (Cacioppo & Petty, 1979b). However, for several of these variables, it is quite possible that the treatment, rather than biasing information processing, serves as a simple acceptance or rejection cue. Specifically, closed-minded personality feedback, horizontal head movements, hecklers, or excessive repetition may not facilitate the production of counterarguments, but may instead induce negative affect that becomes assoicated with the advocacy (see Zajonc & Markus, 1982) or induce a simple inference that leads to rejection (e.g., if the audience is against it, it must be bad; if I shook my head, I must not like it).

For all of the studies that we have described in this section, we favor an interpretation based on biased processing over simple cue association for several reasons, however. First, these treatments have had effects under conditions of relatively high personal relevance. In all of the studies we reported here, students were considering issues with potential personal consequences. As we document fully in the next chapter, positive and negative peripheral cues tend to work best under conditions of low personal relevance.[1] Secondly, in some of the studies there was evidence that subjects actually generated issue-relevant thoughts consistent with biased processing (e.g., Cacioppo & Petty, 1979b; Petty & Brock, 1979). Variables that serve as cues would be less likely to produce significant effects on measures of issue-relevant cognitive activity. In still other studies, the treatments (i.e., headnodding) affected attitudes toward the persuasive message, but not attitudes toward other stimuli in the environment (e.g., the music and headphones; Wells & Petty, 1980). This suggests that the treatment did not serve as a simple affective conditioning cue. Future research that includes

---

[1] In Chapter 8 we will argue that some of these variables may affect information processing when the message has potential personal relevance (as was the case for the studies described in this chapter), but serve as peripheral cues when the elaboration likelihood is low.

these treatments along with message quality and other motivational and ability variables will allow more definitive distinction of whether these variables were effective because they served as peripheral cues, or because they biased information processing. One intriguing possibility, however, is that some of these treatments may induce affect *and* bias information processing. For example, a treatment inducing negative (positive) affect may bias information processing by increasing access to other information linked to negative (positive) states (Bower, 1981; Clark & Isen, 1982).

Retrospective

In this chapter we reviewed evidence consistent with the proposition that some variables affect persuasion by biasing a person's motivation or ability to process the issue-relevant arguments presented. Thus, we have seen that when people's prior knowledge is skewed in an attitude-consistent direction, they tend to cognitively bolster attitude-congruent communications and counterargue opposing ones. We have seen that forewarnings of an involving counterattitudinal message lead to anticipatory counterarguing and subsequent resistance to the message. This anticipatory thinking has been documented with thought-listings and EMG recordings in the speech musculature. Forewarnings of persuasive intent appear to motivate counter-arguing during message exposure. Finally, we ended the chapter with a discussion of a potpourri of variables that appear to bias information-processing activity including personality feedback, excessive message repetition, hemispheric asymmetry, heckling, and recipient head movements. In the next chapter we turn to the postulated tradeoff between message processing (whether relatively objective or biased) and the operation of peripheral cues.

Chapter 6
Message Elaboration versus Peripheral Cues

Introduction

It is now clear that a wide variety of variables can affect a person's motivation and/or ability to consider issue-relevant arguments in either a relatively objective or in a relatively biased manner. However, according to the ELM, extensive issue and argument processing is only one route to persuasion or resistance. When people are relatively unmotivated or unable to process issue-relevant arguments, attitude changes may still occur if peripheral cues are present in the persuasion situation. In fact, the ELM postulates a tradeoff between argument processing and the operation of peripheral cues: as argument scrutiny (whether objective or biased) is reduced, peripheral cues become relatively more important determinants of persuasion, but as argument scrutiny (whether objective or biased) is increased, peripheral cues become relatively less important. In the first part of this chapter we discuss the tradeoff between relatively objective processing and the operation of cues, and in the second part of this chapter we discuss the tradeoff as it applies to biased processing.

Objective Processing versus Peripheral Cues

Investigating the tradeoff between relatively objective processing and the operation of peripheral cues requires establishing two kinds of persuasion contexts: one in which the likelihood of relatively objective argument elaboration is high, and one in which the elaboration likelihood is low. In Chapters 3 and 4 we noted several candidates for varying the elaboration likelihood in a relatively objective manner (e.g., distraction, moderate repetition), but most research pertaining to the tradeoff between elaboration and cues has varied the personal relevance of the communication. Therefore we begin our discussion with the role of issue-importance or personal relevance as a moderator of central and peripheral routes to persuasion.

Personal Relevance and the Operation of Peripheral Cues

In this section we discuss our own work and other studies in which peripheral cues were tested under different personal relevance conditions. We focus first on source cues, then message cues, and then other cues that influence attitudes in the absence of argument scrutiny.

Source Expertise as a Peripheral Cue

If two levels of elaboration are established by varying the personal relevance of a message, one very high and one very low, the ELM expects that attitudes will be determined primarily by argument quality when the elaboration likelihood is high, but primarily by peripheral cues when the elaboration likelihood is low. One simple cue as to the validity of a message is the expertise of the message source (Hovland, Janis, & Kelley, 1953). In our initial study on personal relevance and peripheral cues, we provided a specific test of the view that source expertise becomes more important as a persuasion cue as the likelihood of elaboration decreases, and that argument quality becomes a more important determinant of persuasion as the elaboration likelihood increases (Petty, Cacioppo, & Goldman, 1981).

Method. In this study, 145 students participated in a 2 (Personal relevance: low or high) × 2 (Argument quality: strong or weak) × 2 (Source expertise: expert or inexpert) between-subjects factorial design. The subjects were told that their university was undergoing an academic reevaluation and that the new Chancellor was seeking recommendations about policy changes to be instituted. The subjects were further told that the Chancellor had asked several individuals and groups to audiotape policy statements for possible broadcast on the campus radio station. The subjects were asked to help the psychology department evaluate the tapes for the Chancellor's office. After reading these background comments, all of the students heard a message arguing that seniors should be required to pass a comprehensive exam in their major area.

In the high relevance conditions the subjects were told that the Chancellor was seeking recommendations about policy changes to be instituted the following year, whereas in the low relevance conditions they were told that the Chancellor was seeking recommendations about changes that should be instituted 10 years in the future. Half of the students heard eight cogent arguments in favor of the recommendation and half heard eight weak arguments. Finally, half of the students were told that the tape they would hear was based on a report prepared by a local high school class (low expertise), and half were told that the tape was based on a report prepared by the Carnegie Commission on Higher Education, chaired by a Princeton

University Professor (high expertise). Of course, all subjects actually heard the same speaker. Following message exposure, subjects rated their attitudes concerning comprehensive exams, attempted to recall the message arguments, and completed various ancillary measures.

Results. Manipulation checks revealed that each of the independent variables was manipulated successfully. Specifically, subjects who were exposed to the expert source rated the speaker as more qualified than subjects who were exposed to the inexpert source. Subjects who were exposed to the strong arguments rated the quality of the arguments used to support the position as higher than subjects who received the weak message. In addition, subjects recalled more of the strong than weak arguments and rated the source as more qualified when the arguments were strong rather than weak. Finally, students in the high relevance conditions rated the likelihood that their university would institute comprehensive exams during their tenure as greater than students in the low relevance conditions.

Subjects reported more favorable attitudes toward the comprehensive exam proposal when the arguments were strong rather than weak, and when the arguments were presented by the expert than the inexpert source. More interesting, however, is that two significant interactions on the attitude measure provided support for the ELM. First, a Relevance × Argument quality interaction replicated our previous finding that argument quality was a more important determinant of persuasion for high than low relevance subjects (Petty & Cacioppo, 1979b; see Figure 4-2). In addition, however, a Relevance × Source expertise interaction indicated that the source cue was a more important determinant of attitudes for low than high relevance subjects. The results for all cells of this study are graphed in Figure 6-1. In the top panel (low relevance conditions) it can be seen that increasing source expertise enhanced attitudes regardless of message quality (a cue effect as depicted in the left side of Panel II in Figure 2-3). However, in the bottom panel of Figure 6-1 (high relevance conditions) it can be seen that source expertise had no impact on attitudes; only argument quality was important. In sum, the pattern of data was very supportive of the postulated tradeoff between argument processing and the use of peripheral cues.

Source Likability as a Peripheral Cue
In order to provide evidence for the generality of the proposed tradeoff between argument processing and cue operation, we conducted a conceptual replication of the preceding study employing a different manipulation of relevance, a different issue and arguments, a different source cue, and a different method of message presentation (Petty, Cacioppo, & Schumann, 1983).

Method. A total of 160 undergraduates participated in a 2 (Involvement: low or high) × 2 (Argument quality: weak or strong) × 2 (Source likability: low or high) between-subjects design. All subjects were asked to examine a

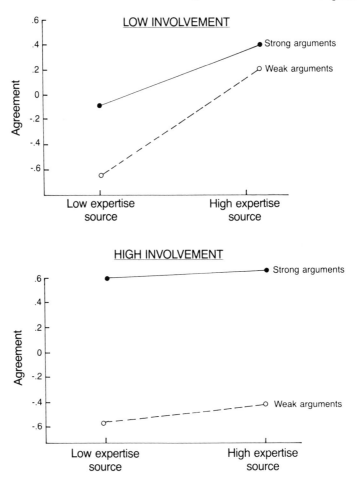

Figure 6-1. Postmessage attitudes as a function of issue-relevance, argument quality, and source expertise. *Top panel* shows that attitudes are affected by source expertise under conditions of low issue-relevance. *Bottom panel* shows that attitudes are not affected by expertise but are modified by argument quality under conditions of high issue-relevance (data from Petty, Cacioppo, & Goldman, 1981).

booklet containing 12· magazine advertisements. Each of the ads was preceded by a brief description of the purpose of the ad. A variety of both familiar and unfamiliar ads appeared in the booklet, but the crucial ad was for a fictitious new product, "Edge disposable razors." Two things were done to either enhance or reduce the personal relevance of the ad for this product. In the high relevance groups, the ad was preceded by a description indicating that the product would be test marketed soon in the subjects' community. In the low relevance groups, the crucial ad was preceded by a description indicating that the product would be test marketed soon in several distant cities. In addition, before subjects examined any ads they were told that at the end of the experiment they would be given a free gift for their participation. In the high relevance groups, they were told that they would be allowed to choose among several brands of disposable razors. In the low relevance groups, they were told that they would be selecting among brands of toothpaste (an ad for toothpaste appeared in the ad booklet). In sum, the high relevance subjects were not only led to believe that the crucial product would be available in their local area soon, but they also believed that they would make a decision about the product class. In contrast, the low relevance subjects believed that the product would not be available in their local area in the forseeable future and did not expect to make a decision about that product class.

Four different versions of the razor ad were constructed. Two featured photographs of two well-known and liked sports celebrities, and two featured middle-aged citizens described as Californians (see Figure 6-2). The product endorsers served as the manipulation of the peripheral cue. Finally, two of the ads contained six persuasive statements about the product (e.g., handle is tapered and ribbed to prevent slipping), and two ads contained six specious or vague statements (e.g., designed with the bathroom in mind). Following examination of the ad booklet, subjects

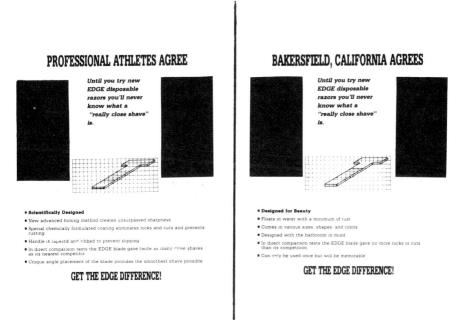

Figure 6-2. Advertising stimuli used in the Petty, Cacioppo, & Schumann (1983) study. *Left panel*—ad containing the positive endorser cue and strong arguments. *Right panel*—ad containing the neutral cue and weak arguments. Pictures of endorsers have been blacked out to preserve propriety and anonymity.

indicated their attitudes about the products depicted, including of course, Edge razors. In addition, they attempted to recall the arguments in the ad, and responded to ancillary measures.

Results. Manipulation checks indicated that each of the treatments was successful. In the high involvement groups, 92.5% recalled that the free gift they were to receive was a razor, whereas in the low involvement groups, 78% correctly recalled that the free gift they were to receive was toothpaste. In addition, subjects reported liking the famous endorsers more than the average citizens, and they rated the strong arguments as more persuasive than the weak ones. Although subjects in the high relevance condition were more likely to recall the brand name of the product, neither relevance nor the other independent variables had an effect on recall of the product-relevant arguments appearing in the ad.

Analyses of subjects' attitudes toward Edge razors revealed main effects for argument quality and relevance (more favorable attitudes with strong than weak arguments and low than high relevance). More importantly, however, two significant interactions paralleled the results of our previous study on source cues (Petty, Cacioppo, & Goldman, 1981). Specifically, a Relevance × Argument quality interaction revealed that the arguments in the ad were a more important determinant of product attitudes for high than low relevance subjects, but a Relevance × Endorser interaction revealed that the status of the product endorsers was a more important determinant of attitudes for low than high relevance subjects. The results of this study are graphed in Figure 6-3. In the top panel it can be seen that the endorsers served as a simple cue under low relevance conditions (enhancing the effectiveness of both messages). The bottom panel indicates that only argument quality affected attitudes in the high relevance conditions.

Conceptual Replication of the ELM Source Cue Studies
In a recent dissertation, Huddleston (1985) undertook a conceptual replication of our application of the ELM to advertising using more naturalistic exposure conditions. In this study, 160 students in introductory speech courses participated in a 2 (Involvement: high or low) × 2 (Argument quality: weak or strong) × 2 (Source cue: negative or positive nonverbal behavior) between-subjects factorial design. All subjects were led to believe that they were assisting a market research firm and that they would view a television program with commercials. Before watching the program (an episode of the mystery/drama, *Quincy*), subjects were informed that they would receive a reward for their participation. Following the procedures of Petty, Cacioppo, and Schumann (1983), two techniques were used to enhance the relevance of the crucial advertised product (the OMEGA III fountain pen). Subjects in the high involvement conditions were told that for their gift, they would be able to select from among several brands of fountain pens, whereas in the low involvement conditions they were told

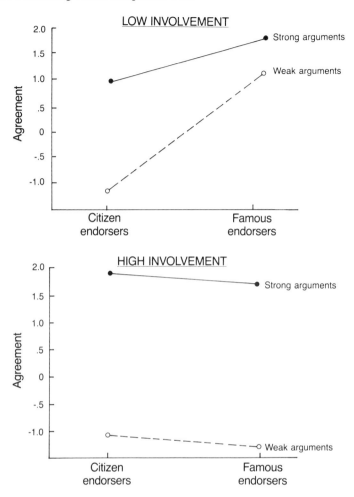

Figure 6-3. Postmessage attitudes as a function of product involvement, argument quality, and endorser attractiveness. *Top panel* shows that attitudes are affected by endorser attractiveness under conditions of low product involvement. *Bottom panel* shows that attitudes are not affected by attractiveness but are modified by argument quality under conditions of high product involvment (data from Petty, Cacioppo, & Schumann, 1983).

that they would select from among several brands of crackers. Next, subjects read several brief product descriptions. In the high relevance conditions these descriptions indicated that the target pen would soon be available in the local area. In the low relevance conditions, these descriptions indicated that the target pen would not be available locally for at least three years.

Four 30-s. versions of a commercial for the OMEGA III pen were prepared. In each, a seated male speaker (a professional actor with commercial experience) presented several arguments in favor of buying the pen that were either strong (e.g., utilizes a special no-smear ink; can be erased with a pencil eraser) or weak (e.g., same type as used by the President to sign bills; floats in water). The nonverbal behavior of the product endorser served as the manipulation of the peripheral cue. In the negative nonverbal behavior conditions, the speaker smiled infrequently, avoided eye contact (i.e., looked above the camera), and shifted his weight in his chair several times. These behaviors, developed in pilot testing, were designed to make the speaker appear insincere and/or low in credibility (see DePaulo, Zuckerman, & Rosenthal, 1980). In the positive nonverbal behavior conditions the speaker smiled, looked in the camera, and did not shift in his chair.

Following exposure to the television program containing the crucial pen ad (and several others), subjects responded to a variety of questions designed to assess the effectiveness of the advertisements. A similar pattern of results was obtained on most of the evaluative measures. One relevant measure that exemplified the overall pattern of results quite well concerned subjects' intentions to try an OMEGA III pen the next time they needed to purchase a pen (measured on a scale of 1 [definitely would not try] to 9 [definitely would try]). An analysis of this measure revealed main effects for each of the manipulated variables (more likely to try with strong than weak arguments, positive than negative cues, and high than low relevance). More importantly, two significant two-way interactions replicated the findings of the Petty, Cacioppo, & Schumann (1983) advertising study. Specifically, a Relevance × Source cue interaction revealed that the nonverbal behavior of the source had a greater impact on subjects' willingness to try the product when it was of low than high relevance. Additionally, a Relevance × Arguments interaction revealed that the nature of the arguments in the ad was a more important determinant of intentions to try the product for high than low relevance subjects. The results for all conditions are graphed in Figure 6-4. In the top panel it can be seen that the nonverbal behavior of the source (positive or negative) served as a simple cue under low relevance conditions, influencing the effectiveness of the message regardless of whether the arguments were strong or weak. The bottom panel indicates that the nonverbal behavior of the source was unimportant under conditions of high relevance. Instead, only argument quality affected intentions to try the product.[1] Importantly, the data patterns depicted in Figures 6-1, 6-2, and 6-4

---

[1]The other measures of evaluation taken in this study generally showed similar effects. Significant Relevance × Source cue interactions of the same form as described in the text were obtained on the measures of attitude toward the pen (good/bad; favorable/unfavorable; satisfactory/unsatisfactory), and more global attitudes toward the product and advertising. Relevance × Argument quality interactions were less plentiful, but occurred on measures of overall ad effectiveness and interest in the product. Interestingly, significant Source cue × Argument quality interactions that appeared on some measures (e.g., good/bad rating of product) indicated that the

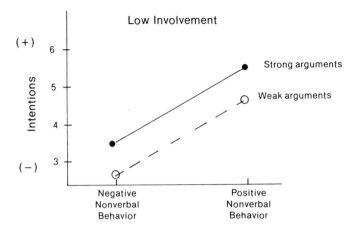

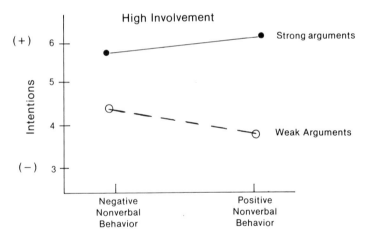

Figure 6-4. Postmessage intentions as a function of product involvement, argument quality, and endorser nonverbal behavior. *Top panel* shows that intentions are affected by the positive or negative nonverbal behavior of the source under conditions of low product involvement. *Bottom panel* shows that intentions are not affected by nonverbal behavior but are modified by argument quality under conditions of high product involvement (data from Huddleston, 1985).

negative nonverbal behaviors disrupted argument processing to some extent, perhaps because the source behaviors of shifting in the seat, failing to make eye contact, etc. were distracting. In any case, separate analyses of the data from only the positive nonverbal behavior conditions revealed significant Relevance × Argument quality interactions on virtually every measure replicating the pattern first observed by Petty & Cacioppo (1979b; see Chapter 4).

are remarkable in their similarity despite the very different topics, settings, and procedures employed in the studies.

Additional Studies on Source Cues

In addition to the research specifically motivated by the ELM which we reported above, other investigations have also provided support for the view that simple source cues are more important determinants of persuasion when personal relevance is low rather than high. For example, in one of the earliest experimental studies on source expertise, Hovland and Weiss (1951) had subjects read a message and then told them about the source. The source was either highly credible or lacked credibility. Four different topics (with appropriate sources) were used in the experiment. Although Hovland and Weiss in collapsing their data across the four topics concluded that the high credibility sources produced more change than the sources of low credibility, an analysis of the credibility effect for individual topics indicates that the credibility effect was reasonably strong for two topics ("Can a practical atomic-powered submarine be built in the present time [1950]?" and "Is the steel industry to blame for the current shortage of steel?"), but was weak and insignificant for two other topics ("Should antihistamine drugs continue to be sold without a doctor's prescription?" and "As a result of TV, will there be a decrease in the number of movie theaters in operation by 1955?"). The availability of cold remedies and the number of movie theaters are issues that have reasonably direct impact on the lives of students. The steel shortage and atomic submarines are much more remote. Thus, consistent with our analysis, the two topics for which source credibility was particularly impactful were the two topics lowest in personal relevance. In addition, it is likely that subjects had more knowledge about the two relevant topics and thus could more easily evaluate these messages without relying on the expertise cue. In short, when the elaboration likelihood was high, source expertise had little effect on persuasion. When the elaboration likelihood was low, however, source expertise was important.

Rhine and Severance (1970) more deliberately examined the impact of source credibility for differentially relevant messages by exposing students to a message on a topic that was either directly relevant to them (raising tuition) or not (increasing park acreage in a distant city). For the tuition message the expert source was a Yale Professor of Economics, and the inexpert source was a Private in the U.S. Army. For the message on parks, the expert source was a Department of Health, Education, and Welfare Committee Report, and the inexpert source was a local hair stylist. Their results indicated that the tuition issue was rated as significantly more important than the parks issue. Separate analyses on the high and low involvement issues indicated that although the expert source was rated as significantly more authoritative than the inexpert source for both messages, the credibility manipulation tended to enhance persuasion only when the topic was of low relevance ($p < 0.07$) and not when the topic was of high relevance ($F < 1$).

Finally, Chaiken (1980, Experiment 2) manipulated the pesonal relevance of an issue by telling students that their university was considering switching from a semester to a trimester system either next year or after they graduated. Subjects either read a message from a likable source who presented one strong argument or from a dislikable source who presented five strong arguments. When the issue was of little relevance, the likable source was significantly more persuasive than the dislikable source (i.e., the source cue was effective). When the issue was of high relevance, however, subjects tended to be more persuaded by the message with five strong arguments than one even though the source was dislikable. In sum, the available evidence is highly consistent with the view that source factors serve as simple acceptance cues when the elaboration likelihood is low, but are unimportant as cues when the elaboration likelihood is high (see also, Das, Roth, & Stagner, 1955; Johnson & Scileppi, 1969).

Number of Message Arguments as a Peripheral Cue
Distinctions between attitude changes based on source factors versus changes based on message factors have a long history in social psychology (e.g., Kelman & Hovland, 1953). In fact, the studies of source cues just described may appear to provide evidence consistent with the distinctions others have made between source and message orientations (e.g., Kelman & Eagly, 1965; McDavid, 1959; Harvey, Hunt, & Schroder, 1961). However, the central/peripheral distinction of the ELM is not equivalent to a source/message dichotomy. Importantly, the ELM holds that both source and message factors may serve as peripheral cues (and both source and message factors may affect information processing; see Chapter 8). As an example of a message factor serving as a cue, consider a person who is not motivated or able to think about the actual merits of the arguments in a message. For this person, it might be reasonable to assume that the more arguments contained in the message, the more meritorious it is. Although the literature on persuasion clearly indicates that increasing the number of arguments in a message is often an effective way to increase persuasion (e.g., Eagly & Warren, 1976; Insko, Lind, & LaTour, 1976; Maddux & Rogers, 1980), most have argued that this is because with more arguments, people generate and/or integrate more favorable issue-relevant beliefs (e.g., Calder, Insko, & Yandell, 1974; Chaiken, 1980). According to the ELM, it would be possible for the number of arguments in a message to affect issue-relevant thinking in some circumstances, but to affect persuasion by serving as a simple cue in other situations. We conducted two studies to test this notion (Petty & Cacioppo, 1984a).

Specifically, we reasoned that the mere number of arguments in a message would serve as a simple peripheral cue as to the validity of the message, but only when the personal relevance of the message was low.

However, increasing the number of arguments in a message might affect persuasion by enhancing issue-relevant thiking when personal relevance was high by providing more information to think about. If this information was cogent (strong arguments), then increasing the amount of information should result in more persuasion, but if the information was specious (weak arguments) then increasing the amount of informaton should result in less persuasion.

Method. A total of 168 students participated in a 2 (Issue relevance: low or high) × 2 (Argument quality: weak or strong) × 2 (Argument quantity: 3 or 9 arguments) between-subjects factorial design. All subjects were led to believe that the study concerned "first impressions." Their task was to look over a sample of what someone had written and to try to form an impression of that person. After these initial instructions, subjects received a written message on the topic of instituting senior comprehensive exams that was described as authored by the faculty chair of the University Committee on Academic Policy. This committee, subjects were told, was charged with advising the Chancellor on changes in academic policy that should be instituted. For some subjects, the proposal was made to have high relevance because the committee chair advocated that the comprehensive exam policy begin at the students' own university next year. For other subjects, the proposal was made to be low in relevance because the chair advocated that the exam policy be instituted in 10 years.

Subjects received one of four messages in favor of the exam proposal. One message contained 9 strong arguments, one contained 3 strong arguments (randomly selected from the 9), one contained 9 weak arguments, and one contained 3 weak ones (randomly selected from the 9). Each argument in the message was presented in a distinct typed paragraph to facilitate the impression of how many arguments were presented. Following exposure to the appropriate message, subjects gave their attitudes on the exam proposal, were asked to list five of their thoughts, and responded to various ancillary questions.

Results. Manipulation checks revealed that all of the manipulations were successful. Subjects generated more favorable thoughts to the strong than the weak message, and more unfavorable thoughts to the weak than the strong message. When asked to estimate how many arguments the message contained, subjects in the 9-argument conditions estimated a greater number than subjects in the 3-argument conditions. Finally, subjects in the high relevance group thought that it was more likely that their university would institute comprehensive exams than subjects in the low relevance group.

Two significant interactions on the measure of subjects' attitudes toward senior comprehensive exams provided support for the predictions of the ELM. A Relevance × Argument quantity interaction revealed that the number or arguments in the message was a more important determinant of persuasion under low than high relevance. However, a Relevance ×

Argument quality interaction revealed that the cogency of the arguments presented was a more important determinant of persuasion under high than low relevance conditions. The attitude data are graphed in Figure 6-5. In the left panel it can be seen that under low relevance, the number of arguments served as a simple cue, increasing agreement regardless of argument quality. In fact, a separate ANOVA on the data for low relevance subjects revealed only a main effect for number of arguments. In the right panel of Figure 6-5, it can be seen that under high relevance, the number of arguments acted to enhance argument processing: when the arguments were strong, increasing their number enhanced persuasion, but when their quality was weak, increasing their number reduced persuasion. A separate ANOVA on the data for high relevance subjects revealed a main effect for argument quality, and an argument quality by argument number interaction.

Further Exploration of the Number of Arguments Effect
In a second study, we provided a conceptual replication of the preceding experiment, and in addition examined the effect of combining strong and weak arguments into one message. According to the ELM, combining strong and weak arguments under low involvement conditions should prove beneficial to persuasion because under these conditions people are likely to be more influenced by the quantity than the quality of arguments. Mixing the messages under high involvement should not prove beneficial, however, because under high involvement, quality is more important than quantity.

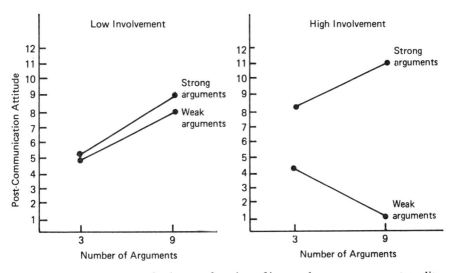

Figure 6-5. Postmessage attitudes as a function of issue-relevance, argument quality, and number of arguments. *Left panel* shows that under conditions of low issue-relevance, attitudes are made more favorable by increasing the number of arguments presented whether the arguments are strong or weak. *Right panel* shows that increasing the number of arguments under conditions of high relevance results in more favorable attitudes if the arguments are strong, but less favorable attitudes if the arguments are weak (data from Petty & Cacioppo, 1984a, Experiment 2).

Method. A total of 46 undergraduates participated in a 2 (Personal relevance: low or high) × 3 (Type of message: 3 strong arguments, 3 weak arguments; or 6 arguments combined message). All subjects were asked to read a message concerning a faculty proposal to increase student tuition. In the high involvement conditions, the message advocated that the tuition be increased at the students' own university, whereas in the low involvement conditions, the message advocated that the tuition be increased at a distant but comparable university. The message that subjects read contained either three strong arguments, three weak arguments, or six arguments (the three strong plus the three weak). After reading the assigned message, the only measure taken was an indication of the subjects' attitudes toward the idea of raising tuition.

Results. Statistical comparison of the messages processed under high and low relevance conditions revealed the following (see data in Figure 6-6). When the issue was of low relevance, 3 strong arguments did not elicit more agreement than 3 weak arguments, but the message with 6 arguments (3 strong and weak) elicited more agreement than either of the 3-argument messages (left panel). When the message was highly relevant, however, 3 strong arguments did elicit more agreement than 3 weak arguments, but the 6-argument message did not enhance persuasion over presenting 3 strong arguments (right panel). Again, argument quantity served as a cue under low relevance, but argument quality was more important under high relevance.

Additional Support for Number of Arguments Serving as a Peripheral Cue
Within the context of a program of research on "mindlessness" (see Chapter 1), Langer and her colleagues have explored the importance of the perception of arguments in an influence situation (Langer, Blank, & Chanowitz, 1978). In a field study on compliance, people who were standing in line to make copies at a Xerox machine served as subjects. A confederate approached the subject with a request to make either 5 (low personal consequences) or 20 (high personal consequences) copies. The request was accompanied by either a valid reason ("I'm in a rush"), a "placebic" reason ("I have to make copies"), or no reason. Both kinds of reasons were more successful in inducing compliance than giving no reason when the personal consequences were low. However, the valid reason was significantly more potent than the placebic reason when the personal consequences were high.

Folkes (1985) provided a partial replication of this effect. In two field studies using the inconsequential request (making 5 copies), respondents were equally willing to comply whether the request contained the valid or the placebic reason. In a third study, however, subjects were asked to guess how they would respond to the requests and to "think carefully before answering." When instructed to think before responding, the valid reason

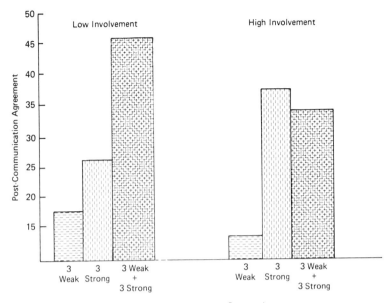

Figure 6-6. Postmessage attitudes as a function of issue-relevance and argument quantity and quality. The data indicate that adding three weak to three strong arguments enhances agreement under conditions of low (*left panel*) but not high (*right panel*) personal relevance (data from Petty & Cacioppo, 1984a, Experiment 1).

produced significantly more anticipation of compliance than the placebic reason. Although these results provide a conceptual replication of some of the conditions conducted by Langer, Blank, and Chanowitz (1978), Folkes takes issue with their assertion that the placebic information is processed "mindlessly." This is because in other conditions conducted by Folkes, she found that providing a *poor* reason for cutting in line (e.g., "because I don't want to wait") was significantly less effective than a valid or placebic reason under low consequences conditions. Folkes argues that if the reasons are truly processed mindlessly under low consequences conditions, a poor reason should be just as effective as the valid and placebic ones. The ELM makes the relative (rather than the absolute) prediction that the validity of a reason should be a more important determinant of compliance when consequences are high rather than low. This was untested in Folkes' study.

Other Variables Serving as Peripheral Cues under Low Relevance Conditions
In addition to the source and message cue studies noted above, additional research has provided support for the view that simple cues are more important determinants of judgments when personal relevance is low rather than high. We note some of these experiments below.

False physiological feedback. In one early study, Taylor (1975) examined the effect of false physiological feedback on attitudes (cf., Valins, 1966). Undergraduate women were led to believe (falsely) that they showed an especially favorable skin resistance response to one of three photographs of men. Following this, subjects were again exposed to the pictures of the three men and were asked to rate their attractiveness. Just prior to this second exposure, some of the women were told that they would be meeting some of the men depicted in the photos and that they would have to choose which ones to invite to the later meeting (high personal relevance). Other subjects were not told this and were simply informed that they would be asked to complete a survey about psychology experiments (low personal relevance). In the high relevance conditions, subjects took longer to rate the pictures (presumably indicative of greater thinking). However, the effects of the false physiological feedback were greater when relevance was low rather than high. Taylor concluded that the simple inference process outlined by Bem's self-perception theory "is most likely to operate when the attitudinal issues involved are relatively unimportant and inconsequential" (p. 126). This conclusion, of course, is consistent with the ELM.

Pleasant music. Gorn (1982) investigated the power of a simple affective cue to modify attitudes toward a product when the personal relevance of an ad was low. Before viewing any ads, subjects in the high relevance conditions were told that their task was to advise an advertising agency as to whether or not they should purchase time on television. In addition, they were told that they would later get to choose a three pen pack of one of the advertised pen brands as a gift. In the low relevance conditions, subjects were provided with little reason to scrutinize the ads. They did not expect to advise the ad agency and were not told about the free pen gift prior to ad exposure. All subjects were exposed to two different ads for a pen. One ad was attribute oriented and provided relevant information about the pen (e.g., "never smudges"), whereas the other ad featured pleasant music rather than information. About one hour after ad exposure, subjects were given a choice between the two brands of advertised pens. Of subjects in the high relevance condition, 71% chose the pen advertised with information, but in the low relevance condition, 63% chose the pen advertised with the pleasant music ($p < 0.001$).

In a conceptually similar study, Park and Young (1986) examined the effects of music on the persuasiveness of shampoo ads presented under high and low involvement conditions. Subjects in the "high cognitive involvement" group were told that shampoos differ in performance characteristics and that they should watch the commercial "as though they were in their living rooms trying to learn about the product's benefits and effectiveness." Subjects in the "low involvement" group were told that shampoos do not differ in their functional performance and that they should watch the commercial "as if you were sitting in your living room, worrying about (a) friend's illness, and knowing that you have no immediate need to purchase shampoo." All subjects saw a television ad for shampoo that contained three major arguments for the product (e.g., has superb cleansing action). The commercial either did or did not contain background music (a popular song ranked #1 by *Billboard* magazine for several months). The authors predicted that the pleasant music would serve as a peripheral persuasion cue only under the low involvement conditions. Although the results were statistically weak, this pattern emerged ($p < .08$, one-tailed). Interestingly, when involvement was high, the effect was reversed ($p < .06$, one-tailed). The authors suggest that under high involvement, the music distracted subjects from processing the strong message arguments (see Chapter 3). In sum, these two consumer studies clearly suggest that simple cues, such as pleasant music, are more likely to have a positive impact on attitudes when the elaboration likelihood is low rather than high (see also, Batra & Ray, 1985).

Visual salience. In another pertinent study, Borgida and Howard-Pitney (1983) examined the impact of personal relevance on attribution rather than attitude judgments. In two experiments they varied the visual prominence of discussants in a videotaped two-person conversation along with the personal relevance of the discussion topic. Previous research had shown that observers' evaluative judgments and attributions of causality tended to be more extreme for visually salient than nonsalient actors, a phenomenon called "top of the head" processing by Taylor and Fiske (1978). Based on the research we reviewed previously showing that personal relevance enhances message processing and reduces cue potency, Borgida and Howard-Pitney reasoned that social perceivers should be less influenced by the seemingly trivial visual salience cue (and presumably more by the content of the observed interaction) when the discussion was on a topic of personal importance.

In their first experiment, personal relevance was manipulated by varying whether subjects believed they would be affected by a proposed change in undergraduate psychology course requirements. In the second experiment, the issue discussed was a statewide change in the drinking age and subjects were divided into high and low relevance groups based on their ratings of issue importance and the extent to which the change would affect them personally. Subjects in both studies viewed a videotape of a pro-con discussion in which only one of the actors faced them. In Experiment 1, subjects exposed to the low relevance discussion rated the visually salient discussant as more causal and more likable. Neither the causality nor liking ratings were affected by salience in the high relevance conditions. In Experiment 2, subjects who found the discussion low in relevance rated the salient discussant as more influential, but subjects who found the discussion high in relevance were unaffected by the visual salience cue.

Summary

The accumulated research on personal relevance that we have just reviewed has provided strong support for the view that the personal relevance of an issue moderates a tradeoff between argument processing and cue utilization. Some studies have shown that various simple cues in the situation (i.e., source credibility, likability, nonverbal behavior, mere number of arguments, physiological feedback, pleasant music, visual salience) have a more powerful effect on judgments when personal relevance is low rather than high. Other studies have shown that the quality of issue-relevant arguments exerts a more powerful effect on judgments when personal relevance is high rather than low. Still other studies have demonstrated both of these effects within the same experiment (e.g., Huddleston, 1985; Petty, Cacioppo, & Goldman, 1981; Petty & Cacioppo, 1984a).

Additional Moderators of Cue Use: Distraction, Need for Cognition, and Others

The research that we have just reviewed clearly indicates that the personal relevance of a message is an important determinant of the route to persuasion. When relevance is high, people are motivated to exert the cognitive effort necessary to evaluate issue-relevant arguments. When relevance is low, simple cues in the persuasion context are more likely determinants of attitudes. According to the Elaboration Likelihood Model, however, other variables should also determine the route to persuasion by affecting a person's motivation and/or ability to process the arguments in a message. In Chapters 3 and 4 we identified several variables that affect motivation and/or ability to process a message in a relatively objective manner. Each of these variables should be capable of moderating the route to persuasion.

Distraction and the Operation of Peripheral Cues

First, consider the effects of external distraction on elaboration. Recall that in a study described previously (Petty, Wells, & Brock, 1976; see Chapter 3), we showed how distraction disrupted argument processing resulting in more agreement when the arguments were weak but less agreement when the arguments were strong. Just as arguments become less important determinants of persuasion as distraction is increased, simple cues should become *more* important determinants of persuasion as distraction is increased. Although this hypothesis has not been tested directly, available research is consistent with this idea.

In one early study, Miller and Baron (1968, Experiment 1; cited in Baron, Baron, & Miller, 1973) varied source credibility along with the manipulation of distraction employed in the original Allyn and Festinger (1961) experiment (see Chapter 3). Women in laundromats were approached to be in the study. Subjects in the distracted conditions were told that the researchers were interested in how well people could judge another person's personality from a voice tape-recording. Subjects in the undistracted conditions were told that the investigators were interested in how people responded to different types of communications. The source of the communication (which took a position against traditional childrearing practices) was either of high credibility (a woman affiliated with the state university who used impressive vocabulary) or not (a woman shopping at a discount store who made grammatical errors). A major result of the study was that distraction enhanced persuasion only when the source of the communication was credible. This interaction has been accounted for in a variety of ways. Consistent with previous theories of distraction (see Chapter 3), some have argued that distraction enhances persuasion only when the source is credible because more credible sources induce more dissonance, or because more credible sources induce more counterarguing (Baron, Baron, & Miller, 1973; Petty & Brock, 1981). Miller and Baron (1968) interpreted their results as indicating that the "personality orientation" manipulation employed in the original distraction research may not really be a manipulation of distraction at all. Instead, it may focus subjects' attention on source attributes and enhance the salience of this manipulation.

The ELM provides a different, yet equally plausible account for the interaction of distraction and source credibility. Rather than emphasizing the finding that distraction enhances persuasion only when credibility is high, the ELM emphasizes that the interaction obtained by Miller and Baron also shows that credibility enhances persuasion only when distraction is high (Petty & Cacioppo, 1984c). In other words, the ELM proposes that when people are disrupted from processing the issue-relevant arguments by distraction, simple cues in the persuasion context become more powerful determinants of influence. Yet, Miller and Baron's argument that there may be something unique about the "personality orientation" manipulation of distraction that focuses attention on the source appears quite reasonable. Stronger support for the ELM interpretation of distraction requires a study in which a manipulation of distraction that does not focus undue attention on the source still enhances reliance on simple cues. In one relevant study, Kiesler and Mathog (1968) exposed undergraduates to a variety of relatively involving messages (e.g., requiring dormitory bed checks) from a source of either high or low credibility under conditions of either distraction or no distraction. Importantly, the manipulation of distraction employed in this study—copying lists of two digit numbers—does not focus attention on the source. Nevertheless, the experiment resulted in a Distraction × Credibility interaction showing that the source cue had a greater impact on attitudes when distraction was present than when it was not (see results in Figure 6-7). This, of course, is consistent with the ELM analysis of distraction.[2]

---

[2] In a study described partially in Chapter 3, Tsal (1984) varied distraction, argument quality, and the likability of pictures associated with an ad for a product. Although argument quality became a less important determinant of persuasion when

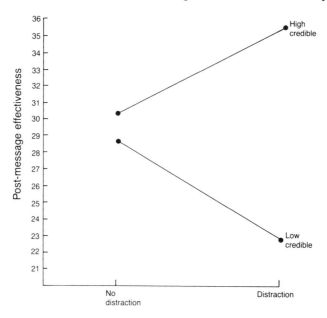

Figure 6-7. Postmessage attitudes as a function of distraction and source credibility (data from Kiesler & Mathog, 1968).

Need for Cognition and the Operation of Peripheral Cues
In addition to personal relevance and distraction, the other variables discussed in Chapters 3 and 4 should also be moderators of the route to persuasion. For example, we have already noted that argument quality becomes a more important determinant of persuasion as people feel more personal responsibility for message evaluation (Petty, Harkins, & Williams, 1980), and for individuals high rather than low in need for cognition (Cacioppo, Petty, & Morris, 1983). Thus, the ELM predicts that peripheral cues in the persuasion context should generally be more important for group than individually responsible message evaluators, and for individuals low rather than high in need for cognition (NC).

In a first attempt to examine the differential use of peripheral cues by people low (LNC) and high (HNC) in need for cognition, we exposed undergraduates to a videotape in which either an attractive or an unattractive source presented 8 strong arguments for the imposition of senior comprehensive exams (Cacioppo, Petty, Kao, & Hargitt, cited in Cacioppo &

---

distraction was increased (see Figure 3-3), the picture manipulation was equally effective under distraction and no distraction conditions. Unfortunately, subjects in this study were *instructed* to "extract meaning" from the pictures. Thus, it is not clear what would have happened if this artificial processing strategy (demand) had not been imposed.

Petty, 1984b). Attractiveness was manipulated by varying the clothing and make-up used by the source. Subjects initially indicated their attitudes toward the topic prior to message exposure and did so again immediately following the message. In addition, subjects rated the source along various dimensions. A manipulation check for attractiveness indicated that the manipulation was equally successful for HNC and LNC individuals. Two results from the study indicated that LNC subjects made greater use of the attractiveness cue than HNC subjects. First, low but not high NC subjects used attractiveness for judging other source characteristics such as trust-worthiness. More interestingly, a Source attractiveness × Need for Cognition interaction on the measure of attitude change (post-pre score) showed that the unattractive communicator affected HNC and LNC subjects similarly, but the attractive source had a significantly greater impact on LNC than HNC individuals.

In a more recent study, we examined the differential susceptibility of HNC and LNC subjects to cues in a situation in which no arguments actually were presented (Haugtvedt, Petty, & Cacioppo, 1986). In order to examine the relative impact of cues on attitude issues for which the elaboration likelihood would normally be high or low, we first conducted a survey of opinions to assess students' overall motivation and ability to think about several different topics. Students showed equivalent agreement with statements supporting stiffer penalties for drunk driving and the dangers of nuclear power plants, but indicated that they "knew more" about the first issue and that it was more "personally important" to them. Thus, these issues were selected for the experiment. The study was conducted as part of a mass testing in an introductory psychology class. Subjects first responded to a battery of personality tests including NC, and then completed a student opinion survey. To manipulate a simple peripheral agreement/disagreement cue, subjects were informed that " ... over 80% of college students com-pletely *agreed* with ... " or "completely *disagreed* with" stiffer penalties for drunk driving or the dangers of nuclear power plants immediately prior to asking for their own opinions (which were indicated on 5-point agree/disagree scales). Separate analyses for the two issues indicated that the simple cue had no effect on the attitudes of either HNC or LNC individuals when the issue was one of high perceived relevance and knowledge. However, for the low relevance/knowledge issue, a significant NC (above median or below median) × Peripheral cue (agreement or disagreement) interaction emerged (see top panel of Figure 6-8). Individual cell com-parisons revealed that LNC subjects were affected by the simple agreement cue, but HNC subjects were not.

Two recent studies by Chaiken and her colleagues have provided ad-ditional support for the idea that LNC subjects are more susceptible to peripheral cues than HNC individuals. In one study (Chaiken, Axsom, Hicks, Yates, & Wilson; cited in Chaiken, in press), students who scored high or low on the need for cognition scale (Cacioppo & Petty, 1982) were

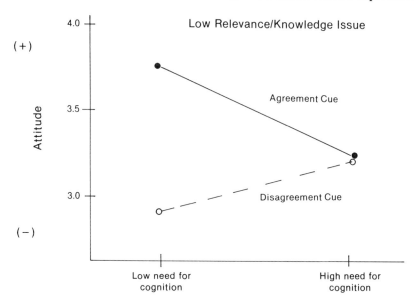

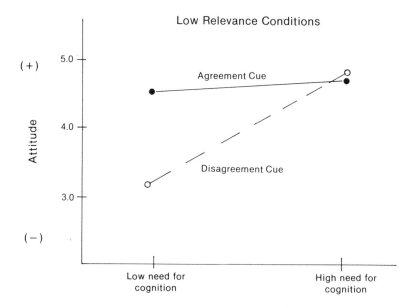

Figure 6-8. *Top panel*—attitudes on a low relevance/low knowledge issue as a function of need for cognition and the presence of peripheral agreement/disagreement cues (data from Haugtvedt, Petty, & Cacioppo, 1986). *Bottom panel*—postmessage attitudes on a low-relevance issue as a function of need for cognition and the presence of peripheral agreement/disagreement cues (data from Axsom, Yates, & Chaiken; cited in Chaiken, in press).

exposed to a message arguing that seniors should be required to pass a comprehensive exam in their major as a requirement for graduation. Although all students heard a message containing 6 arguments in favor of the exam proposal, in one version of the tape the speaker announced that he would present 10 arguments whereas in another version he announced that he would present only 2 arguments. A significant Need for cognition $\times$ Number of arguments interaction revealed that low but not high need for cognition subjects agreed more with the comprehensive exam proposal when the speaker announced that it contained 10 rather than 2 arguments. In short, LNC subjects were influenced by the simple message cue, but HNC subjects were not.

In a second study, Axsom, Yates, and Chaiken (cited in Chaiken, in press) examined the relative effectiveness of simple audience cues for high and low NC subjects under conditions of high and low personal relevance. High and low NC subjects were exposed to a taped speaker who advocated probation as an alternative to imprisonment. In the positive audience cue conditions, the tape contained an audience that responded to the speaker with loud bursts of applause. In the negative audience cue conditions, the audience was largely indifferent with only a few audience members clapping. The speaker presented either 6 strong or 6 weak arguments in favor of probation. In the high relevance conditions, subjects were told that the probation issue was being considered for adoption in their own state and that the experiment was important. In the low relevance conditions they were told that the probation issue was being considered in a distant state and that the study was "only preliminary." The major result of this study was a three-way interaction between need for cognition, audience cue, and the relevance of the issue. When the issue was high in personal relevance, neither HNC nor LNC subjects were influenced by the audience reactions. However, when the issue was low in personal relevance, LNC subjects were affected by the audience cue, although HNC subjects were still not affected (see bottom panel of Figure 6-8).

The research reported in this section clearly indicates that people low in their need for cognition are more influenced by various simple cues in the persuasion context than are people high in need for cognition. This effect has been observed with cues such as source attractiveness, the mere number of arguments believed to be in the message, and simple indications of what other people think, whether presented as statistical data or more vividly as applause. This research complements the studies detailed in Chapter 4, which indicated that people who are high in need for cognition are more influenced by the quality of the arguments in a message than are people low in need for cognition. Taken together, these studies provide compelling evidence for the notion that need for cognition is an important moderator of the route to persuasion.

Message Modality and the Operation of Peripheral Cues
In Chapter 3 we noted that one variable that appears to affect the extent of issue-relevant thinking is the modality of message presentation. In general,

audio and video presentations compared with print give people less opportunity to process issue-relevant arguments because exposure is forced rather than self-paced. Thus, presenting messages in written form should be especially important when the arguments are complex and difficult to process rapidly (Chaiken & Eagly, 1976). On the other hand, if it is generally more difficult to process issue-relevant arguments when exposure is forced rather then self-paced, simple cues in the persuasion context should be more powerful determinants of persuasion in the former than in the latter modality. Studies in which the medium of presentation and source cues have been manipulated have supported this proposition. Thus, both source credibility (Andreoli & Worchel, 1978) and likability (Chaiken & Eagly, 1983) have had a greater impact on attitudes when a message was presented on video or audio tape rather than in written form.

The Nature of the Message and the Operation of Peripheral Cues
Interestingly, the nature of the message itself has also been implicated as a determinant of whether a person processes mostly issue-relevant arguments, or searches for simple cues to determine message acceptability. Pallak, Murroni, & Koch (1983), for example, exposed subjects to different messages and sources for a brand of aspirin. In one message the arguments were supported by facts and the language was neutral in tone. In another message the facts were replaced by vague generalities and more emotional language. Presumably, the latter message would be more difficult to judge on its merits. Consistent with this reasoning, a manipulation of source attractiveness affected the brand attitudes of subjects exposed to the vague but not the factual message.

Going one step further, Yalch and Elmore-Yalch (1984) took a generally factual message about bank teller machines and added a large amount of quantitative information (e.g., "From only a small portion of total transactions handled by the bank, they are expected to grow to a significant amount" was changed to "From only 5% of total transactions handled by the bank, they are expected to grow to over 45%"). Based on previous research suggesting that over-quantification may reduce a person's motivation to process a message (Witt, 1976), the authors used the ELM to predict that source credibility would be a more important determinant of persuasion for the quantified than the regular version of the message. A significant Source expertise × Message quantification interaction on the attitude measure provided support for this hypothesis. It appears then that messages that are either overly vague (Pallak, Murroni, & Koch, 1983) or overly quantified (Yalch & Elmore-Yalch, 1984) may induce reliance on peripheral cues because these messages reduce subjects' ability (vague message) or motivation (overly quantified message) to process issue-relevant arguments.

In sum, the accumulated evidence is quite consistent with the ELM view that there is a tradeoff between argument processing and the operation of peripheral cues. Specifically, any variable that generally reduces a person's ability and/or motivation to process issue-relevant arguments to low levels also increases the likelihood of observing an effect for simple peripheral cues that may reside in the source, message, recipient, or context. Conversely, any variable that generally increases a person's motivation and/or ability to process issue-relevant arguments to high levels reduces the potency of peripheral cues.

Biased Processing versus Peripheral Cues

In the previous section we reviewed evidence for the tradeoff between relatively objective processing and the operation of peripheral cues. As we noted in Chapter 1, the ELM posits an identical tradeoff between biased processing and the operation of cues. In this section we review research on the biasing variable that has been studied the most—the effects of prior knowledge or issue-relevant schemata.

Effects of Schemata on the Use of Peripheral Cues

In Chapter 5 we saw that an issue-relevant schema facilitates information processing, resulting mostly in a bolstering of the original attitude position. Research is also generally consistent with the complementary principle expressed by the ELM that simple cues or decision rules are more likely to affect susceptibility to influence when prior knowledge is low rather than high. In this section we review the evidence for this proposition.

Gender as a Cue under Low Knowledge Conditions
One cue that we have studied in the context of previous issue-relevant knowledge is gender. Previous studies of sex differences in persuasion have provided some support for the view that females are more susceptible to influence than males in certain contexts (see reviews by Cooper, 1979; Eagly & Carli, 1983), and one explanation for this effect is based on the idea that females may have been socialized to be more agreeable (i.e., concerned with social harmony) than males (e.g., Eagly, 1978). To the extent that females have learned to be more agreeable and less dominant than males, the invocation of this socialized female gender role or category (cf., Deaux, 1984) could lead to a sex difference in influenceability. However, according to the ELM, attitude expression based on the female gender role should be more likely when women have little ability to process the issue-relevant information presented than when ability is high. We conducted a study that tests this reasoning (Cacioppo & Petty, 1980b).

Method. In this research, 32 undergraduates participated in a 2 (Gender: male or female) × 2 (Type of stimulus: male or female knowledge) × 3 (Type of advocacy: factual description, accurate evaluation, or inaccurate evaluation) mixed model factorial design with prior knowledge and type of advocacy serving as within-subjects factors. All of the students were led to believe that their task was to assist in the development of stimulus materials for a subsequent study. Each subject was given a stack of 36 photographs and 36 one-page questionnaires and was told to inspect each photograph and to read the comments that accompanied each picture. Participants were led to believe that previous subjects had written these comments. The photos that we employed were relevant to domains for which men and women in a pretest had rated their knowledge differently. Half of the photos depicted football tackles (high male knowledge) and half depicted current fashions (high female knowledge). The comments that accompanied each picture were either completely factual and descriptive (e.g., the dress is blue, the runner's feet are off the ground) or included an evaluation (e.g., that's a great tackle) that was either accurate or inaccurate. After examining each picture, subjects were instructed to rate the extent to which they agreed with the comments made by the other subject.

Results. Table 6-1 presents the data for each of the individual cells in the design along with cell comparisons based on the Duncan Multiple Range Test. The ELM suggests that to the extent that gender roles provide simple rules as to how one should behave (e.g., "As a woman, I should maintain harmony"), such rules should operate mostly when ability (and/or motivation) to evaluate the stimuli are low. In our study, when the comments were completely factual and easily verifiable, both males and females should be equally able to evaluate the comments whether they concerned fashions or football; thus, there should be no sex differences in extent of

Table 6-1. Mean Agreement as a Function of Sex of Subject, Type of Stimulus, and Type of Comment

	Sex of Subject	
Type of Stimulus	Men	Women
Inaccurate evaluation		
Tackle	3.54[1]	4.30[23]
Fashion	4.90[3]	4.02[12]
Accurate evaluation		
Tackle	6.38[4]	7.26[5]
Fashion	6.74[45]	7.26[5]
Factual description		
Tackle	6.81[45]	7.21[5]
Fashion	7.26[5]	7.49[5]

Note: Responses were made on scales where "1" indicated "disagree completely" and "9" indicated "agree completely." Entires with dissimilar superscripts differ at the 0.05 level (by the Duncan Multiple Range Test). Data from Cacioppo and Petty (1980b).

agreement. Our data were consistent with this expectation. When the comments were evaluative rather than descriptive, however, knowledge is required to confidently evaluate the statements. For football tackles, then, the invocation of the female gender role should lead to women showing more agreement than men whether the evaluations were accurate *or* inaccurate. Actual accuracy should make little difference because in both cases women would have little confidence (owing to low knowledge) in their judgments. Our data were also consistent with this expectation. Finally, when the judgments concerned fashions, women do have the requisite knowledge and confidence to make judgments. Thus, they should be more accepting of the accurate evaluations, but less accepting of the inaccurate evaluations than men. Our data revealed that women were significantly less accepting of the inaccurate characterizations of fashions, but were only marginally more accepting of the accurate evaluations of the fashions. Overall, then, the data are quite compatible with the ELM analysis. Other research has also supported the view that prior knowledge is an important determinant of sex differences in influenceability (e.g., Karabenick, 1983; Sistrunk & McDavid, 1971).

Behavioral Cues under Low Knowledge Conditions
In addition to simple rules based on gender, another simple principle that people sometimes use is based on observation of their own behavior and the situational constraints imposed upon it (i.e., the "self-perception principle"; Bem, 1967, 1972). For example, if an initially agreeable behavior is overjustified, people may reason that their behavior is governed more by the reward than their attitude and come to evaluate the behavior less positively (e.g., Lepper, Greene, & Nisbett, 1973; see Deci & Ryan, 1980).

Wood (1982, Experiment 2) reasoned that this relatively simple inference process based on a behavioral cue should be a more potent determinant of attitudes for people who have relatively little knowledge on a topic. To test this hypothesis, she assessed the prior knowledge and experience people had on the issue of environmental preservation by asking subjects to list their beliefs and previous behaviors concerning the topic. As in her previous study (Wood, 1982, Experiment 1, see description in Chapter 5), subjects were divided into high and low belief and behavior retrieval groups based on a median split of the number of beliefs and behaviors about environmental preservation listed. One to two weeks later when subjects returned, they were asked to deliver a proattitudinal message (in favor of enviornmental preservation) to two other people on campus and to seek their signatures on a petition. Subjects were either informed that they would receive five dollars or no reward for this task. After a brief rehearsal time, subjects committed themselves to delivering the message, and they completed an attitude measure. In addition to main effects for money and prior knowledge, a Prior knowledge (behavior retrieval) × Incentive interaction was obtained: the incentive had no effect on the attitudes of subjects with high knowledge, but the incentive reduced the pro-environmental attitudes of low knowledge subjects. The low knowledge subjects apparently used the incentive to make an inference about their attitudes (as self-perception theory would expect), but the attitudes of high knowledge subjects were unaffected by this simple cue.

In a conceptually similar study, Chaiken and Baldwin (1981) used Rosenberg's (1960) affective-cognitive consistency model to separate subjects who were likely schematic or aschematic on the issue of environmental preservation. Subjects completed semantic differential scales (affective) and expectancy-value scales (cognitive) on the issue. Subjects who had low discrepancies between the attitudes assigned by each method were considered to have attitudes that were more highly articulated or thought out than subjects whose discrepancies were large. Two weeks after assessment of affective-cognitive consistency, the subjects completed a questionnaire in which either pro or anti-environmental behaviors were made salient. This was accomplished by using the procedure of Salancik and Conway (1975) in which subjects are asked to endorse statements about the environment. The likelihood of a subject endorsing a pro or anti-environmental position is manipulated by varying whether the behavior is described as "frequent" or "occasional" (i.e., subject will more likely endorse the statement "I occasionally litter" than "I frequently litter"). Following completion of this behavioral salience questionnaire, subjects rated their own attitudes on being an environmentalist. The major result of this study was that the manipulation of behavioral salience affected the ratings of people who had poorly articulated attitudes, but not the ratings of people whose attitudes were more highly articulated. In sum, the work of Wood (1982) and Chaiken and Baldwin (1981) has shown that people with poorly developed attitude schemas are more susceptible to simple inferences (such as self-perception, Bem, 1972) based on behavioral cues than are people whose attitudes are more highly articulated. Thus, just as self-perception (behavioral cue) processes are more likely to affect attitudes when *motivation* to process is low rather than high (see discussion of Taylor (1975) earlier in this chapter), these same cue processes appear more likely to operate when *ability* to process is low rather than high.

Cognitive Cues under Low Knowledge Conditions
In a study on political cognition, Fiske, Kinder, & Larter (1983) showed that people who had low knowledge about politics were more likely to use simple cues in rendering judgments about an obscure country than people who had high political knowledge. Students in this study were divided into high and low political knowledge groups based on a pretest. Later they read details about the country, Mauritius. For some subjects the country was described as "democratic" but for others it was described as "communist" (a simple label or cue that could guide inferences and evaluations). The story about the country contained information that was consistent with both possible characterizations. Following the story, subjects were asked to make a variety of inferences about the country (e.g., "To what extent would you expect the

leaders to be inhuman, cruel, cold?"). The inferences of low knowledge subjects were consistent with the initial labeling of the country as communist or democratic, but the inferences of the high knowledge subjects were more even handed and consistent with the informational description of the country that was provided. In short, the judgments of the low knowledge subjects were influenced by this simple democratic/communist cue, but the judgments of high knowledge subjects were tied more to their analysis of the information provided.

In another relevant study, Srull (1983b, Experiment 3) examined the extent to which high and low knowledge subjects would judge the validity of statements based on simple cues. Previous research in cognitive psychology had shown that people's confidence in relatively unfamiliar factual statements (e.g., Montana has a greater range in temperature than any other state in the U.S.) could be increased by mere repetition of the statements (Bacon, 1979; Hasher, Goldstein, & Toppino, 1977). Srull reasoned that the simple familiarity cue should have a greater impact on the validity judgments of people whose knowledge on the topic was relatively low. To test this idea, undergraduates rated their self-knowledge of automobiles in relation to the rest of the population and a median split was used to classify subjects into high and low knowledge groups. Over the three sessions that subjects attended in a two-week period, statements about cars (e.g., The Cadillac Seville has the best repair record of any American made automobile) were presented either one, two, or three times. Although no statistical analyses were presented, Srull reported that the increase in credibility associated with familiarity (repetition) was "consistently less" for the high than the low knowledge subjects (p. 574).[3] In sum, the studies by Fiske, Kinder, and Larter (1983) and Srull (1983b) indicate that simple cognitive cues have a greater impact on judgments for people who are low rather than high in their knowledge of a topic.

Affective Cues under Low Knowledge Conditions
Finally, we note that simple affective cues may be a more important determinant of attitudes when prior knowledge is low rather than high. In a series of studies, Srull (1983a) induced a positive or negative mood in subjects by asking them to privately recall everything possible from a past affectively toned event in their personal life. Following this, they were exposed to various print advertisements and were asked to evaluate them and the products they depicted. A consistent result was that subjects evaluated the products more positively when they were in a positive than neutral mood at endcoding, and more negatively when they were in a negative than neutral mood at encoding. To test the view that this affective

---

[3]Batra and Ray (1986) have recently suggested and provided some evidence for the view that a simple "familiarity heuristic" may enhance attitudes toward a consumer product under conditions of low elaboration likelihood.

assimilation should have a greater impact on the attitudes of low than high knowledge subjects, Srull (1983b, Experiment 4) exposed students to an attribute oriented ad for a new car after they had been placed in a positive, negative, or neutral mood. Subjects were divided into high and low knowledge groups based on a median split on a self-report index of automobile knowledge. The major result was that the attitudes of the low knowledge subjects were affected significantly by the mood manipulation as expected, but the attitudes of the high knowledge subjects were not modified. Thus, just as affective cues appear to be more important determinants of attitudes when *motivation* to process a message is low (e.g., Gorn, 1982; described earlier in the chapter), affective cues may have greater impact when *ability* to process is low.

Testing the ELM Analysis of Prior Knowledge

In general, research on prior knowledge has provided support for the ELM view that when prior knowledge is low, simple behavioral, cognitive, and affective cues in the persuasion context affect influence. When prior knowledge is high, these simple cue processes are relatively unimportant. Instead, as we reviewed in Chapter 5, when attitudes are well articulated, message processing typically is biased because previous knowledge generally enables the counterarguing of incongruent messages and the bolstering of congruent ones. However, more definitive support for the ELM analysis of prior knowledge requires a study in which knowledge is examined along with argument strength and a peripheral cue.

Fortunately, Wood, Kallgren, & Priesler (1985) have reported such a study. In this study, Wood and her colleagues asked undergraduates to list their beliefs and behaviors relevant to environmental preservation. Subjects were divided into three groups based on a combination of the total number of beliefs and behaviors listed (creating high, medium, and low knowledge groups). One to two weeks later, subjects returned and were exposed to one of four persuasive messages. The messages differed in both the strength and length of the arguments presented. Two of the messages contained three strong arguments in favor of an anti-preservation view and two messages contained three weak arguments. Two versions of each argument were developed, however. One version contained short concise statements of the arguments, and the other contained longer more wordy versions of essentially the same information. The long and short versions were equated in terms of strength and ease of comprehension.

After exposure to one of the versions of the message, subjects indicated their attitudes on the topic of environmental preservation. Overall, a main effect for knowledge was obtained indicating that as knowledge increased, subjects were more resistant to the counterattitudinal appeal. In addition, individual cell comparisons revealed that the attitudes of high knowledge subjects were affected by argument quality, but the attitudes of low

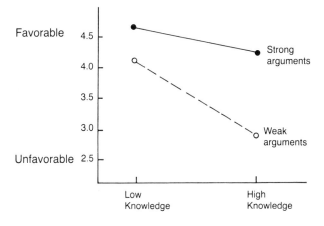

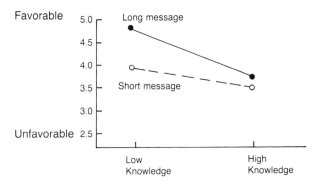

Figure 6-9. Postmessage attitudes as a function of prior knowledge, argument quality, and argument length. *Top panel* shows that attitudes are affected more by argument quality when prior knowledge is high than low. *Bottom panel* shows that attitudes are affected more by argument length when knowledge is low than high. Both panels show attitudes are less favorable when knowledge is high than low (data adapted from Wood, Kallgren, & Priesler, 1985; see footnote 4).

knowledge subjects were not. A closer inspection of this interaction pattern (graphed in the top panel of Figure 6-9) indicates that although high knowledge subjects were generally more resistant to both messages than low knowledge subjects, this was especially true for the message containing weak arguments. As noted previously, this particular interaction pattern suggests that high knowledge subjects were better able (and perhaps more motivated) to counterargue the incongruent message, but that it was more difficult to counterargue the strong than the weak version of it (compare with Panel IV in Figure 2-3). In addition, planned comparisons indicated that the attitudes of low knowledge subjects were affected by argument length, but the attitudes of high knowledge subjects were not (see bottom panel of Figure 6-9). In sum, low knowledge subjects' attitudes were affected by the simple cue of message length, but high knowledge subjects' used their prior knowledge in an attempt to defend their attitudes. They were more successful in doing this when the arguments in the message were weak rather than strong.[4]

Retrospective

In this chapter we explored the tradeoff between argument processing (whether relatively objective or biased) and the operation of peripheral cues. We have seen that when a person's ability and/or motivation to process issue-relevant arguments is attenuated, peripheral cues in the persuasion context become more important determinants of influence. Affective, cognitive, and behavioral cues have all proven effective when the elaboration likelihood was low. Futhermore, these cues have resided in the source (e.g., credibility, likability), the message itself (e.g., mere number of arguments), the recipient (feedback of bodily responses, mood), and the persuasion context (e.g., pleasant music, audience reactions). As the elaboration likelihood is increased, however, peripheral cues become less important. In short, in this chapter we have seen how a wide variety of individual (e.g., prior knowledge, need for cognition) and situational (e.g., distraction, message modality) variables moderate the route to persuasion by affecting the likelihood of issue-relevant elaboration and the reliance on peripheral cues. In the next chapter we examine the differential consequences of these two routes to persuasion.

---

[4]For ease of exposition we have graphed the data based on a median split on prior knowledge (Wood, personal communication, October 18, 1984) rather than the three-way split reported in the published article. As might be expected, the three-way split only enhances the differences between high and low knowledge groups, though the median split is based on a larger sample per cell.

Chapter 7

Consequences of the Route to Persuasion

Introduction

In the preceding chapters of this monograph we have outlined how the Elaboration Likelihood Model accounts for the initial attitude changes induced by persuasive messages, and we have reviewed the evidence for the ELM. We have seen that there are two qualitatively different routes to persuasion, which are moderated by a continuum of elaboration likelihood. When the elaboration likelihood is high, people follow the central route to persuasion as they attempt to scrutinize the issue-relevant information presented. This processing may proceeed in either a relatively objective or a relatively biased manner. When the elaboration likelihood is low, people follow the peripheral route to persuasion. Under this second route, attitudes are influenced by relatively simple cues in the persuasion context that either become directly associated with the advocacy or allow an inference as to the likely correctness or desirability of a particular attitude position without necessitating a personal evaluation of the issue-relevant arguments presented. The last postulate of the ELM proposes that there are at least three important consequences of the route to persuasion: attitudes formed or changed via the central route will show greater temporal persistence, resistance to counterpropaganda, and prediction of behavior than attitudes formed or changed via the peripheral route. In Chapter 1 we provided the justification for this postulate. In this chapter we review the evidence for this proposition.

Persistence of Persuasion

Enhanced Thinking Produces Persistence

If extended issue-relevant thinking increases the temporal persistence of opinion change, then conditions that foster issue-relevant elaboration should be accompanied by greater attitudinal persistence than conditions that minimize elaboration. In this section we review some evidence bearing on this notion.

Research on Role Playing

Among all the ways to change attitudes, one of the influence paradigms requiring the most issue-relevant thinking to produce persuasion is "role playing." In role playing research people are required to generate or improvise their own arguments for a message (e.g., King & Janis, 1956). Importantly, research indicates that to the extent that people have sufficient knowledge and skill to generate their own messages, the attitude changes induced by these messages are especially persistent.

In an illustrative study, Watts (1967) had subjects read a communication or actively generate a passage on an assigned topic. The persuasive messages employed in the experiment were developed in pretesting so that they would produce the same amount of initial attitude change as would the self-generation of a communication. The pretesting was apparently successful in that subjects who passively read the communication showed an amount of initial attitude change equivalent to that of subjects who generated their own messages. Both groups showed significantly more attitude change than controls. On a delayed measure of attitudes, taken 6 weeks later, however, subjects in the self-generation conditions showed total persistence of attitude change, whereas subjects in the passive reading conditions showed total decay.

Elms (1966) conducted a conceptually similar study. After reading a brief anti-smoking pamphlet, some subjects were asked to play the role of a person who had a serious disease and quit smoking. These subjects were told that it was their job to generate a message that would convince their best friend to quit. These subjects were also told to write down all of the reasons they could think of for giving up smoking. Another group of subjects, playing the role of the best friend, passively listened to the message generated by the active subjects after they too had read the anti-smoking pamphlet. Finally, the passive subjects also wrote down all of the reasons they could think of to stop smoking. On the immediate test of opinion, both active and passive subjects showed equivalent amounts of attitude change in the anti-smoking direction. On a measure taken 3 weeks later, however, the active subjects were significantly more anti-smoking than the passive group. Since the role playing subjects engaged in a more active and effortful issue-relevant elaboration than passive subjects, the ELM would expect their attitude changes to show greater temporal persistence. One factor that is a likely contributor to this greater persistence is that self-generated arguments are more accessible than arguments generated by others (Greenwald & Albert, 1968; Slameka & Graf, 1978).

Research on Anticipatory Shifts

Although in the role playing studies, subjects are instructed to think about an issue position, in other research the experimental conditions elicit issue-relevant thought spontaneously. For example, in research on anticipatory attitude shifts, subjects are induced to expect to discuss an issue or receive a message on some topic, and attitudes are measured prior to the discussion or message presentation (Cialdini & Petty, 1981). In one anticipatory change study relevant to persistence (Cialdini, Levy, Herman, Kozlowski, & Petty, 1976), college students were led to believe that they would discuss a campus issue with another student who held a position opposite to their own. Subjects were told that the discussion would take place either immediately or one week later, and the issue to be discussed was either one that was personally important to the students or unimportant. While waiting for the discussion to begin, subjects listed their thoughts on the issue and then reported their attitudes. Although subjects in all conditions showed some anticipatory shifting of their positions, only one group of subjects maintained their new issue positions after they had been informed that the discussion was cancelled. This group, subjects who expected to immediately discuss a personally important issue, was presumably the most motivated to undertake the cognitive work necessary to prepare for the discussion. Consistent with this analysis, these subjects listed significantly more thoughts that supported their own positions in anticipation of the discussion than subjects in the other cells.

Testing the ELM Analysis of Persistence

In both the role playing research and the research on anticipatory shifts, attitude changes that were accompanied by considerable issue-relevant cognitive activity led to more persisting shifts than changes induced with less issue-relevant thinking. However, in both of these paradigms, no persuasive messages were presented. According to the ELM, the same result should hold if the attitude changes resulted from exposure to a persuasive communication. Specifically, the greater the elaboration of the message arguments, the more persistent the resulting attitude change should be. The accumulated persuasion literature is quite consistent with the idea that conditions that foster people's ability or motivation to engage in issue-relevant cognitive activity also enhance the persistence of persuasion. Thus, research has shown that using more interesting or involving issues about which subjects have more knowledge (e.g., Ronis, Baumgardner, Leippe, Cacioppo, & Greenwald, 1977), providing more time to think about the message (Mitnick & McGinnies, 1958), leading people to believe that they will be interviewed on the attitude issue (Chaiken, 1980), increasing message repetition (Johnson & Watkins, 1971), and reducing distraction (Watts & Holt, 1979), all are associated with increased temporal persistence of attitude change (see Cook & Flay, 1978; Petty, 1977; for reviews). To provide a more direct test of the ELM view of persistence, however, we attempted to induce comparable attitude changes under the central and the peripheral routes, and then track attitude persistence over time (Petty, Cacioppo, Haugtvedt, & Heesacker, 1986; Experiment 1).

Method. In our study on attitude persistence, 100 students participated in a 2 (Personal relevance: high or low) × 2 (Message type: strong arguments–positive cue or weak arguments–negative cue) × 2 (Time of assessment: immediate or delayed) mixed model factorial design. All of the subjects in the experimental conditions listened to three persuasive messages. Each message began with a description of the origin of the message and provided a brief biography of the message source. The first two messages served as filler material and were identical for all subjects. The third message contained the experimental manipulations. Half of the subjects were led to believe that the advocacy concerned an imminent change in policy (the institution of senior comprehensive exams) at their own university (high relevance), and half were led to believe that the advocacy concerned the same proposed policy change at a distant university (low relevance). Half of the students received a message from a very prestigious and credible source, which provided six strong arguments in support of instituting senior comprehensive exams, and half of the students received a message from a low prestige, inexpert source, which provided six weak arguments in support of the exams. An additional group of 25 subjects received an irrelevant third message and served as an attitude-only control. Subjects' attitudes were first assessed immediately after the message presentation. Then, from 10 to 14 days following message exposure, subjects were called and asked their opinions concerning a number of campus issues, including the general idea of senior comprehensive exams.

Based on our previous research on personal relevance (Petty & Cacioppo, 1979b; Petty, Cacioppo, & Goldman, 1981; see Chapters 4 and 6) and additional pilot testing of the sources and messages under high and low relevance conditions, we expected that both the high and low involvement groups who received the positive source-strong arguments message would show equivalent amounts of initial persuasion. However, the change in the high relevance group should be based mostly on a careful evaluation and elaboration of the strong issue-relevant arguments (central route), whereas the change in the low relevance group should be based mostly on the positive source cue (peripheral route). Similarly, the rejection of the advocacy in the high and low relevance groups exposed to the negative source-weak arguments message should be equivalent initially, but in the high involvement group the rejection should be based mostly on scrutiny of the weak arguments, whereas in the low relevance group the rejection should be based mostly on the negative source. Our major prediction was that attitudes changed via the central route (high relevance conditions) would show greater temporal persistence than attitudes changed to the same degree, but via the peripheral route (low relevance conditions).

Results. An analysis of subjects' immediate and delayed attitudes provided support for the ELM predictions regarding persistence. On the immediate measure of attitudes, both high and low relevance groups of subjects exposed to the positive message/source were more favorable than controls, and both groups of subjects exposed to the negative message/source were less favorable than controls. More interestingly, however, the degree of personal relevance had an impact on whether or not these initial attitudes persisted. Specifically, an analysis of variance on the initial and delayed attitudes of high relevance subjects revealed only a main effect for type of communication. The positive source-strong arguments message was more effective than the negative source-weak arguments message both initially and at the delayed testing. An analysis on the attitudes of low relevance subjects, however, revealed a Message type × Time of measurement interaction (see Figure 7-1). For these subjects, the initial difference between the two message conditions was no longer apparent at the delayed testing. Specifically, low involvement subjects exposed to the positive

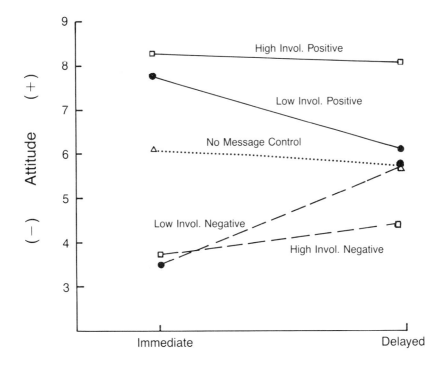

Time of Attitude Measurement

Figure 7-1. Immediate and delayed postmessage attitudes as a function of personal relevance (involvement) and type of communication. The figure shows that attitude changes, whether induced by a positive (strong arguments, high credible source) or a negative (weak arguments, low credible source) communication, persist longer when initially processed under high rather than low involvement (elaboration) conditions (data from Petty, Cacioppo, Haugtvedt, & Heesacker, 1986, Experiment 1).

message/source were less favorable at the delayed than the initial assessment, but those exposed to the negative message/source were more favorable at the delayed than the initial assessment. In short, those subjects who formed their initial attitudes based on a careful consideration of issue-relevant arguments showed greater persistence of attitude change (whether favorable or boomerang) than those subjects whose initial attitudes were based primarily on the source cue.

Alternative Models of Attitude Persistence

Message Learning Model

Before proceeding with other consequences of the route to persuasion, it would be useful to compare the ELM to other models of the persistence of attitude change. Perhaps the most widely studied model is the "Yale" message learning approach as pioneered by Carl Hovland and his colleagues (e.g., Hovland, Lumsdaine, & Sheffield, 1949; Hovland, Janis, & Kelley, 1953) and elaborated by William McGuire and others (e.g., Watts & McGuire, 1964; see also, Miller & Campbell, 1959; Eagly, 1974; Eagly & Himmelbarb, 1974). As McGuire (1968) indicates, use of the message learning approach involves "predicting how any independent variable in the communication situation (such as order of presentation, source credibility, . . . etc.) will be related to attitude change by analyzing that variable's likely impact on learning the message contents. Hence, if there is a primacy effect in learning, then one is predicted also in retention of message content; if there is a negatively decelerated decay in retention of message content, a like function is predicted as regards the persistence of induced attitude change." (p. 179).

However, reviewers of the literature on retention of message content and persistence have concluded that there appears to be little link between retention of specifc message arguments and persistence of persuasion (e.g., Brock & Shavitt, 1983; Fisk, 1981; Greenwald, 1968; McGuire, 1969; Miller & Colman, 1981). As Cook and Flay (1978) summarized: "It seems unlikely that retention of message details and delayed attitude are related in any simple way" (p. 23). Studies examining correlations between message retention and delayed attitude have found the correlations to be very modest, nonsignificant, or even negative (e.g., Cacioppo & Petty, 1979b; Insko, 1964; Watts & McGuire, 1964). Furthermore, studies examining the decay function of attitudes and message retention have revealed that the two measures may not follow the same temporal pattern (e.g., Papageorgis, 1963). In his comprehensive review of the attitudes literature in 1969, McGuire concluded that the "learning theory approach to attitude change seems to us to be acquiring more the status of a fertile error" (p. 266).

Cognitive Response Model

In an attempt to salvage a learning model of persistence, Greenwald (1968) proposed a "cognitive response" model which argued that just as initial persuasion depended upon the cognitive responses (idiosyncratic associations) to the message content, persistence of persuasion depended upon the learning and retention of these cognitive responses. In a test of this idea, Love and Greenwald (1978) had undergraduates complete an opinion pretest, read one of two messages, list their cognitive reactions to each argument in the message, complete an opinion posttest, and then attempt to recall the arguments in the message and their reactions. One week later, subjects again completed an opinion posttest and attempted to recall the message arguments and their cognitive responses. Analyses employing partial correlations (initial pretest was partialed out) revealed that although the delayed opinion measure could be predicted on the basis of the cognitive responses recalled at the delayed testing session (number of favorable minus unfavorable reactions recalled), the measure of number of message arguments recalled was not significantly related to delayed opinion. Although this study provides evidence consistent with Greenwald's cognitive response hypothesis, the evidence is correlational and therefore questions about causal direction remain (Cook & Flay, 1978).

In a study designed to provide an experimental test of the cognitive response hypothesis, Petty (1977) exposed undergraduates to one of two messages on the topic of increasing the legal driving age to 21. One message presented 5 highly persuasive (strong) arguments and the other contained 5 less persuasive (weak) arguments in favor of the proposal. A third (control) group of subjects read 5 neutral statements about driving. Each of the arguments and statements was only one sentence long (14 to 28 words). After reading the appropriate message, subjects were asked to list five of their own thoughts about the proposal to raise the driving age. The major manipulation in this study was whether subjects were asked to memorize the specific arguments in the message or their own thoughts on the issue with all subjects being given as much time as was needed to memorize the material close to verbatim. One measure of attitudes was taken right after the initial memorization task, and a second measure was taken one week later. At the delayed session, subjects were also requested to recall the arguments/ statements and the thoughts generated the previous week.

The results of this study revealed that subjects receiving the strong arguments generated more favorable thoughts and fewer unfavorable thoughts than subjects receiving the weak arguments or neutral statements. In addition, subjects receiving the strong arguments were more favorable toward raising the driving age than the remaining subjects on the initial measure of opinion (see top panel of Figure 7-2). More interestingly, when attitudes were assessed one week later, only those subjects who were exposed to the strong arguments and who memorized their cognitive responses persisted in their new opinions. Subjects who were exposed to the strong arguments but who memorized the exact message statements rather than their own reactions to the message were no longer different from the controls or subjects who received the weak arguments (see bottom panel of

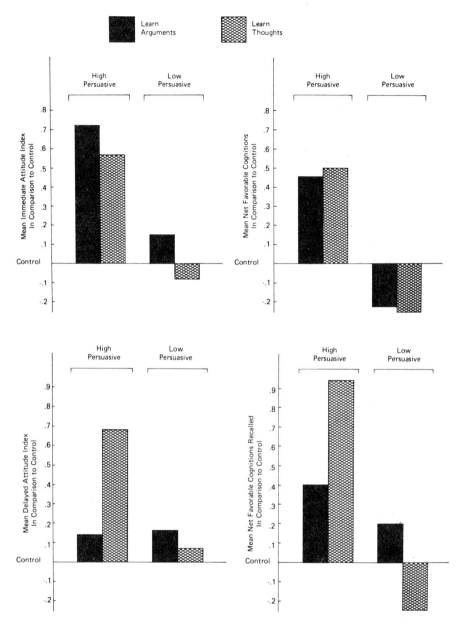

Figure 7-2. Immediate and delayed postmessage attitudes and thoughts as a function of message persuasiveness and learning of arguments and thoughts. *Top panel* shows that subjects were significantly persuaded by the highly persuasive arguments (*left*) and generated more favorable cognitions than controls to these arguments (*right*). Whether subjects learned the arguments or their own thoughts did not affect these initial measures. *Bottom panel* shows that only subjects who memorized their own thoughts to the persuasive arguments persisted in their attitude change (*left*) and recalled more favorable cognitions than controls (*right*). Subjects who memorized the message arguments showed decay of attitudes and favorable cognitions (data from Petty, 1977).

Figure 7.2). In sum, when the initial favorable cognitive responses to the strong message arguments were rehearsed, rendering them more accessible within the attitude schema, the initial attitude change was more enduring then when the specific message arguments were the more accessible component of the attitude schema.

The ELM endorses the cognitive response view that to the extent that the initial message elaborations remain salient, the initial attitude change will persist. However, there are several important differences between the ELM and the cognitive response approach. Perhaps the most crucial concerns the determinants of *initial* persuasion. According to the cognitive response approach, the effects of "most of the traditional independent variables of persuasion . . . (on attitudes) . . . are mediated strictly through their effects on cognitive responses to persuasion" (Greenwald, 1968, p. 168; see also Perloff & Brock, 1980; Petty, Ostrom, & Brock, 1981b). The ELM, of course, postulates *two* routes to persuasion and indicates that attitudes can change in the absence of extended issue-relevant thinking if salient cues are provided in the persuasion context and people lack the requisite motivation and/or ability to engage in message scrutiny. Although the ELM and the cognitive response model share a similar conceptual basis regarding the persistence of persuasion, the ELM does not require the continued salience of the initial message-relevant thoughts for persistence. As we noted in Chapter 1, persistence may also result from a person's perception that a great deal of thinking accompanied attitude formation which induces a reluctance to abandon one's position. Also, relative persistence may result from the repeated pairing of a peripheral cue with a person, object, or issue (e.g., Johnson & Watkins, 1971; Weber, 1972); although these attitudes would still likely be highly susceptible to counterpersuasion because the person would have great difficulty defending his or her position if attacked with strong arguments.

Dissociative Cue Model
In addition to their focus on message learning, Hovland, McGuire, Cook, and others have addressed the operation of augmenting and discounting cues as they relate to the persistence of persuasion. In order to account for the "sleeper effect" (an increase in persuasion over time that may occur when a message is initially paired with a weak source or other discounting cue), Hovland, Lumsdaine, and Sheffield (1949) argued that two independent processes may be involved in persuasion. One process involves *learning* the message arguments (based on message attention and comprehension), but the other involves *accepting* the arguments or the message conclusion (incorporated as "reception" and "yielding" in McGuire's, 1968, model).[1] According to this two-component view, attitude change in response to a persuasive message may be the result of two separate processes:

---

[1]The most recent version of McGuire's information processing model incorporates 12 steps from "exposure" to "post-action" (McGuire, 1985).

learning the message arguments associated with the message conclusion, and associating an acceptance cue with the message conclusion. An acceptance (augmenting) cue (e.g., credible source) is postulated to enhance initial agreement over and above that produced by learning the message arguments alone, whereas a discounting cue (e.g., inexpert source) is thought to initially inhibit the persuasion produced by message learning. It was assumed that over time the link between the cue and the conclusion would decay faster than the link between the message arguments and the conclusion. Because of this, the joint operation of the learning and cue processes could produce a sleeper effect. Specifically, the positive impact of learning message arguments would endure longer than the negative impact of the discounting cue leading to more agreement over time (Cook & Flay, 1978).

The dissociative cue hypothesis and the ELM differ in at least three important respects. The first significant difference has to do with the ELM's focus on issue-relevant *elaboration* rather than message *learning*. The two formulations become somewhat more similar if message "elaboration" is substituted for message "learning" in the dissociative cue formulation. However, at least two essential differences remain.

First, although both models highlight positive and negative cues, the dissociative cue formulation presumes that in a typical persuasion situation, attitudes are affected *jointly* (additively) by salient cues *and* message processing (learning). In contrast, the ELM highlights the fact that in various persuasion situations (where source and other cues are available prior to or during message presentation) there is a *tradeoff* between message processing and the operation of cues. Thus, attitudes may be affected mostly by cues *or* by message processing (elaboration). As detailed in Chapter 6, people's attitudes will be affected primarily by various peripheral cues in the persuasion context when motivation and/or ability to process issue-relevant arguments is low. However, people's attitudes will be affected primarily by the quality of the issue-relevant arguments presented when motivation and ability are high. The differential conditions under which either peripheral cues or message processing dominate (e.g., high/low personal relevance, high/low distraction, prior knowledge, need for cognition, etc.) are not considered by the dissociative cue model. The ELM proposes a tradeoff between argument processing and the operation of cues that is moderated by the elaboration likelihood continuum. At the high end of the continuum, argument processing dominates and simple cues have little effect. At the low end of the continuum, cues dominate and little argument processing occurs. In contrast, the dissociative cue model assumes that both cues and argument processing typically operate jointly and additively (Cook, Gruder, Hennigan, & Flay, 1979).

Another important difference between the ELM and the dissociative cue model is that the ELM holds that it is possible for salient contextual factors (including source variables), to affect the manner in which the message arguments are processed (Petty & Cacioppo, 1981a). In other words, message arguments and certain contextual variables may not have indepdent effects, but as we have seen previously, various contextual factors may affect the nature of information processing. Specifically, the ELM holds that source and message factors may have *interactive* rather than *additive* effects in some contexts. For example, in Chapter 4 we saw that increasing the number of message sources could increase a person's motivation to process the issue-relevant arguments (see the next chapter for further discussion). In sum, the ELM focuses on message elaboration rather than message learning, postulates a tradeoff between cues and message processing, and suggests that source factors may affect message processing rather than contributing independently to persuasion (i.e., source and message factors may interact).

Although we have just argued that in the typical persuasion situation attitudes are unlikely to be affected in an additive fashion by argument processing and peripheral cues, it is possible for both cues and arguments to affect attitudes *independently* (as specified by the discounting cue model) in certain narrowly defined situations. For example, if the source is identified *after* the message arguments have been processed, then it would be possible for a source cue to affect persuasion over and above the influence of the message. Interestingly, the best evidence for a sleeper effect comes from studies in which a discounting cue is presented *after* rather than prior to message exposure (Gruder, Cook, Hennigan, Flay, Alessi, & Halamaj, 1978; Hovland & Weiss, 1951; Pratkanis & Greenwald, 1985). However, according to the ELM, a sleeper effect should still be very difficult to produce even if a negative cue follows a message. This is because if the message is on a topic of low personal relevance or knowledge, for example, the postmessage cue may be effective, but the message will have induced insufficient processing to lead to persistence. If the message is on a topic of high personal relevance or knowledge, however, although the message may induce considerable processing, many negative cues (e.g., an unattractive source) presented after the message may be judged irrelevant and therefore ignored. Although the sleeper effect is of considerable conceptual significance, obtaining it may require conditions that are infrequently present in either the "real world" or in persuasion research.

Three Process Model
Kelman (1958, 1961) has developed a theory of attitude persistence that is based on specifying the antecedents and consequents of three different attitude change processes. In Kelman's typology, attitudinal *compliance* occurs when attitudes change as a result of a person wanting to obtain rewards or avoid punishments under the control of some powerful source. Change is postulated to persist only to the extent to which the powerful source can monitor the person's attitudes. Attitudinal *identification* occurs when attitudes change as a result of a person wanting a satisfying

relationship with or wanting to view him or herself as similar to some attractive source. Change is thought to persist only to the extent to which the person's relationship with the attractive source remains a salient goal. Attitudinal *internalization* occurs when attitudes change as a result of a person accepting new information that is perceived to be inherently conducive to the maximization of preexisting values. According to Kelman (1961), a crucial dimension for acceptance of such information, and thus for internalization, "is the agent's credibility, that is his relation to the (message) content" (p. 65). Since attitude change through internalization is independent of the power of, or one's personal relationship with a source, it is believed to persist. Although Kelman (1958) has conducted one study that is consistent with the three process theory (see discussion in Chapter 8), other research has not been as supportive. In particular, there is little evidence for the view that source credibility generally enhances persistence (Cook & Flay, 1978).

The ELM shares the view that attitude changes based on "internalization" of issue-relevant information are more likely to persist than those based on certain cues (e.g., source attractiveness), but the formulations differ in the antecedents of these different processes. Kelman ties the type of persuasion mostly to the nature of the message source. Thus, expert sources produce internalization, attractive sources produce indentification, and powerful sources produce compliance. According to the ELM, expertise, attractiveness, and power may all serve as simple cues under some circumstances, producing short-lived agreement resulting from little issue-relevant thinking. Under other circumstances, however, issue-relevant thinking may induce relatively enduring persuasion regardless of source expertise, attractiveness, or power. According to the ELM, the crucial determinant of persistence is not the source of the message, but the person's general motivation and ability to process issue-relevant arguments (see Figure 1-1). Also, although Kelman's internalization is similar to what we have called persuasion via the "central" route, and "identification" and "compliance" would qualify as peripheral approaches, the ELM does not tie the effectiveness of sources to these particular processes. For example, in some situations the use of an attractive source may induce persuasion via the process of identification as Kelman suggests. In others, an attractive source may induce change by invoking the balance principle (Insko, 1981), or may influence agreement by triggering an attractiveness heuristic (Chaiken, 1986). Although it is important to specify why attractiveness serves as a cue in different situations (e.g., Mills & Harvey, 1972), the ELM views all of these processes as peripheral in that they are postulated to operate under similar conditions (i.e., low elaboration likelihood) and have similar consequences (e.g., relative lack of persistence compared with changes based on issue-relevant argumentation).

Attitude-Behavior Link

Enhanced Thinking Produces Attitude-Behavior Consistency

In the previous section we provided support for the view that attitude changes based primarily on thoughtful consideration (or self-generation) of issue-relevant arguments produced more enduring persuasion than changes based primarily on simple cues in the persuasion context. Research is also consistent with the view that attitudes formed or changed via the central route are more predictive of behavior than attitudes based on peripheral cues.

As we noted previously, one effortful form of issue-relevant processing occurs when attitude change results from the self-generation of arguments, as in research on role playing (e.g., Watts, 1967). These changes, then, should be especially predictive of behavior. In a relevant program of research, Fazio and Zanna (1981) have explored the consequences of attitudes formed via direct rather than indirect experience. When an attitude is formed through direct personal experience, the attitude is necessarily based on self-generated information. When an attitude is based on indirect experience (i.e., a message from others), less effortful processing typically may be involved. In some sense then, the distinction between direct and indirect experience is analogous to the distinction between attitudes based on role playing (i.e., self-generation of arguments) versus passive exposure.

In a prototypical study on direct versus indirect experience with the attitude object, Regan and Fazio (1977, Experiment 2) varied the manner in which subjects' attitudes toward five intellectual puzzles were formed. Half of the subjects were presented with previously solved examples of each puzzle by an experimenter who explained the directions and solutions (indirect experience). A second group of subjects was given the opportunity to work the puzzles themselves. These subjects had direct behavioral experience, but presumably also had to self-generate the positive or negative attributes of the puzzles because the experimenter did not supply them. Subsequently, all subject rated how much they liked the puzzles, and then were given 15 min. to work any puzzles they desired. The attitudes of subjects in the direct experience (self-generation) group proved better predictors of behavior toward the puzzles than the attitudes of subjects with only passive exposure to information. For example, attitudes of the direct experience subjects predicted the order in which the puzzles were attempted ($r = 0.51$) better than the attitudes of subjects with indirect experience ($r = 0.22$). Other research employing different attitude objects and behaviors has also supported the view that attitudes formed via direct experience with the attitude object predict behavior better than attitudes based on indirect information (see review by Fazio, 1985). The ELM suggests that one reason for this is that attitude formation based on direct experience may typically require greater elaboration of the merits of the object (e.g., puzzle) than attitude formation based on passive exposure.

Consider another study by Sivacek and Crano (1982), which explored the attitude-behavior relationship in groups of people who either did or did not have a personal stake in an issue. The attitudes of interest in their study concerned an impending statewide referendum to raise the legal drinking age from 19 to 21. One group of subjects studied would be personally affected by the proposal (i.e., those who would not be 21 by the time the proposed law went into effect), and one group would not be affected personally. Even though both groups of subjects expressed equally strong attitudes against the proposal, more people who would be personally affected by the proposal agreed to engage in behaviors consistent with their negative attitudes than people who would not be personally affected. If we can assume that the attitudes of the high relevance group were more likely formed via the central route (i.e., extensive issue-relevant thought), whereas the attitudes of those who would not be affected were more likely formed via the peripheral route (e.g., identifying with the opinions of their friends), then the results of this study are consistent with the view that attitudes formed via the central route are more predictive of behavior than attitudes formed via the peripheral route.

Finally, consider a series of studies by Davidson, Yantis, Norwood, and Montano (1985) that examined the attitude-behavior relation in groups of people who differed in the amount of information they possessed about the attitude object. In one study, subjects' voting intentions toward the two candidates for mayor in a local election were assessed 4 to 14 days prior to the election. In addition, the subjects were asked to list the information and beliefs that they possessed about the candidates. Then, following the election, subjects were telephoned and asked whether they voted in the election, and if so, for whom. Analyses were confined to people who said they voted. The major result of this study was that the amount of information a person had about the candidates moderated the relationship between preelection intentions and reported voting in the election. Specifically, regression analyses indicated that as the amount of information about the candidates increased, so did the correlation between intentions and behavior. These results were replicated in two additional studies in which the amount of information people had about an attitude object was assessed in a self-report format (7-point scale ranging from "completely uninformed" to "completely informed") rather than with a thought-listing. Furthermore, in these studies, the amount of information remained a moderator of intention-behavior consistency even after controlling for previous experience with the attitude object and confidence in one's intentions. If we make the reasonable assumption that people with more information about an attitude object were more likely to have formed their attitudes and intentions via the central rather than the peripheral route, these results are consistent with the ELM.

Testing the ELM Analysis of Attitude-Behavior Consistency

Enhanced Elaboration Increases Attitude-Behavior Consistency
In general, the accumulated attitude-behavior research is consistent with the view that the more cognitive effort that is involved in attitude formation, the greater the utility of the attitude in predicting behavior (Cialdini, Petty, & Cacioppo, 1981). In our own research, we have also found that conditions fostering a high elaboration likelihood produce higher attitude-behavior correlations than conditions in which the elaboration likelihood is low. In one study described in Chapter 6, for example, we exposed subjects to mock magazine advertisements for a disposable razor under conditions of either high or low personal relevance, (Petty, Cacioppo, & Schumann, 1983). Recall that under high relevance, attitudes were affected primarily by the issue-relevant arguments presented for the product, but under low relevance attitudes were affected more by peripheral source cues (see Figure 6-3). Importantly, in additon to assessing product attitudes in this study, we also asked subjects to rate how likely they were to purchase the product (behavioral intentions). Overall, the attitude-intention correlation under high relevance was 0.59, whereas under low relevance it was 0.36 (p <0.07).

Just as increasing motivation to process issue-relevant arguments should enhance the utility of attitudes in predicting behavior, so too should enhancing ability to process the message. In one relevant study, we exposed subjects to advertisements containing strong arguments for a new pen either 1, 4, or 8 times in the context of a simulated television program (Schumann, Petty, & Cacioppo, 1986). Each repetition of the message gives subjects an additional opportunity to consider the product-relevant information (see Chapter 3). After message exposure, subjects rated their attitudes toward the advertised pen, their likelihood of purchasing this brand in the near future, and the amount of time they spent thinking about the product during the program. Subjects reported engaging in more thought about the product as repetition increased, and the attitude-intention correlation also improved significantly with repetition. Specifically, attitudes and intentions toward the pen product correlated 0.65 with one exposure. By four exposures, the correlation increased to 0.78 and remained at this high level at eight exposures (0.75).

Need for Cognition and Attitude-Behavior Consistency
The ELM holds that situational variables can moderate the attitude-behavior relationship by affecting the likelihood that attitudes are formed or changed via the central or peripheral routes. Relevant dispositional

variables should operate in a similar manner. For example, we have provided considerable evidence for the view that the need for cognition scale (NCS; Cacioppo & Petty, 1982) allows at least gross distinctions to be made between individuals who differ chronically in their tendency to engage in and enjoy effortful cognitive endeavors (see Chapter 2). Furthermore, the cumulative research on NC and persuasion indicates that as expected, the attitudes of high need for cognition (HNC) individuals are more likely to be affected by issue-relevant thinking (central route; see Chapter 4), whereas the attitudes of low need for cognition (LNC) individuals are more likely to be affected by peripheral cues (see Chapter 6). Because of this, it would be expected that the attitudes of HNC individuals would be more predictive of their behavior than the attitudes of LNC persons. In order to test this hypothesis, we conducted a study during the 1984 presidential campaign (Cacioppo, Petty, Kao, & Rodriguez, in press, Experiment 2).

Method. A survey was administered to a large number of undergraduates 8 weeks prior to the 1984 presidential election. The survey included measures of attitudes toward the presidential tickets (Mondale/Ferraro; Reagan/Bush), reported thought and knowledge about the candidates, voting intentions, and level of need for cognition. A subset of individuals differing widely in their NC scores (falling in the top and bottom thirds of the distribution) were selected for further study. Of these subjects, 61 constituted the "knowledge subsample," and 108 constituted the "attitude-behavior subsample."

Subjects in the knowledge subsample group were invited to the laboratory either 3 to 5 weeks prior to the election (N = 33) or 3 to 5 weeks after the election (N = 28). During the session, subjects were asked to list everything they knew about the presidential candidates. Subjects were given 5 min. to list one fact per line and were told that spelling and grammer were unimportant. The number of unique items of information listed by the subject served as the primary dependent measure of knowledge.

Subjects in the attitude-behavior subsample were contacted by telephone from 1 to 3 days following the election. Subjects were asked if they had voted, and if so, for whom. Subjects who indicated that they had not voted were asked to indicate for whom they would have voted. Of the 56 LNC individuals who were contracted, 41 (73%) reported having voted, and 43 (83%) of the 52 HNC individuals reported having voted (n.s.).

Results. A 2 (Need for cognition: high or low) × 2 (Time of measurement: before or after election) between-subjects ANOVA on the amount of information possessed by subjects in the knowledge subsample revealed only a main effect for NC. As expected, HNC individuals generated more facts about the presidential candidates (M = 8.13) than LNC persons (M = 6.10).

Similar mixed model ANOVAS on the data from subjects in the attitude-behavior subsample revealed main effects for both Time and NC. Subjects reported having thought more about the candidates, having more knowledge about, and more confidence in their selections after than before the election. Also, HNC individuals reported having thought more about the candidates and knowing more about them than LNC persons. One interaction revealed that HNC individuals reported more thinking about the candidates before the election than LNC persons, but after the election both groups reported similar amounts of thinking. Finally, HNC individuals reported more favorable attitudes toward the Mondale/Ferraro ticket than LNC individuals.

To test our major hypothesis that the preelection attitudes of HNC, in contrast to LNC, subjects would be more predictive of subsequent reports of voting, the correlation between a relative preference index (difference score between attitudes toward the two tickets; positive numbers favored Mondale/Ferraro) and reported voting (1 = Reagan/Bush; 2 = Mondale/Ferraro) was calculated separately for the HNC and the LNC groups. The preelection preference index predicted postelection reports better for HNC ($r = 0.87$) than LNC ($r = 0.46$) individuals. Because these correlations included all subjects, whether they reported actually voting or not, the correlations were recomputed for the subsample that reported actually voting. Again, attitudes predicted behavior better for HNC ($r = 0.86$) than LNC ($r = 0.41$) individuals.

Conclusions

Before proceeding to the next consequence of elaboration, it is noteworthy that our argument that the more issue-relevant elaboration involved in attitude formation or change, the greater the attitude-behavior correlation, appears to conflict with a recent claim by Wilson, Dunn, Bybee, Hyman, and Rotondo (1984) that analyzing reasons for one's attitudes *reduces* attitude-behavior consistency. In the research suporting the contention of Wilson et al., however, one effect of having subjects think about the reasons behind their attitudes was to produce a change in attitudes. Thus, Wilson and his colleagues have compared the ability of an *initial* attitude to predict behavior with the ability of a *changed* attitude. Their results indicated that the new attitude was less predictive than the old one. Importantly, the ELM addresses a comparison between two initial attitudes (one formed via the central route and one formed via the peripheral route) *or* two newly changed attitudes (one changed via the central and one changed via the peripheral route). The ELM predicts that the central attitudes will predict behavior better than comparable attitudes formed or changed via the peripheral route.[2] As we have seen, the available evidence is consistent with the view

---

[2]Wilson (1986) argues that analyzing reasons may also reduce attitude-behavior consistency even if attitudes are not changed, however. He further argues that this effect may occur primarily when (a) the attitudes in question are affectively based

that when the experimental conditions or dispostional factors enhance people's motivation or ability to elaborate issue-relevant information, the attitudes formed or changed predict intentions and behaviors better than when the elaboration likelihood is low (see also, Kallgren & Wood, 1985; Pallak, Murroni, & Koch, 1983; Sandelands & Larson, 1985).

Resistance to Counterpersuasion

Enhanced Thinking Produces Resistance

A third consequence of the route to persuason postulated by the ELM is that attitudes formed or changed via the central route should be more resistant to counterpropaganda than attitudes formed or changed via the peripheral route. Importantly, the *resistance* of an attitude to attack is conceptually distinct from the temporal *persistence* of an attitude. Thus, some attitudes may be highly persistent, but only if they are not challenged. Other attitudes may be very transient even in a vacuum. Likewise, it is possible for some attitudes to be very resistant to change, but only in the short term. Despite the conceptual independence of persistence and resistance, we have already outlined the reasons why the ELM holds that usually these two qualities will go together. Attitudes based on extensive issue-relevant thinking will tend to be both persistent and resistant, whereas attitudes based on peripheral cues will tend to be transient and susceptible to counterpersuasion.

Attitudes for which persistence and resistance do *not* go together provide an intriguing target of study. Perhaps the most dramatic example of the possible independence of persistence and resistance is found in cultural truisms. Truisms such as "you should brush your teeth after every meal" tend to be highly persistent in a vacuum, but very susceptible to influence if attacked. As McGuire (1964) noted, people have very little practice in defending these beliefs because they have never been attacked. Furthermore, the ELM would contend that these beliefs are highly susceptible to persuasion because they were probably formed with very little issue-relevant thinking. It is likely that people come to accept unquestioningly the various cultural truisms sometime during childhood. The truisms are presented many times during development by powerful, likable, and expert sources (e.g, parents, teachers, television characters) with little or no justification. This continual pairing of a belief with a positive source cue may result in a relatively persistent attitude, but one that cannot be defended when subsequently attacked.

(e.g., attitude toward a dating partner) rather than cognitively based (e.g., attitude toward a presidential candidate), and (b) the cogitative analyses are conducted on a short-term rather than a long-term basis. These very interesting suggestions warrant further investigation.

Most research on attitudinal resistance has focused on how various "treatments" can help bolster an attitude that a person already has. In an important program of research, McGuire (1964) has provided impressive evidence for the view that attitudes toward truisms can be made more resistant by providing people with the requisite motivation and/or ability to counterargue opposing messages. For example, in an early study on the "inoculation effect," McGuire and Papageorgis (1961) provided subjects with a "supportive defense" (which presented arguments supporting subjects' original beliefs) on one cultural truism, a "refutational defense" (which presented and refuted arguments *against* subjects' beliefs) on another truism, and no defense on a third truism. Two days later, subjects were exposed to messages that attacked their initial beliefs on all three truisms. The results showed that both defenses were helpful in inducing resistance to the counterpropaganda, but the refutational defense (inoculation treatment) was significantly more effective. The underlying logic of McGuire's inoculation theory is that a threat to a previously unchallenged belief, provided in the refutational defense, motivates the person to defend that belief when it is assailed in the future. People have probably never heard certain truisms impugned, and may not be able to conceive of them as being susceptible to attack. A refutational defense disabuses people of this notion, motivating them to bolster the assailed belief and giving them practice in defending it.

Research employing cultural truism topics has replicated McGuire's finding that refutational defenses are superior to supportive defenses in conferring resistance (e.g., Suedfeld & Borrie, 1978). However, research not employing cultural truisms has tended to find that refutational and supportive defenses confer similar degrees of resistance (e.g., Adams & Beatty, 1977; Pryor & Steinfatt, 1978). When the issue employed is not a cultural truism, and people are therefore not operating under the assumption that their belief is invulnerable, the refutational defense should not have any unique motivating power, and thus would not necessarily be more effective than a supportive defense.

Testing the ELM Resistance Predictions

Importantly, the work on resistance using McGuire's inoculation paradigm and others (e.g., Burgoon, Cohen, Miller, & Montgomery, 1978; see review by Smith, 1982) has focused on how an initial belief held by a person can be made more resistant by providing some treatment that enhances the person's motivation and/or ability to counterargue a subsequent opposing communication. This work is consistent with the ELM in that it demonstrates that attitudes can be made more resistant by motivating or enabling people to engage in additional thought about the reasons or arguments supporting their attitudes. However, the ELM makes unique predictions about the differential resistance of attitudes formed via different routes.

Specifically, the ELM postulates that people who come to accept an initial position because of a peripheral cue (e.g., source expertise) should be generally more susceptible to an attacking message than people who adopt the same initial position based on a careful scrutiny and elaboration of the message arguments. We tested this prediction in a recent study (Petty, Cacioppo, Haugtvedt, & Heesacker, 1986; Experiment 2).

Method. A total of 113 students participated in the study. The experimental conditions comprised a 2 (Extent of elaboration: low or high) × 2 (Message direction: pro or anti) mixed design with extent of processing serving as a between-subjects variable and message direction serving as a within-subjects factor. Several control groups were also included (see below). Undergraduate students were recruited to participate in a "media evaluation" study. Upon arriving at the lab they were told that the psychology department was helping the Journalism School obtain ratings of audiotapes submitted by applicants to the broadcasting program. They were further told that in order to obtain ratings simulating those that would be obtained under normal radio listening conditions in which distractions were present, they would be asked to monitor the quadrant in which an X appeared on a screen before them. Subjects expected to listen to and rate five different announcers during the session.

All experimental subjects initially listened to an irrelevant message and then to a message attributed to three college professors from prestigious universities that presented seven strong arguments for the imposition of comprehensive exams as a requirement for college graduation (pro-exam communication). Following this, subjects were exposed to another irrelevant message, and then to a message containing seven arguments against the imposition of senior comprehensive exams that was attributed to another prestigious college professor (anti-exam communication).

Half of the experimental subjects were randomly assigned to hear the first key (pro-exam) message under conditions that would inhibit message elaboration. These subjects were told, via an introduction on the tape, that the announcer for the message was from a distant university and that the proposal to insititute the exams was proposed for this distant school (i.e., low personal relevance conditions that were designed to reduce motivation to process the message; Petty & Cacioppo, 1979b; see Chapter 4). In addition, for these subjects the Xs flashed on the screen once every 5 s (a high distraction task that was designed to disrupt processing; Petty, Wells, & Brock, 1976; see Chapter 3). The remaining experimental subjects were assigned to hear the pro-exam message under conditions that were designed to be more facilitative of argument processing. For these subjects, the announcer for the message was from their own university and they were led to believe that the proposal would affect students at their own school (high personal relevance). Furthermore, the Xs flashed on the screen once every 15 s (low distraction). For all subjects, the anti-exam message was attributed to an announcer from a distant school, and Xs flashed during this message at the low distraction rate. Based on the previous research reported in this volume and pilot testing for this study, we expected subjects in the low elaboration conditions to be influenced primarily by the positive source cues associated with the issue; but subjects in the high elaboration conditions were expected to be influenced primarily because of their processing of the strong issue-relevant arguments.

Following each message, experimental subjects rated the student announcer, the source of the information contained in the communication (i.e., the college professors), and also provided their own opinions about each of the issues "since your own opinion on the issue discussed may influence your ratings of the announcer." Thus, subjects gave their opinions about senior comprehensive exams twice—once following the pro-exam message and once following the anti-exam message. After the final communication was presented, all subjects were given a brief period of time to list the thoughts they recalled having to the pro-exam message and then the anti-exam message. A no message control group was also included in the study to assess the effectiveness of the pro-exam message conditions in producing absolute attitude change.[3]

Results. Subjects in both the high and the low elaboration experimental groups were significantly (and equally) more favorable toward senior comprehensive exams after exposure to the pro-exam message than were control subjects who did not receive the pro-message. Importantly, correlational analyses supported the view that even though the amount of change was similar in both groups, the processes inducing change were different and as expected. Specifically, the attitudes of high elaboration subjects were correlated with the number of favorable issue-relevant thoughts that they generated about senior comprehensive exams ($r = .38, p < .10$) but were unrelated to their ratings of the source of the information ($r = .22$). In contrast, the attitudes of low elaboration subjects were uncorrelated with the number of favorable thoughts generated ($r = .11$), but were predicted by their ratings of the source of the information about the exams ($r = .59, p < .01$).

The major attitude results from the study are depicted in Figure 7-3. A 2 (Extent of elaboration) × 2 (Message direction) ANOVA on attitudes revealed two significant effects. First, a main effect for message indicated

---

[3]Additional groups of control subjects heard the initial pro-exam message under high or low elaboration conditions, provided their opinions, and then responded to the senior comprehensive exam issue again *without* hearing the anti-exam message. The results from these controls (graphed in the bottom panel of Figure 7-3) revealed only a main effect for time indicating that both groups of subjects showed a very small decay on the second attitude assessment.

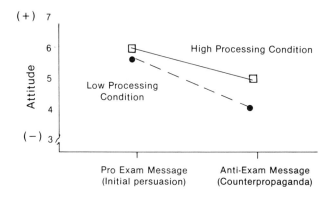

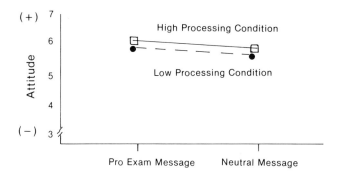

Figure 7-3. Attitudes after an initial message and subsequent counterpropaganda as a function of the initial level of message processing. *Top panel* shows that attitude changes induced under high processing conditions (high relevance, low distraction) showed greater resistance to counterpropaganda than comparable attitude changes induced under low processing conditions (low relevance, high distraction). *Bottom panel* depicts control conditions showing that in the absence of counterpropaganda, the attitude changes induced under high and low processing conditions showed a similar small amount of decay (data from Petty, Cacioppo, Haugtvedt, & Heesacker, 1986, Experiment 2).

that subjects became less favorable toward the exams after exposure to the anti-exam message. However, an Extent of elaboration × Message direction interaction provided support for our major hypothesis: subjects whose attitudes were changed under high elaboration conditions were more resistant to the counterpersuasive message than subjects who initially changed the same amount, but under low elaboration conditions. In short, subjects who became more favorable toward senior comprehensive exams because they elaborated the issue-relevant arguments maintained their favorable positions in the face of counterpropaganda better than did subjects who formed quantitatively similar attitudes on the basis of the positive source cues.

Conclusions
Although there has been considerable interest in McGuire's (1964) program of research on different types of treatments that increase the likelihood that an already existing attitude will resist attack, little attention has been paid to the factors that determine whether a newly formed attitude will or will not prove resistant to subsequent propaganda. The ELM clearly indicates that attitude changes that take place when situational (e.g., high relevance) or individual difference (e.g., high need for cognition) factors foster issue-relevant elaboration should prove more resistant in the face of counter-propaganda than comparable attitude changes that result from simple cues under low elaboration conditions. Interestingly, and consistent with the ELM, recent research has suggested that high knowledge subjects who form an initial judgment about some material may even be more resistant to conflicting messages that they generate themselves than are people who have low knowledge on the issue (Hirt & Sherman, 1985).

Retrospective

In this chapter we discussed three major consequences of the route to persuasion. First, evidence was reviewed that was consistent with the view that the more issue-relevant thinking accompanying attitude formation or change, the more likely the attitude was to persist over time. This prediction and others from the ELM was contrasted with three alternative models of attitude persistence. Second, research was reviewed which indicated that attitudes based on issue-relevant thinking or extensive issue-relevant information were more predictive of behavior than attitudes based on peripheral cues. Finally, we noted that the available evidence supported the view that issue-relevant thinking induces resistance to subsequent counter-attitudinal propaganda. Now that we have addressed the major antecedents and consequences of the two routes to persuasion, in the next chapter we examine some complicating factors in the ELM.

Chapter 8

Intricacies of the Elaboration Likelihood Model

Introduction

We have now presented the major postulates of the Elaboration Likelihood Model and the evidence for these postulates. In reviewing the evidence for the ELM we have focused deliberately on variables and instances that were straightforward and relatively unambiguous in interpretation. Although it would be nice if we could have provided an exhaustive list of variables that serve as peripheral cues and variables that affect message processing in either a relatively objective or a biased manner, we have already seen that this is not possible. For example, we have argued that the effects on information processing of some variables may shift from relatively objective to relatively biased as the variable reaches very high levels. Thus, although increasing personal relevance and message repetition may generally enhance subjects' motivation and/or ability to see the merits of strong arguments and the flaws in weak ones, we have suggested that when personal relevance or message repetition reach very high levels, the initially objective processing may become biased as the person becomes motivated to reject the advocacy (Cacioppo & Petty, 1979b; Petty & Cacioppo, 1979b). In short, some variables have multiple effects on information processing. In addition, we have seen that some variables may affect information processing under certain conditions, but serve as peripheral cues in other contexts. For example, we reviewed evidence in Chapter 6 that a manipulation of the number of arguments in a message could serve as a peripheral cue when the personal relevance of the message was low, but that increasing the number of arguments in a message could increase the amount of information processing activity when the personal relevance of the message was high (Petty & Cacioppo, 1984a). In this chapter we will comment on these and other intricacies of the ELM.

Variables with Multiple Effects on Elaboration

In most of the research that we have discussed so far, we have examined the isolated effects of different source, message, recipient, and channel factors on information processing. However, in most natural persuasion situations, many variables combine to create the overall persuasion context. For example, consider a high need for cognition person who is part of a jury whose members share responsibility for evaluating an expert witness who presents weak arguments in a corporate tax case in a courtroom with noisy distractions. All of the many variables present in this situation must be considered jointly to determine the probable persuasive impact of the testimony. Normally, sharing cognitive responsibility with a group reduces information processing activity (Petty, Cacioppo, & Harkins, 1983), but our message recipient dispositionally tends to like to think (Cacioppo, Petty, & Morris, 1983) and is therefore less susceptible to motivation loss in groups when the task is an interesting cognitive one (Petty, Cacioppo, & Kasmer, 1985). Therefore, *motivation* to process the message is likely high despite the group responsibility. However, due to a lack of prior knowledge about corporate taxes and the distractions inherent in the situation, our message recipient may have little *ability* to process the message arguments (Petty, Wells, & Brock, 1976; Wood, Kallgren, & Priesler, 1985). Thus, the perceived expertise of the witness may serve as a potent influence cue (Kiesler & Mathog, 1968).[1]

Our example relies mostly on the idea that each of the features of the persuasion situation (e.g., distraction, group responsibility) can be considered separately and independently regardless of the levels of the other variables with which it is combined. If so, one can roughly add (subtract) the effects of each variable to determine the overall elaboration likelihood. Although this is sometimes possible, as we discuss next, it is also possible for one variable to have very different effects on information processing depending on the level of other variables.

Variables that Enhance and Reduce Message Processing

The Effect of Rhetorical Questions
Some variables may increase information processing at one level of another factor, but may actually decrease processing at a different level of that factor.

---

[1]Just as any one persuasion context may contain many variables that affect the elaboration likelihood, any one persuasion context may contain multiple peripheral cues. We assume that the less motivated a person is to scrutinize an advocacy, the fewer the cues that will have an impact on attitudes. When motivation is very low, the most salient cue will likely have the largest impact on attitudes. On the other hand, if motivation is high, but ability to process issue-relevant arguments is low, people may scrutinize the message and persuasion context very carefully and consider all relevant cues in order to evaluate the advocacy.

For example, we hypothesized that the use of rhetorical questions could operate in this manner. Zillmann (1972) reported the first experimental investigation of rhetorical questions. In his study, subjects heard a defense attorney's closing arguments in a second degree murder case. The subjects either heard the summary presented completely in statement form or with 10 argument-condensing persuasive statements transformed to rhetorical form (e.g., "Johnny was a peaceful boy," to "Johnny was a peaceful boy, wasn't he?"). Subjects hearing the rhetorical version were more favorable to the defense than those hearing the statement version. Zillmann proposed that rhetorical questions tended to be used with strong arguments and that through socialization, rhetorical questions would come to "mark relatively powerful arguments" for most people (i.e., rhetoricals served as a positive peripheral cue). We suggested, on the other hand, that given people had the ability to process the issue-relevant arguments in the message, that the use of rhetorical questions would motivate thinking about the argument associated with the rhetorical question. If people attempted to covertly respond to the rhetorical questions in a message, then the use of rhetoricals would likely enhance agreement only if the message arguments were strong. If the arguments were weak, people would likely disagree with the rhetorical questions and show less agreement than if the message contained no rhetoricals. According to the positive cue hypothesis, rhetoricals should enhance persuasion for both strong and weak messages.

If the elaboration view is correct, however, another point to consider is that the use of rhetorical questions should be most effective in enhancing thinking when recipients are not naturally devoting much effort to scrutinizing the message. If the message was naturally eliciting a great deal of thought, it would be unlikely that the use of rhetoricals could enhance elaboration further. Under these conditions, rhetoricals might have no further effect on elaboration and persuasion, or the use of rhetoricals might actually interfere with subjects' thought processes. Based on pilot work, we favored the latter possibility. Specifically, in a preliminary study, subjects were exposed to a personally relevant audiotaped message that either did or did not contain rhetorical questions. When the message contained rhetoricals, subjects reported that although they were trying very hard to think about the message, the questions asked by the speaker disrupted their ongoing chain of thoughts. This distraction effect of rhetoricals is likely confined to situations in which the presentation rate of the message is controlled externally rather than by the subject. If the presentation rate was controlled by the subject (e.g., a print message), then the disruption effect should be eliminated. In any case, to test our view that rhetorical questions might enhance processing when the motivation to elaborate was low, but inhibit ongoing processing when motivation was already high (as least for audio messages), we conducted a study in which we varied the use of rhetorical questions and argument quality along with a variable known to affect subjects' motivation to process issue-relevant arguments—the personal relevance of the message (Petty, Cacioppo, & Heesacker, 1981).

Method. A total of 160 students participated in a 2 (Message form: statement or rhetorical) × 2 (Personal relevance: low or high) × 2 (Argument quality: strong or weak) between-subjects factorial design. Subjects believed that their task was to evaluate radio editorials and they heard one of four versions of an audiotaped editorial advocating that seniors be required to pass a comprehensive exam in their major as a requirement for graduation. Subjects in the high relevance conditions were led to believe that the president of their university had recommended that the exam proposal begin at their university in the next year. Subjects in the low relevance conditions were led to believe that the president of a distant university had recommended that the exam proposal be initiated at his institution in 10 years. Subjects heard either a strong or a weak editorial containing eight major arguments in favor of instituting comprehensive exams. In the regular editorials, each of the major arguments ended with a summary sentence in the form of a declarative statement (e.g., Thus, instituting a comprehensive exam would be an aid to those who seek admission to graduate and professional schools). In the rhetorical versions of the message, six of the eight argument summarizing statements were transformed into rhetorical questions (e.g., Wouldn't instituting a comprehensive exam be an aid to those who seek admission to graduate and professional schools?). Following exposure to the appropriate editorial, subjects completed attitude measures, were given 2.5 min to list their thoughts, and responded to various ancillary measures.

Results. Analyses of the listed thoughts revealed that the strong and weak messages differed in the profile of thoughts elicited as expected. Of greater interest, however, was a three-way interaction on the measure of attitude toward senior comprehensive exams. This interaction revealed that when personal relevance was low, attitudes in response to the strong and weak messages were more extreme with the rhetorical than the statement version of the advocacy (see top left panel of Figure 8-1), but when personal relevance was high, attitudes in response to the strong and weak messages were more extreme with the statement than the rhetorical version of the communication (see top right panel of Figure 8-1). In addition, subjects were asked how distracted they were from thinking about the message. A significant Message form × Personal relevance interaction revealed that low relevance subjects felt less distracted with the rhetorical than the statement advocacy, but high relevance subjects felt more distracted with the rhetorical than the statement message. This pattern of data is consistent with the view that the use of rhetorical questions increased elaboration when subjects were not naturally motivated to process the issue-relevant arguments, but inhibited elaboration of the arguments when processing was already high. In sum, it appears that summarizing arguments as rhetorical questions can either increase or decrease elaboration of audio communications depending upon the normal level of processing elicited by the message.

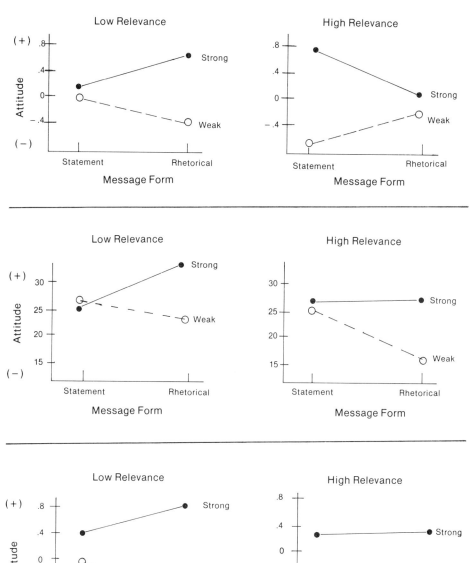

Figure 8-1. Postmessage attitudes as a function of personal relevance, argument quality, and the use of rhetorical questions. Figure shows that across three replications, the use of rhetorical questions enhanced message processing under conditions of low personal relevance. The effects of rhetoricals under high relevance were less clear (see text for discussion). (*Top panel*—data from Petty, Cacioppo, & Heesacker, 1981. *Middle panel*—data from Burnkrant & Howard, 1984. *Bottom panel*—data from Swasy & Munch, 1985.)

Additional Research on Rhetorical Questions

Recently, Burnkrant and Howard (1984) conducted a replication of our rhetoricals study making a few key changes. Subjects were presented with the strong or weak version of our senior comprehensive exam message that was made either high or low in personal relevance. Instead of hearing the message over headphones, however, subjects were presented with the message as a written communication. In addition, instead of summarizing each message argument as a rhetorical question after the argument was presented, all rhetorical questions *preceded* the presentation of the arguments. Burnkrant and Howard argued that these changes should eliminate the distraction effect that we observed under high involvement. First, as we noted earlier, presenting the message in print rather than orally gives subjects time to stop the message to consider the arguments fully. Thus, the rhetoricals need not disrupt processing even if subjects are highly involved. Second, placing the rhetorical questions at the beginning rather than at the end of the arguments has the advantage of generating interest and curiosity while avoiding the disadvantage of interrupting the train of thought concerning the argument just presented. The results of their study were consistent with this reasoning. The use of introductory rhetorical questions in print enhanced argument elaboration regardless of the personal relevance of the issue (see middle panel of Figure 8-1). Interestingly, despite the similar pattern of attitude data observed under high and low relevance conditions, there was some hint in their thought-listing data that rhetorical questions enhanced elaboration of the message more under low than high relevance conditions. Specifically, an analysis of the total number of thoughts subjects listed about the issue revealed that under low relevance, the rhetorical versions of the message elicited significantly more thoughts than the statement versions, but under high relevance conditions it did not.

Swasy and Munch (1985) conducted a closer replication of our rhetoricals study. In this experiment, all subjects heard our strong or weak senior comprehensive exam message in either the statement or the rhetorical form under conditions of high or low personal relevance. The message in this study was presented on audiotape as in our original experiment. Under low relevance, the use of rhetorical questions clearly enhanced elaboration replicating our result and that of Burnkrant and Howard (see bottom left panel of Figure 8-1). However, under high relevance conditions, the attitude measure revealed no evidence for the view that rhetorical questions disrupt processing. In fact, there was little evidence for any effect of rhetoricals (bottom right panel of Figure 8-1). Nevertheless, on the question asking subjects how distracted they were from thinking about the arguments, an Involvement × Message form interaction appeared—subjects reported that the rhetorical questions caused more distraction than statements in the high but not the low involvement conditions. Recall that this was the same pattern that we observed in our initial study (Petty, Cacioppo, & Heesacker, 1981). Swasy and Munch account for the discrepancy between their subjects' own reports that rhetoricals were distracting under high involvement and the failure to find evidence for this on the attitude measure by "raising concerns about the validity of a self-report distraction measure" (p. 883). An alternative possibility is that the self-reports of distraction are valid, and the attitude results may be attributed to the different procedures used in the studies. Specifically, one potentially important procedural difference between our study and that of Swasy and Munch is that we had subjects complete the thought-listing measure *after* responding to the attitude scales, but Swasy and Munch had subjects respond to the thought-listing measure *before* completing the attitude scales. Subjects may therefore have been motivated and able under high relevance to use the thought-listing period to think about the message and issue prior to completing the attitude measure. Thus, even though the rhetoricals may have distracted subjects from processing during the message (as revealed in the subjects' self-reports), the thought-listing period provided an opportunity for thought after message exposure. The result of this, of course, would be to attenuate any difference between the statement and the rhetorical versions of the advocacy under high relevance.[2]

In sum, the research on rhetorical questions has produced consistent support for our view that under conditions of low motivation to process a message, the use of rhetoricals enhances argument scrutiny. With rhetoricals, strong arguments become more persuasive but weak arguments become less persuasive (see left column of Figure 8-1). The effect of rhetorical questions under conditions of high relevance is less clear. One possibility is that under conditions of high relevance, the enhancing effect of rhetoricals on elaboration may be attenuated or even reversed if the message presentation is externally paced. The studies on rhetorical questions provide interesting examples of how an independent variable can have different but explicable effects on elaboration depending on the level of other variables with which it is combined such as personal relevance, modality of message presentation, and postmessage opportunity for thought.

---

[2]One unexplained aspect of both replications of our rhetoricals study is the failure of the high relevance manipulation to induce greater argument processing. Since this effect has been found several times in independent investigations (e.g., Huddleston, 1985; Leippe & Elkin, in press; Petty & Cacioppo, 1979b, 1984a), it is not clear why it was not obtained in these studies. In any case, the failure of the involvement manipulation to enhance argument processing undoubtedly also contributed to the failure of these studies to find a disrupting effect for rhetorical questions in the high relevance conditions.

Shifting Processing from Objective to Biased

We have seen that some variables, such as the use of rhetorical questions, may enhance elaboration at one level of another factor, but reduce elaboration at a second level of that factor. A second way in which the impact of one variable can depend on the level of another factor is in whether the variable induces relatively objective or relatively biased information processing. For example, we have demonstrated that increasing the degree of personal relevance of a message can enhance a person's motivation to process the message in a relatively objective manner (Petty & Cacioppo, 1979b). However, we have also seen that this processing may become biased if personal relevance is combined with a threat such as that induced by a forewarning of persuasive intent (Petty & Cacioppo, 1979a). In short, the personal relevance may motivate increased processing, but the threat directs this processing in the defense of one's initial position.

Other variables may also interact similarly with personal relevance. For example, we previously noted that all else equal, people would prefer their preexisting attitudes to be correct. Thus, people tend to want to accept proattitudinal messages and reject counterattitudinal ones. In our own research, we have not employed messages that were extremely counter or proattitudinal. If a strongly counterattitudinal message was combined with personal relevance, the net result might well be intensified *unfavorable* processing, whereas if a strongly proattitudinal message was combined with personal relevance, the net result might well be intensified *favorable* processing. In sum, although personal relevance per se may normally enhance a person's motivation to consider the merits of an advocacy in a relatively objective manner, if the message position is either extremely negative or positive, enhanced relevance may still increase processing, but the processing may shift from relatively objective to relatively biased.

Variables that Affect Message Processing and Serve as Peripheral Cues

In the last section we argued that whether or not a particular variable enhances or diminshes processing, or motivates relatively objective or relatively biased processing, may depend on the level of other variables in the persuasion context. Similarly, whether a variable affects information processing or serves as a peripheral cue may depend on the level of other elements in the persuasion context. We discuss this feature of the ELM below.

Multiple Effects of Source Expertise and Attractiveness

In our introductory chapter, we noted that one aspect of persuasion research that has disappointed reviewers of the field is that even variables that were expected to be quite simple in their effects on attitude change have instead proven to be quite complex. We also noted that perhaps the most dramatic example of this was provided by the conflicting research on features of the message source (Eagly & Himmelfarb, 1974). Postulate 3 of the ELM outlines the several different ways in which source (and other) factors can affect persuasion: they can serve as arguments, they can serve as cues, or they can affect argument processing. In the research that we have reviewed so far, we have focused on how source factors operate when the overall elaboration likelihood is either very high or very low. We have seen that when people are unmotivated and unable to process a message, they rely on simple cues in the persuasion context such as the expertise or attractiveness of the message source, although other cues may be used if they are more salient (see Chapter 6). Importantly, since subjects are either unmotivated or unable to evaluate message arguments, a positive source tends to enhance persuasion and a negative source tends to reduce persuasion regardless of message quality (e.g., see top panels in Figures 6-1, 6-3, and 6-4).

On the other hand, when people are highly motivated and able to process message arguments, strong arguments are more effective than weak ones despite the presence of peripheral cues such as source credibility and attractiveness (e.g., see bottom panels in figures 6-1, 6-3, and 6-4). When motivation and ability to process are high, people are concerned with evaluating the true merits of the advocacy. In order to do this, they will scrutinize all available and inferred information in the immediate persuasion context and attempt to relate it to information stored previously in memory. Importantly, a consideration of source factors may be part of a person's attempt to evaluate issue-relevant information when the elaboration likelihood is high. For example, under some circumstances a source may serve as a persuasive argument (e.g., a physically attractive source may provide persuasive visual testimony as to the effectiveness of a beauty product; Kahle & Homer, 1985; Petty & Cacioppo, 1981b). Additionally, a consideration of source information might help a person in evaluating the true merits of any given argument. For example, consider an expert source (Professor of Education at Princeton) who suggests that tuition be increased at his university. When elaboration likelihood is low (e.g., as a result of low personal relevance or high distraction), this prestigious source might serve as a simple positive cue. When elaboration likelihood is high, however, a subject considering the source and message together might realize that the expert source is biased or has a vested interest in the presentation of some arguments (e.g., an argument to raise tuition to increase faculty salaries). The important point is that when the elaboration likelihood is high, source information does not serve as a simple acceptance or rejection cue, but rather it is considered along with all other available information in the subject's attempt to evaluate the true merits of the arguments and position advocated.

Our conclusions about the impact of source factors under conditions of high and low elaboration likelihood are only part of the story of how source factors impact on persuasion. As we noted in Chapter 1, we view elaboration likelihood as a continuum anchored at one end by the peripheral route to persuasion, and at the other end by the central route. In all of our research described in the previous sections, we have attempted to create and describe relatively clear instances of central and peripheral routes to persuasion. Thus, for example, in our research on motivation to process, subjects were either highly involved with the topic or very uninvolved. In the high involvement conditions, subjects were confronted with an advocacy that had immediate personal implications for their own graduation (Petty, Cacioppo, & Goldman, 1981) or their finances in attending college (Cacioppo, Petty, & Morris, 1983). In the low involvement conditions, subjects were confronted with a message about a change in university policy that they were *certain* would not affect them, or they were faced with an ad for a product that they were certain would not be available in their local area for a long time (Petty, Cacioppo, & Schumann, 1983). The extreme high and low elaboration likelihood conditions have been quite useful for theory testing purposes and in explicating the two routes to persuasion. However, these conditions represent only part of the elaboration likelihood continuum.

Specifically, many day-to-day persuasion contexts are unlikely to be as high or as low in elaboration likelihood as the conditions we have deliberately created in our initial research. For example, people are sometimes uncertain as to the personal relevance of an issue, or have moderate rather than very high or very low knowledge on a topic. It is important to specify the operation of source (and other) factors when the elaboration likelihood is moderate rather than extreme. We have proposed that under more moderate conditions, people use source (and other) factors to determine how much thinking to do about the message (Petty & Cacioppo, 1981a, 1984c). When a message is on a topic of high personal relevance and people have considerable knowledge on the issue, they know that they want to evaluate the merits of the arguments presented and that they have the ability to do so. Under these conditions, source factors are unimportant in their role as simple cues. When a message clearly is on a topic of very low relevance and/or people have very little issue-relevant knowledge, people know that they either do not want or are not able to think about the message and they seek a simpler way to evaluate the recommendation if a judgment is required. Source cues provide one such simple means of evaluation. However, when the personal consequences or prior knowledge are moderate or unclear, people may not be sure whether the message is worth thinking about. Under these circumstances, characteristics of the message source can help a person decide if the message is worth (or needs) considering. For example, when people have the option of whether or not to think about a message or the proposal is *potentially* relevant, they may reason that it is more worthwhile to think about what an expert has to say than an inexpert. Why waste precious time thinking about information that is likely to be specious? Or, people may believe that proposals by experts are more likely to be carried out, and are therefore more worthy of thought. A similar case could be made for attractive sources because attractive people are thought to possess a wide variety of positive traits including intelligence (Berscheid & Walster, 1974). On the other hand source expertise may sometimes decrease processing. For example, if people anticipate that others will ask for their opinions, but the issue is one on which they have only moderate knowledge, they may feel that it is relatively risk-free to identify with an expert's opinion but that the arguments of a source whose credibility is suspect require scrutiny. In any case, we have proposed that in many situations people use source cues to determine whether or not a message is worthy of (or needs) scrutiny. Although we have made some suggestions (e.g., Petty & Cacioppo, 1981a, p. 237), future research will be needed to identify the precise conditions under which sources enhance and reduce motivation to process a message.

We have now conducted several studies in which source factors were studied at moderate levels of motivation to process rather than at levels that were very high or very low. We will describe two studies in which we employed the same topics and messages as used in our previous research on personal relevance (see Chapters 4 and 6) to facilitate comparison. Recall that in one study described previously (Petty, Cacioppo, & Goldman, 1981), we told high relevance subjects that a change in academic policy was being considered for next year at their own university (in which case most subjects certainly would be affected personally), and low relevance subjects were told that the policy was being considered for 10 years in the future (in which case current students certainly would not be affected). In our studies on moderate or ambiguous relevance, all subjects were led to believe that a change in policy was being advocated for their university, but they were not told when or if this policy ever would be implemented. Thus, subjects could not be certain whether or not the change in policy would affect them, although there was some potential that if implemented soon, it would. What is the effect of source factors when personal relevance is possible, but uncertain? We have studied both source expertise and source attractiveness under these conditions.

Source Attractiveness Can Affect Message Processing

Method. In an initial study on how attractive sources can affect message processing, 220 undergraduates were randomly assigned to the cells of a 2 (Source attractiveness: high or low) × 2 (Source age: old or young) × 2 (Argument quality: strong or weak) between-subjects factorial design (Puckett, Petty, Cacioppo, & Fisher, 1983). The subjects were told that many universities were considering instituting comprehensive exams for seniors and that students in an evening undergraduate continuing education course had written essays on this topic. Each subject was given a folder that contained a typed essay in favor of the exam proposal along with a card containing a picture and a brief description of the author of the essay. The social attractiveness of the author was manipulated by varying the physical attractiveness of the photograph contained in the folder along with the background information provided: socially attractive authors were described as having better family backgrounds and more prestigious hobbies than the socially unattractive authors. The age of the essay author, was also manipulated (21 vs. 68 years old), but this factor had no effect on persuasion. After subjects examined the folder containing the strong or weak senior comprehensive exam message and the source information, they were asked to rate the essay author and to provide their own opinions about the exam proposal.

Results. Not surprisingly, subjects were more persuaded by the strong than the weak essays. The major result of this study, however, was a significant Argument quality × Source attractiveness interaction on the measure of subjects' attitudes toward senior comprehensive exams (see Figure 8-2). This interaction was due to the fact that subjects scrutinized the arguments more when they were attributed to the socially attractive sources. In fact, the impact of argument quality on attitudes was significant only for the attractive sources. As depicted in Figure 8-2, this interaction was due to the joint tendencies for attractiveness to enhance agreement with the proposal when the arguments presented were strong, but for attractiveness to reduce agreement when the arguments presented were weak. The latter effect (an attractive source reducing agreement), of course, is opposite to what one normally would expect the effect of attractive sources to be (cf., Chaiken, 1979). Interestingly, a measure of source perceptions indicated that the attractive sources were rated more positively on a number of dimensions (e.g., intelligence, likability, etc.) only when they presented strong arguments. When the attractive sources presented weak arguments, they were derogated relative to the unattractive sources who presented weak argu-

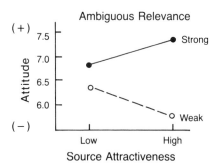

Figure 8-2. Postmessage attitudes as a function of source attractiveness and argument quality under conditions of ambiguous personal relevance (data from Puckett, Petty, Cacioppo, & Fisher, 1983).

ments. This follows directly from the fact that the information presented by the attractive sources was processed more carefully.

Source Expertise Can Affect Message Processing
In a study that was similar conceptually to the Puckett et al. study on source attractiveness, we attempted to determine if source expertise could affect message processing (Heesacker, Petty, & Cacioppo, 1983).

Method. A total of 354 undergraduates were randomly assigned to the cells of a 2 (Source expertise: high or low) × 2 (Argument quality: strong or weak) × 2 (Field dependence: field dependent or independent) between-subjects factorial. As in the study on source attractiveness, we again left the degree of personal relevance ambiguous. This time, however, subjects heard rather than read the strong or weak message on senior comprehensive exams. Some subjects were led to believe that the advocacy was based on a six-month study by the Carnegie Commission on Higher Education which was chaired by a Professor of Education at Princeton University (high expertise). Other subjects were led to believe that the advocacy was based on a report of a local high school journalism class chaired by a student in the class (low expertise). The subjects were told that these reports were submitted to the university Chancellor who was seeking recommendations about policy changes to be instituted at their university. Subjects were further told that they were rating the professional broadcast quality of audiotapes that were prepared from written reports by the committees. Finally, subjects in this study were divided into those who were relatively field dependent or independent as assessed by the embedded figures test (Ekstrom, French, & Harmon, 1962). Following exposure to the appropriate message, subjects rated their own attitude on the senior comprehensive exam issue.

Results. Overall, subjects showed more agreement to the strong than the weak message arguments. In addition, however, a three-way interaction was obtained on the measure of subjects' attitudes toward senior comprehensive exams. To understand this interaction, separate 2 × 2 ANOVAS were computed for field dependent and field independent subjects. The data for field dependent subjects showed the main effect for Argument quality and an Argument quality × Source expertise interaction ($p < 0.08$; see Figure 8-3). Similar to the effect observed for social attractiveness, the interaction revealed that the arguments were more carefully processed when they were presented by the expert than by the inexpert source. In fact, simple main effects tests indicated that field dependent subjects differentiated the arguments only when the source was highly credible. As depicted in Figure 8-3, this interaction pattern was due to the joint tendencies for strong arguments to be more persuasive when presented by an expert, but for weak arguments to be less persuasive when presented by an expert, and again the latter effect is opposite to what one normally would expect the effect of

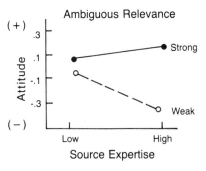

Figure 8-3. Postmessage attitudes for field dependent subjects as a function of source credibility and argument quality under conditions of ambiguous personal relevance (data from Heesacker, Petty, & Cacioppo, 1983).

expertise to be. Field independent subjects, on the other hand, showed only a main effect for argument quality, probably because these subjects are generally more motivated and/or able to extract meaning from stimuli (Witkin, Goodenough, & Oltman, 1979). If field independent subjects generally have a higher elaboration likelihood than field dependent subjects, then they would be more likely to process the message arguments regardless of the source.

Summary and Discussion
In sum, although the operation of source factors may seem quite simple on the surface, the ELM indicates that their operation, although orderly and predictable, is quite complex. In separate experiments, we have seen that when personal relevance is high, source factors can serve as persuasive arguments or assist in the evaluation of arguments; when personal relevance is low, source factors can serve as simple cues; and when personal relevance is moderate or ambiguous, source factors can affect the extent of message processing (see also Heesacker, 1986; Stoltenberg & Davis, in press). Since these source effects are obtained under different conditions, it is not surprising that a great diversity of results has been observed in the literature. For example, we noted that most research on source expertise has indicated that although expertise effects are rather easy to demonstrate for relatively uninvolving issues, expertise and other simple source effects are less likely for more personally relevant topics (e.g., Chaiken, 1980; Kelman & Hovland, 1953; Petty, Cacioppo, & Goldman, 1981; Rhine & Severance, 1970). Furthermore, the persuasive impact of sources high in expertise has tended to be very short lived (Cook & Flay, 1978). These results are consistent with the ELM in that when an issue is on a topic of low personal relevance, source expertise is postulated to serve as a simple acceptance cue inducing favorable attitudes with little issue-relevant thinking. The consequence is that the attitude formed has little temporal persistence and resistance, and few implications for behavior.

On the other hand, a few studies have shown that expert sources may sometimes produce relatively persisting attitude changes. For example, in a test of his three-process model of persistence (see Chapter 7), Kelman (1958) showed that attitude change induced by an expert source persisted for one to two weeks. In this study, Black college students were presented with a message arguing in favor of maintaining some private all-Black colleges even if the Supreme Court declared segregation unconstitutional. The subjects heard the message just prior to the impending 1954 announcement of the Supreme Court decision on desegregation. Since it was not clear what the Supreme Court would decide about the future of all-Black schools at the time subjects heard the message, whether a new policy would be implemented or not was unclear. These are precisely the conditions under which we have argued that expert sources enhance information processing. If so, then the relative persistence of the attitude changes induced by the expert source in Kelman's study may be attributed to the fact that the expert source enhanced argument elaboration resulting in a well-articulated and persisting attitude.

Other Variables with Multiple Effects

We have now seen how some source variables can serve as arguments in some contexts, cues in other contexts, and affect argument processing in still other situations. This general principle, which is stated explicitly in ELM Postulate 3 (see Table 1-1), was applied mostly to separate variables elsewhere in this volume. However, it should now be clear that any *one* variable can serve in all of these roles. A few more examples should help to elucidate how one variable can serve in multiple roles depending on the specific features of the persuasion context.

Multiple Sources
First, consider the impact of the number of other people who endorse a particular attitudinal position. As we noted in Chapter 4, traditional analyses of the number of message sources have assumed that the more people who are perceived to advocate a position, the more conformity pressure that is induced, and the more agreement that results (e.g., Asch, 1951). Whether or not the sources presented arguments in support of their positions was unimportant. People agreed with multiple sources out of a desire to be correct (Festinger, 1954) or at least to appear correct (Jellison & Arkin, 1977). However, more recent analyses have argued that multiple sources may enhance information-processing activity (e.g., Burnstein & Sentis, 1981; Harkins & Petty, 1983). For example, recall from Chapter 4 that Harkins and Petty (1981a) found that having three sources present strong arguments enhanced persuasion but that having three sources present weak arguments reduced persuasion over that achieved when the same information was presented by one source (see Figure 4-5).

Importantly, the Harkins and Petty (1981a) study was conducted under conditions of ambiguous personal relevance and the results obtained were similar to the effects we reported in this chapter for source attractiveness and expertise under similar conditions (see Figures 8-2 and 8-3). According to the ELM, however, what would be expected to happen if message relevance was very high or very low? When the elaboration likelihood is very low (such as when personal relevance or prior knowledge are very low, distraction is very high, etc.), people will be unmotivated and/or unable to engage in the cognitive work necessary to evaluate the issue-relevant arguments. Under these conditions, people may use the number of people who support the issue as a simple cue as to the worth of the proposal. Therefore, judgments would be based primarily on this cue—the more people who supported the proposal, the more agreement that would result regardless of whether the arguments presented were strong or weak. When the elaboration likelihood is very high, however, message recipients will undertake a deliberate assessment of the message arguments and the number of endorsers will have little value as a simple acceptance cue. In short, the ELM holds that the number of people supporting a message may serve as a simple conformity cue under some conditions (low elaboration likelihood), act to enhance processing in other conditions (moderate elaboration likelihood), and have no power as a simple cue in still other conditions (high elaboration likelihood). These different predicted effects are depicted in the top three panels of Figure 2-3. No experiment to date, however, has examined the impact of the number of sources across the full elaboration likelihood continuum.

Message Variables
Factors associated with the message source, of course, are not the only variables that can both serve as cues and affect message processing. Message variables can likewise serve in both roles. We have already discussed in Chapter 6 how the number of arguments could serve as a simple cue when personal relevance was low, but affect information processing when personal relevance was high (Petty & Cacioppo, 1984a). Other message variables may operate similarly.

For example, earlier in this chapter we argued that the use of rhetorical questions could increase elaboration when personal relevance was low, but reduce elaboration when personal relevance was high (for audio messages). Can rhetorical questions also serve as simple cues? Since some research suggests that people may make various inferences about the message source depending upon the kind of language used (Ryan & Giles, 1982), rhetorical questions have the *potential* to serve as cues. Research has suggested that sometimes the use of rhetorical questions makes the speaker appear more polite (a positive cue; e.g., Bates, 1976), but sometimes the use of rhetorical questions makes the speaker appear less confident (a negative cue; e.g., Newcombe & Arnkoff, 1979). If a communication were on a very esoteric or unfamiliar topic for which the audience had few or no preexisting message-relevant beliefs, it would be unlikely that the use of rhetoricals could affect message elaboration. For such issues, to the extent that some evaluation was required, rhetorical questions might serve as simple cues. To the extent that the rhetoricals made the speaker or the arguments appear more favorable, more agreement would result (cf., Zillmann, 1972), but to the extent that the rhetoricals made the speaker or arguments appear less favorable, less agreement would result.

Recipient and Context Factors

In addition to source and message variables, recipient and context variables may also serve in multiple roles. For example, in Chapter 3 we saw how the physical posture of a message recipient (reclining or standing) could affect the extent of elaboration under moderate involvement conditions (see Figure 3-7; Petty, Wells, Heesacker, Brock, & Cacioppo, 1983). If subjects were presented with a message they were unable to elaborate, then posture or other factors related to comfort during message exposure might serve as simple positive or negative affective cues (e.g., Griffit & Veitch, 1971).

In Chapter 6 we saw how false physiological feedback could serve as the basis of a simple inference about the desirability of a picture when the personal consequences of doing so were low (Taylor, 1975). However, in other situations, physiological feedback may cause a person to ruminate about *why* a picture (or other stimulus) has affected bodily processes. This may involve extensive processing of the attributes of the stimulus and lead to attitude changes that are induced by the central rather than by the peripheral route (cf., Liebhart, 1979). In any given situation, depending on the nature of the stimulus employed (e.g., involving or not), the type of bodily response detected (felt or not), the amount of time provided to think, and other factors, the change induced may either be the result of a simple inference or may result from more extensive processing of the stimulus (Petty & Cacioppo, 1983b).

The Role of Affect in the ELM

Although persuasion researchers over the past few decades have focused on the cognitive foundations of attitudes, investigators are beginning to show renewed interest in the affective bases of attitudes and other judgments (e.g., Cacioppo & Petty, 1981a; Clark & Fiske, 1982; Zajonc & Markus, 1982). Importantly, the ELM holds open the same possibilities for affect that it does for the other source, message, recipient, and context variables that we have already discussed. For example, we noted in Chapter 1 that for some people or in some situations, a determination of the central merits of an attitude object might entail an analysis of one's *feelings* rather than one's beliefs or behaviors. Thus, the affective state (e.g., love) induced by an attitude object (e.g., a person) might serve as a persuasive argument for or against the merits of the object when the elaboration likelihood is high (e.g., when the person is a potential spouse). This process is most likely when the affect is perceived to be directly relevant to the central merits of the object or issue under consideration (e.g., the salivating joy one feels when considering the merits of consuming a sizzling steak when famished, or the disgust one feels after realizing that the steak is rancid). In short, according to the ELM, relevant affective states should serve as persuasive arguments or help in assessing the cogency of arguments when the elaboration likelihood is high (e.g., fear may contribute to a person's assessment of the danger inherent in not following a specific recommendation; cf. Rogers, 1983). When the elaboration likelihood is high but *irrelevant* affective states are induced, it is likely that the affect will bias issue-relevant thinking by making affectively consonant thoughts and ideas more accessible in memory (Bower, 1981; Clark & Isen, 1982). As we noted in Chapter 5, this process may explain the increased negative thinking that is observed when strong arguments are repeated an excessive number of times (cf., Cacioppo & Petty, 1985).

In contrast to the postulated impact of affective states when the elaboration likelihood is high, when people are either relatively unmotivated or unable to engage in the cognitive work necessary to evaluate the central merits of an attitude object or issue, then affect, whether relevant or irrelevant, should serve as a simple peripheral cue. As a cue, affect should enhance attitudes when it is pleasant, but have a negative effect when it is unpleasant. In Chapter 6 we reviewed research that was consistent with this principle. For example, recall that Gorn (1982) found that pleasant music had a favorable impact on attitudes toward a consumer product but only under conditions of product relevance. Similarly, Srull (1983b) found that mood had an impact on attitudes for people who were low in issue-relevant knowledge, but did not influence attitudes when knowledge was high.

Finally, we note that when people are uncertain as to whether or not they wish to scrutinize a persuasive communication (moderate elaboration likelihood), one's affective state may determine whether or not the communication is processed. Specifically, people may be more willing to undertake the cognitive effort necessary to process a message if they are feeling good rather than bad. The basis for this reasoning stems from previous research suggesting that disphoric states tend to dampen one's level of activity including the tendency to engage in effortful cognitive endeavors (e.g., see Castillo, 1985). Interestingly, the Petty, Wells, Heesacker, Brock, and Cacioppo (1983) study on recipient posture (graphed in Figure 3-7) can be interpreted in this context. To the extent that standing was less pleasant than lying during the message, this relative discomfort might have contributed to the diminished processing observed when people were placed in this posture. In sum, although research on the role of affect in persuasion is sparse at present, the ELM provides a guiding framework for analyzing its role in attitude change.[3]

---

[3]Our analysis of affect presumes a *moderate* level of this construct (i.e., not so low as to be imperceptible, but not so high as to be alarming or disruptive of all processing).

Summary

It is important to note that even though the ELM holds open the possibility that variables can affect agreement either by having an impact on information processing or by serving as simple cues, the ELM specifies, in a general manner at least, the conditions under which each process is likely to operate. Thus, a whole list of source (e.g., credibility, attractiveness, number of sources), message (e.g., number of arguments, use of rhetoricals, discrepancy), audience (e.g., affective states, presence of hecklers, false physiological feedback), and other variables may affect attitudes by modifying information processing under certain conditions (e.g., moderate to high personal relevance), but affect attitudes by serving as simple cues in other contexts (e.g., low prior knowledge).

Processing When No Message or Both Sides Are Presented

Throughout most of this volume we have focused on the typical persuasion situation in which various arguments on only one side of an issue are presented to a recipient. Other persuasion contexts occasionally arise, however, and in this final section we briefly address the implications of the ELM for two of them.

First, in some situations a position is advocated, but no arguments are presented for the person to evaluate. Still, according to the ELM, motivation and ability to think will be important determinants of the route to persuasion. However, when no arguments are presented, thinking cannot be guided by the message arguments. Instead, thinking can be guided either by the person's initial attitude, or by the topic of the advocacy itself. In the former case, people will engage in a biased scanning of arguments in memory supporting their initial positions, and attitude polarization may result (see Tesser, 1978). In the latter case, people will search memory in a more objective manner for information and arguments that are consistent with the advocated position. To the extent that supportive information and arguments are available, change in the direction of the advocacy may occur (see Burnstein & Vinokur, 1977; King & Janis, 1956). Importantly, in each of these cases, the attitudes formed are the product of issue-relevant thinking and will have the characteristics of other attitudes induced via the central route. Of course, if no arguments are presented, and people lack the requisite motivation or ability to think about the issue, then peripheral cues associated with the advocacy may determine the extent and direction of influence.

A second atypical situation occurs when people are presented with arguments on both sides of an issue. Again, motivation and ability to think about the issue will determine the route to persuasion. If motivation and/or ability are low, but a judgment is required, people will examine both sides in a cursory manner and will likely favor the position associated with the more favorable cues. For example, the side with the greater number of arguments, or the side endorsed by the more prestigious source will be selected. However, if people have the necessary motivation and ability to evaluate the issue in a relatively objective manner, then the side presenting the highest quality arguments will be favored. If both sides present equally compelling positions, people may be motivated to resolve the ambiguity by using the available information to bolster their initial positions. Also, if one's previous knowledge on a issue is biased in favor of one's initial position, as will often be the case, then people will likely have greater ability to cognitively bolster their side but counterargue the opposing side. This process can lead to attitude polarization (e.g., Lord, Ross, & Lepper, 1979; see Chapter 5).

Retrospective

In this chapter we have examined and addressed some of the complications that arise in the Elaboration Likelihood Model. Among the complications are that variables can have one effect on elaboration when they are paired with some variables, but have different, even opposite, effects on elaboration when they are paired with other variables. Thus, some variables enhance elaboration at one level of a factor, but disrupt elaboration at another level of the same factor. Additionally, some variables affect information processing in a relatively objective manner when combined with some factors, but affect information processing in a more biased fashion when combined with other factors. Finally, we noted that the same factor can serve in any one of the three major roles postulated for variables by the ELM. That is, any one factor (e.g., source attractiveness) can serve as a persuasive argument in one context, act as a peripheral cue in another, and affect message elaboration in still a third situation. Fortunately, the ELM provides guidance as to when each of these processes is likely. In the final chapter, we offer some concluding remarks about the ELM.

Chapter 9
Epilogue

Introduction

We began this monograph with questions about the likely effectiveness of televised speeches given on New Year's Day by the American president and the Soviet premier to national audiences in each other's countries. The research and theory presented in this volume have indicated that communications such as these can produce persuasion via two fundamentally different routes. One route is based on the thoughtful (though sometimes biased) consideration of arguments perceived central to the merits of the issue under consideration, whereas the other is based on affective associations or simple inferences tied to peripheral cues in the persuasion context. When variables in the persuasion situation render the elaboration likelihood high, the first kind of persuasion occurs (central route). When variables in the persuasion situation render the elaboration likelihood low, the second kind of persuasion occurs (peripheral route). Importantly, there are different consequences of the two routes to persuasion. Attitude changes via the central route appear to be more persistent, resistant, and predictive of behavior than changes induced via the peripheral route (see Figure 1-1).

In outling the antecedents and consequences of the two routes to persuasion, the Elaboration Likelihood Model provides a framework from which to analyze the speeches of the U.S. and Soviet leaders. For example, a fundamental question is: How much thinking were the audiences likely to be doing about the communications? First, recall that the American president appeared during a news program in the Soviet Union, whereas the Russian premier appeared during televised coverage of a holiday parade in the United States. Thus, the elaboration likelihood was probably higher for the former than the latter speech. Because of this, the American leader may have been more likely to be judged on the quality of his arguments, whereas peripheral cues may have had a greater impact on attitudes toward the

Soviet leader's speech. Of course, this analysis is a gross oversimplification, and even if it was accurate, it would only be a starting point in the analysis. As we documented elsewhere in this monograph, a large number of factors must be considered in assessing the impact of the speeches (e.g., Did the President present strong or weak arguments? Was the processing of his speech objective or biased? Were the cues surrounding the Premier's speech positive or negative?). Despite these complexities, the ELM provides a unique and focusing perspective from which to analyze the situation. In this brief epilogue chapter, we will first discuss the elaboration likelihood concept in somewhat greater detail, and then we will consider the integrative potential of ELM.

Determinants of Elaboration Likelihood

In the preceding chapters we surveyed a wide variety of variables that proved instrumental in affecting the likelihood that a person would elaborate a persuasive communication, and thus the route to persuasion. In fact, one of the basic postulates of the ELM, that variables may affect persuasion by increasing or decreasing issue-relevant thinking proved useful in accounting for the effects of a seemingly diverse list of variables (see Chapters 3–5). The effects of these variables had been explained with many different theoretical accounts in the accumulated persuasion literature. The ELM was successful in tying the effects of these variables to one underlying process. We have also seen that many different variables could serve as peripheral cues, affecting persuasion without issue-relevant thinking. Again, the operation of a diverse list of variables is integrated by the common antecedents and consequents of their operation (see Chapters 6 and 7). Finally, we have seen that some variables were capable of serving in multiple roles, enhancing or reducing thinking in some contexts, and serving as simple acceptance or rejection cues in others (see Chapter 8).

In Figure 9-1 we present a general framework for thinking about the determinants of argument processing.[1] As we explained previously in Chapter 1, the likelihood that elaboration occurs can be viewed as being a function of the separable elements of motivation and ability.[2] By *motivation*, we mean the factor that propels and guides people's information processing and gives it its purposive character. We have seen that there are many

---

[1] The important influence of Heider (1958) in this figure should be apparent.

[2] Luck might also be considered a contributing factor. Luck refers to the transient and random circumstance in which an individual's ongoing ruminations bear upon an unanticipated attitude object or issue. As such, luck is not a particularly important determinant of elaboration likelihood. Hence, this factor is not considered further.

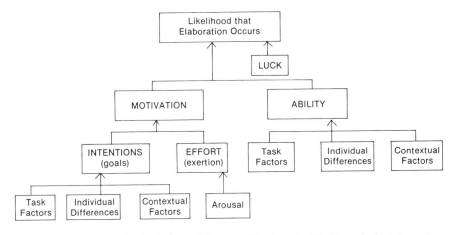

Figure 9-1. Schematic depiction of factors affecting the likelihood of elaboration.

variables that can affect a person's motivation to elaborate upon the content of a message. For instance, individuals have been found to be more motivated to think about the issue and message arguments when they are: (a) the only one rather than one of many assigned to evaluate the recommendation (e.g., Petty, Harkins, & Williams, 1980); (b) personally affected rather than unaffected by the adoption of the recommendation (e.g., Petty & Cacioppo, 1979b); (c) exposed to multiple sources rather than a single source espousing the virtues of a recommendation (e.g., Harkins & Petty, 1981a); and (d) high rather than low dispositionally in need for cognition (e.g., Cacioppo, Petty, & Morris, 1983). What these variables (and others affecting motivation) seem to have in common is that they act upon a directive, goal-oriented component which might be termed *intention,* and a nondirective, energizing information processing component which might be termed *effort* or exertion. As we have seen, many variables can influence a person's intention to think about the message arguments or issue. The *task variables* of personal relevance and responsibility, the *individual difference variable* of need for cognition, and the *contextual variable* of number of sources all influence an individual's intention to think about the persuasive communication presented.[3]

Intention is not sufficient for motivation, however, since one can want to think about a message or issue, but not exert the necessary effort to move from "intending" to "trying." For example, a person who is dispositionally

---

[3]We do not mean to suggest that these "intentions" are always conscious or deliberate in the sense that a person carefully plans to process the message. Instead, the goal of elaborating the message may be invoked quite spontaneously and naturally in certain situations or in certain people (cf., Sherman, in press).

Table 9-1. Factors Affecting Motivation and Ability to Process a Persuasive
Communication in a Relatively Objective and Biased Manner

	Motivational Factors	Ability Factors
Relatively Objective Processing	Personal relevance (Petty & Cacioppo, 1979b)	External distraction (Petty, Wells, & Brock, 1976)
	Personal responsibility (Petty, Harkins, & Williams, 1980)	Transient heart rate (Cacioppo, 1979)
	Number of sources (Harkins & Petty, 1981a)	Recipient Posture (Petty, Wells, Heesacker, Brock, & Cacioppo, 1983)
	Need for cognition (Cacioppo, Petty, & Morris, 1983)	Moderate message repetition (Cacioppo & Petty, 1985)
Relatively Biased Processing	Forewarning of message content (Petty & Cacioppo, 1977)	Self-schemata (Cacioppo, Petty, & Sidera, 1982)
	Forewarning of persuasive intent (Petty & Cacioppo, 1979a)	Hemispheric asymmetry (Cacioppo, Petty, & Quintanar, 1982)
	Excessive message repetition (Cacioppo & Petty, 1979b)	Vertical/horizontal head movements (Wells & Petty, 1980)

high in need for cognition may have the general goal of thinking, but may
not exert the effort on a particular day due to mental fatigue. Little research
has been directed explicitly at specifying what variables affect this stage,
although effort has been linked previously to drive and arousal (e.g.,
Kahneman, 1973). The data obtained using measures of autonomic and
skelotomotor activation have not provided clear support for this connection,
however, and interesting questions remain regarding exactly which variables act on cognitive effort and whether more sophisticated conceptualizations and measures of arousal will yield evidence for the hypothetical link
outlined in Figure 9-1 (e.g., see Cacioppo & Petty, in press).

If both intention and effort are present, then motivation to think about the
advocacy will exist. Message elaboration, however, also requires that the
individual have the *ability* to process the message. As we have seen
elsewhere in this monograph, there are a variety of variables that can affect
elaboration ability. *Task variables* such as message comprehensibility (e.g.,
Eagly, 1974), *individual difference variables* such as intelligence (e.g., Eagly &
Warren, 1976) and relative hemispheric activation (e.g., Cacioppo, Petty, &
Quintanar, 1982), and *contextual variables* such as distraction (e.g., Petty,
Wells, & Brock, 1976) and moderate message repetition (e.g., Cacioppo &
Petty, 1979b) all influence an individual's ability to think about message

arguments. It can be seen that all factors affecting the person's *opportunity* to process message arguments, such as external distraction, would fall under the headings of either task or contextual factors.

Figure 9-1 does not address what happens next, but rather the ELM as outlined in Figure 1-1 does. If task, individual, and contextual factors in the persuasion situation combine to render motivation and ability to process high, then the arguments in the persuasive communication will be elaborated. The nature of this elaboration will be determined by whether the motivational and ability factors combine to yield relatively objective or relatively biased processing. If the processing is relatively objective, elaboration will be governed mostly by the subjective cogency of the issue-relevant arguments contained in the message. If the processing is relatively biased, issue-relevant thoughts will be governed more by factors such as the person's initial attitude schema. Table 9-1 summarizes some of the major variables examined in our research that affect motivation and ability to elaborate in a relatively objective or biased manner.

Integrative Potential of the ELM

We noted early in this monograph that reviewers of the attitude change literature have been disappointed by the fact that many conflicting effects have been observed even for ostensibly simple variables. For example, manipulations of source expertise have sometimes increased persuasion, sometimes had no effect, and sometimes decreased persuasion. Similarly, studies testing different theories of persuasion have sometimes found the theory to be useful in predicting attitude change, and other times have found the theory to be unpredictive. For example, self-perception processes appear to operate under some conditions, but not others.

The Elaboration Likelihood Model represents an attempt to place these many conflicting results and theories under one conceptual umbrella by specifying the major processes underlying persuasion and indicating how many of the traditionally studied variables and theories relate to these basic processes. Thus, we have seen that a seemingly simple variable like source credibility is actually capable of affecting persuasion in rather complex ways. The ELM, however, elucidates the general conditions under which these different effects are likely to operate. Specifically, we have seen that source expertise acts as a simple peripheral cue when the elaboration likelihood is very low, but not when it is very high (e.g., Petty, Cacioppo, & Goldman, 1981). When the elaboration likelihood is moderate, source expertise affects a person's motivation to think about the issue-relevant arguments provided (e.g., Heesacker, Petty, & Cacioppo, 1983).

Similarly, the ELM may prove useful in specifying the domains of different attitude theories. Theories proposing that attitudes change because of simple affective cues (e.g., Staats & Staats, 1957, 1958; Kelman, 1958), or cognitive heuristics (e.g., Bem, 1972; Chaiken, in press) should operate mostly when the elaboration likelihood is low. On the other hand, persuasion models emphasizing issue-relevant cognitive activity (e.g, Ajzen & Fishbein, 1980; McGuire, 1964; Petty, Ostrom, & Brock, 1981) should operate mostly when the elaboration likelihood is high. Consider the decade-long controversy regarding the viability of dissonance and self-perception theories. Both conceptualizations predicted the same pattern of attitude results in many situations, though for different reasons (Greenwald, 1975). Self-perception theory postulated that attitude change resulted from a simple inference based on the observation of one's own behavior (Bem, 1972). Dissonance theory, on the other hand, postulated a much more cognitively active process. As a result of dissonance, people were believed to engage in rationalizing thoughts that would justify their attitude-inconsistent action (i.e., biased elaboration; Festinger, 1957). In the language of the ELM, self-perception proposes a peripheral route to persuasion, whereas dissonance is more central. Thus, dissonance processes should be more likely to operate when the elaboration likelihood is relatively high (i.e., conditions of high issue relevance, consequences, personal responsibility, prior knowledge, etc.) rather than low. Research is generally supportive of this view (e.g., Fazio, Zanna, & Cooper, 1977; Cooper & Fazio, 1984). On the other hand, self-perception processes should be more likely to operate when the elaboration likelihood is relatively low (i.e., conditions of low issue relevance, consequences, responsibility, knowledge, etc.) rather than high. Research also supports this proposition (e.g., Chaiken & Baldwin, 1981; Taylor, 1975; Wood, 1982).[4] If our analysis is correct, then a number of interesting (and so far untested) consequences follow. For example, if Person A becomes more favorable toward some behavior because of a dissonance producing experience, and Person B become equally more favorable toward the same behavior because of an instance of self-perception, the attitude of Person A should show greater resistance to counterpersuasion (see Chapter 7).

   In proposing that certain variables can increase persuasion in some situations but decrease persuasion in others, and that some theories operate in some situations but not others, the ELM is broadly consistent with McGuire's (1983) "contextualist" epistemology for social psychology. In short, the ELM proposes that many of the effects and theories uncovered by persuasion researchers over the years are valid, but their domain of operation is limited (Petty & Cacioppo, 1981a). Importantly, the ELM specifies two general categories of persuasion processes (central and peripheral) and elucidates their antecedents and consequences. In doing this, the ELM suggests *when* many of the traditionally studied variables will

---

[4]Of course, even self-perception requires some *minimal* thought sufficient for an inference to be made (e.g., Scott & Yalch, 1978). The same applies to the operation of many other peripheral cues.

work and *how* they will work. It also helps to specify the domains of many of the extant mini-theories of persuasion.

Finally, we note that although we have confined our discussion (and our own research) in this monograph mostly to the traditional influence situation in which a persuasive communication on one side of an issue (e.g., raising tuition) is presented to a message recipient, we believe that the ELM also has more general applicability to other topics studied by social psychologists. For example, in research on majority versus minority influence, subjects do not hear one message but rather receive conflicting viewpoints from both a majority and a minority group (e.g., Moscovici, 1980). Researchers in this area have suggested that under certain conditions, minorities induce influence via the central route whereas the influence of majorities is more peripheral (Maass & Clark, 1984; Nemeth, 1986). Interpersonal attraction might be governed by both central and peripheral processes as well. For example, early in a relationship when prior knowledge and involvement are relatively low, peripheral physical cues such as attractiveness (e.g., Berscheid & Walster, 1974), or contextual cues such as room temperature (e.g., Griffit & Vietch, 1971) may be influential. As prior knowledge and involvement increase, these cues should become less important as the central merits of the person are processed.[5] Likewise, attitudes toward oneself might be similarly influenced. Specifically, there may be both central and peripheral aspects of the self-concept with the first being formed because of extensive processing of self-relevant information and the second resulting from relatively minimal processing of various cues. In addition, not only may attitudes and beliefs be affected via the central and peripheral routes, but so too may other judgments such as causal attributions (see discussion of Borgida & Howard-Pitney, 1983, in Chapter 6).

Conclusions

Perhaps the greatest strength of the Elaboration Likelihood Model is that it specifies the major ways in which variables can have an impact on persuasion, and it points to the major consequences of these different

---

[5]Importantly, as we noted in Chapter 1, the dimensions that are central to the merits of an attitude object can vary from person to person (e.g., Cacioppo, Petty, & Sidera, 1982; Snyder & DeBono, 1985) and from situation to situation. Thus, for some people, attractiveness may be a central merit (employed when personal involvement is relatively high) whereas intelligence is a peripheral cue (used in evaluation when personal involvement is relatively low). For other people, the opposite may hold. In addition, different situations may render different attributes as central. For example, in judging a person's prospects for graduate school, intelligence is central but attractiveness is peripheral. In judging a person for a modeling career, the opposite may hold.

mediational processes. In one sense, the ELM is rather simple. It indicates that variables can affect persuasion in a limited number of ways: a variable can serve as a persuasive argument, serve as a peripheral cue, or affect argument scrutiny in either a relatively objective or a relatively biased manner. In confining the mediational processes of persuasion to just these possibilities, the ELM provides a unique simplifying and organizing framework that may be applied to many of the traditionally studied source, message, recipient, and context variables. The postulates of the ELM in its present state of development do *not* ultimately indicate *why* certain arguments are strong or weak, why certain variables serve as cues, or why certain variables affect information processing. Instead, the ELM limits the mediational processes of persuasion to a finite set and specifies, in a general way at least, the conditions under which each mediational process is likely to occur and the consequences of these processes. In doing this, the ELM may prove useful in providing a guiding set of postulates from which to interpret previous work, and in posing an interesting set of hypotheses to be explored in future studies.

References

Abelson, R. (1972). Are attitudes necessary. In B. T. King & E. McGinnies (Eds.), *Attitudes, conflict, and social change.* New York: Academic Press.

Adams, J. S. (1959). Advice seeking of mothers as a function of need for cognition. *Child Development, 30,* 171-176.

Adams, W. C., & Beatty, M. J. (1977). Dogmatism, need for social approval and the resistance to persuasion. *Communication Monographs, 44,* 321-325.

Ahlering, R., & McClure, K. (1985). *Need for cognition, attitudes, and the 1984 Presidential election.* Paper presented at the Midwestern Psychological Association, Chicago, IL.

Ajzen, I., & Fishbein, M. (1977). Attitude-behavior relations: A theoretical analysis and review of empirical research. *Psychological Bulletin, 84,* 888-918.

Ajzen, I., & Fishbein, M. (1980). *Understanding attitudes and predicting social behavior.* Englewood Cliffs, NJ: Prentice-Hall.

Allport, G. W. (1935). Attitudes. In C. Murchison (Ed.), *Handbook of social psychology* (Vol. 2). Worchester, MA: Clark University Press.

Allyn, J., & Festinger, L. (1961). The effectiveness of unanticipated persuasive communication. *Journal of Abnormal and Social Psychology, 62,* 35-40.

Anderson, N. (1981). Integration theory applied to cognitive responses and attitudes. In R. Petty, T. Ostrom, & T. Brock (Eds.), *Cognitive responses in persuasion.* Hillsdale, NJ: Erlbaum.

Andreoli, V., & Worchel, S. (1978). Effects of media, communicator, and message position on attitude change. *Public Opinion Quarterly, 42,* 59-70.

Appel, V., Weinstein, S., & Weinstein, C. (1979). Brain activity and recall of TV advertising. *Journal of Advertising Research, 19,* 7-15.

Apsler, R., & Sears, D. O. (1968). Warning, personal involvement, and attitude change. *Journal of Personality and Social Psychology, 9,* 162-166.

Argyle, M., & Kendon, A. (1967). The experimental analysis of social performance. In L. Berkowitz (Ed.), *Advances in experimental social psychology* (Vol. 3). New York: Academic Press.

Asch, S. (1948). The doctrine of suggestion, prestige, and imitation in social psychology. *Psychological Review, 55,* 250-276.

Asch, S. (1951). Effects of group pressure upon the modification and distortion of judgment. In H. Guetzkow (Ed.), *Groups, leadership, and men.* Pittsburgh: Carnegie.

Bacon, F. T. (1979). Credibility of repeated statements: Memory for trivia. *Journal of Experimental Psychology: Human Learning and Memory, 5,* 241-252.

Bargh, J. A. (1984). Automatic and conscious processing of social information. In R.

S. Wyer & T. K. Srull (Eds.), *Handbook of social cognition* (Vol. 3. pp. 1–43). Hillsdale, NJ: Erlbaum.

Baron, R. A., Baron, P., & Miller, N. (1973). The relation between distraction and persuasion. *Psychological Bulletin, 80,* 310–323.

Bates, E. (1976). *Language and context: The acquisition of pragmatics.* New York: Academic Press.

Batra, R., Ray, M. (1984). Advertising situations: The implication of differential involvement and accompanying affective responses. In R. J. Harris (Ed.), *Information processing research in advertising.* Hillsdale, NJ: Erlbaum.

Batra, R., & Ray, M. (1985). How advertising works at contact. In L. Alwitt & A. Mitchell (Eds.), *Psychological processes and advertising effects: Theory, research and application.* Hillsdale, NJ: Erlbaum.

Batra, R., & Ray, M. (1986). Situational effects of advertising repetition: The moderating influence of motivation, ability, and opportunity to respond. *Journal of Consumer Research, 12,* 432–445.

Belch, G. E. (1982). The effects of television commerical repetition on cognitive responses and message acceptance. *Journal of Consumer Research, 9,* 56–65.

Bem, D. J. (1967). Self-perception: An alternative interpretation of cognitive dissonance phenomena. *Psychological Review, 74,* 183–200.

Bem, D. J. (1972). Self-perception theory. In L. Berkowitz (Ed.), *Advances in experimental social psychology* (Vol. 6). New York: Academic Press.

Berscheid, E., & Walster, E. (1974). Physical attractiveness. In L. Berkowitz (Ed.), *Advances in experimental social psychology,* (Vol. 7). New York: Academic Press.

Bettman, J. R. (1986). Consumer psychology. *Annual Review of Psychology, 37,* in press.

Birnbaum, M. H., & Mellers, B. (1979). Stimulus recognition may mediate exposure effects. *Journal of Personality and Social Psychology, 37,* 391–394.

Bobrow, D. G., & Norman, D. A. (1975). Some principles of memory schemata. In D. G. Bobrow & A. Collins (Eds.), *Representation and understanding: Studies in cognitive science.* New York: Academic Press.

Borgida, E., & Howard-Pitney, B. (1983). Personal involvement and the robustness of perceptual salience effects. *Journal of Personality and Social Psychology, 45,* 560–570.

Bower, G. H. (1981). Mood and memory. *American Psychologist, 11,* 11–13.

Brehm, J. W. (1966). *A theory of psychological reactance.* New York: Academic Press.

Brehm, J. W. (1972). *Responses to loss of freedom: A theory of psychological reactance.* Morristown, NJ: General Learning Press.

Brickner, M. A., Harkins, S. G., & Ostrom, T. M. (in press). The effects of personal involvement: Thought provoking implications for social loafing. *Journal of Personality and Social Psychology.*

Britton, B. K., & Tesser, A. (1982). Effects of prior knowledge on use of cognitive capacity in three complex cognitive tasks. *Journal of Verbal Learning and Verbal Behavior, 21,* 421–436.

Brock, T. C. (1967). Communication discrepancy and intent to persuade as determinants of counterargument production. *Journal of Experimental Social Psychology, 3,* 269–309.

Brock, T. C. (1968). Implications of commodity theory for value change. In A. Greenwald, T. Brock, & T. Ostrom (Eds.), *Psychological foundations of attitudes.* New York: Academic Press.

Brock, T. C., & Shavitt, S. (1983). Cognitive-response analysis in advertising. In L. Percy & A. Woodside (Eds.), *Advertising and consumer psychology.* Lexington, MA: D. C. Heath.

Burgoon, M., Cohen, M., Miller, M., & Montgomery, C. (1978). An empirical test of a model of resistance to persuasion. *Human Communications Research, 5,* 27–39.

Burnkrant, R. E., & Howard, D. J. (1984). Effects of the use of introductory rhetorical questions versus statements on information processing. *Journal of Personality and Social Psychology, 47,* 1218–1230.

Burnkrant, R. E., & Sawyer, A. (1983). Effects of involvement on information processing intensity. In R. J. Harris (Ed.), *Information processing research in advertising.* Hillsdale, NJ: Erlbaum.

Burnstein, E., & Schul, Y. (1982). The informational basis of social judgments: Operations in forming an impression of another person. *Journal of Experimental Social Psychology, 18,* 217–234.

Burnstein, E., & Sentis, K., (1981). Attitude polarization in groups. In R. Petty, T. Ostrom, & T. Brock (Eds.), *Cognitive responses in persuasion* (pp. 197–216). Hillsdale, NJ: Erlbaum.

Burnstein, E., & Vinokur, A., (1977). Persuasive argumentation and social comparison as determinants of attitude polarization. *Journal of Experimental Social Psychology, 13,* 315–332.

Cacioppo, J. T. (1979). The effects of exogenous changes in heart rate on the facilitation of thought and resistance to persuasion. *Journal of Personality and Social Psychology, 37,* 487–496.

Cacioppo, J. T., Harkins, S. G., & Petty, R. E. (1981). The nature of attitudes and cognitive responses and their relationships to behavior. In R. Petty, T. Ostrom, & T. Brock (Eds.), *Cognitive responses in persuasion.* Hillsdale, NJ: Erlbaum.

Cacioppo, J. T., Losch, M. E., Tassinary, L. G., & Petty, R. E. (in press). Properties of affect and affect-laden information processing as viewed through the facial response system. In R. Peterson, W. Hoyer, & W. Wilson (Eds.), *The role of affect in consumer behavior: Emerging theories and applications.* Lexington, MA: D.C. Heath.

Cacioppo, J. T., & Petty R. E. (1979a). Attitudes and cognitive response: An electrophysiological approach. *Journal of Personality and Social Psychology, 37,* 2181–2199.

Cacioppo, J. T., & Petty. R. E. (1979b). Effects of message repetition and position on cognitive responses, recall, and persuasion. *Journal of Personality and Social Psychology, 37,* 97–109.

Cacioppo, J. T., & Petty, R. E. (1980a). Persuasiveness of communications is affected by exposure frequency and message quality: A theoretical and empirical analysis of persisting attitude change. In J. H. Leigh & C. R. Martin (Eds.), *Current issues and research in advertising.* Ann Arbor, MI: University of Michigan Graduate School of Business Administration.

Cacioppo, J. T., & Petty, R. E. (1980b). Sex differences in influenceability: Toward specifying the underlying processes. *Personality and Social Psychology Bulletin, 6,* 651–656.

Cacioppo, J. T. & Petty, R. E. (1980c). The effects of orienting task on differential hemispheric EEG activation. *Neuropsychologia, 18,* 675–683.

Cacioppo, J. T., & Petty, R. E. (1981a). Electromyograms as measures of extent and affectivity of information processing. *American Psychologist, 36,* 441–456.

Cacioppo, J. T., & Petty, R. E. (1981b). Electromyographic specificity during covert information processing. *Psychophysiology, 18,* 518–523.

Cacioppo, J. T., & Petty, R. E. (1981c). Social psychological procedures for cognitive response assessment: The thought listing technique. In T. Merluzzi, C. Glass, & M. Genest (Eds.), *Cognitive assessment.* New York: Guilford.

Cacioppo, J. T., & Petty, R. E. (1982). The need for cognition. *Journal of Personality and Social Psychology, 42,* 116–131.

Cacioppo, J. T., & Petty, R. E. (1984a). The Elaboration Likelihood Model. *Advances in Consumer Research, 11,* 673–675.

Cacioppo, J. T., & Petty, R. E. (1984b). The need for cognition: Relationship to attitudinal processes. In R. McGlynn, J. Maddux, C. Stoltenberg, & J. Harvey (Eds.), *Social perception in clinical and counseling psychology*. Lubbock, TX: Texas Tech Press.

Cacioppo, J. T., & Petty, R. E. (1985). Central and peripheral routes to persuasion; The role of message repetition. In A. Mitchell & L. Alwitt (Eds.), *Psychological processes and advertising effects*. Hillsdale, NJ: Erlbaum.

Cacioppo, J. T., & Petty, R. E. (in press). Stalking rudimentary processes of social influence: A psychophysiological approach. In M. P. Zanna, J. M. Olson, & C. P. Herman (Eds.), *Social influence: The Ontario symposium* (Vol. 5). Hillsdale, NJ: Erlbaum.

Cacioppo, J. T., Petty, R. E., & Kao, C. (1984). The efficient assessment of need for cognition. *Journal of Presonality Assessment, 48,* 306–307.

Cacioppo, J. T. Petty, R. E., Kao, C., & Rodriguez, R. (in press). Central and peripheral routes to persuasion: An individual difference perspective. *Journal of Personality and Social Psychology*.

Cacioppo, J. T., Petty, R. E., Losch, M. E., & Kim, H. S. (1986). Electromyographic activity over facial muscle regions can differentiate the valence and intensity of affective reactions. *Journal of Personality and Social Psychology, 50,* 260–268.

Cacioppo, J. T., Petty, R. E., & Marshall-Goodell, B. (1984). Electromyographic specificity during simple physical and attitudinal tasks: Location and topographical features of integrated EMG responses. *Biological Psychology, 18,* 85–121.

Cacioppo, J. T., Petty, R. E., & Morris, K. (1983). Effects of need for cognition on message evaluation, recall, and persuasion. *Journal of Personality and Social Psychology, 45,* 805–818.

Cacioppo, J. T., Petty, R. E., & Morris, K. (1985). Semantic, evaluative, and self-referent processing: Memory, cognitive effort, and somatovisceral activity. *Psychophysiology, 22,* 371–384.

Cacioppo, J. T., Petty, R. E., & Quintanar, L. (1982). Individual differences in relative hemispheric alpha abundance and cognitive responses to persuasive communications. *Journal of Personality and Social Psychology, 43,* 623–636.

Cacioppo, J. T., Petty, R. E., & Sidera, J. (1982). The effects of a salient self-schema on the evaluation of proattitudinal editorials: Top-down versus bottom-up message processing. *Journal of Experimental Social Psychology, 18,* 324–338.

Cacioppo, J. T., Petty, R. E., & Stoltenberg, C. (1985). Processes of social influence: The elaboration likelihood model of persuasion. In P. Kendall (Ed.), *Advances in cognitive behavioral research and therapy* (Vol. 4). New York: Academic Press.

Cacioppo, J. T., Sandman, C., & Walker, B. (1978). The effects of operant heart rate conditioning on cognitive elaboration and attitude change. *Psychophysiology, 15,* 330–338.

Calder, B. J., Insko, C., & Yandell, B. (1974). The relation of cognitive and memorial processes to persuasion in a simulated jury trial. *Journal of Applied Social Psychology, 4,* 62–93.

Calder, B. J., & Sternthal, B. (1980). Television commercial wearout: An information processing view. *Journal of Marketing Research, 17,* 173–186.

Cantor, G. N. (1968). Children's "like-dislike" ratings of familiarized and non-familiarized visual stimuli. *Journal of Experimental Child Psychology, 6,* 651–657.

Cantor, N., & Mischel, W. (1979). Prototypes in person perception. In L. Berkowitz (Ed.), *Advances in experimental social psychology (Vol. 12)*. New York: Academic Press.

Carlsmith, J. M., Ellsworth, P. C., & Aronson, E. (1976). *Methods of research in social psychology*. Reading, MA: Addison-Wesley.

Castillo, D. T. (1985). *Affective responding by depressives: An application of the mere exposure paradigm.* Unpublished doctoral dissertation, University of Iowa, Iowa City, IA.

Chaiken, S. (1979). Communicator physical attractiveness and persuasion. *Journal of Personality and Social Psychology, 37,* 1387-1397.

Chaiken, S. (1980). Heuristic versus systematic information processing and the use of source versus message cues in persuasion. *Journal of Personality and Social Psychology, 39,* 752-756.

Chaiken, S. (1986). Physical appearance and social influence. In C. P. Herman, M. P. Zanna, & E. T. Higgins (Eds.), *Physical appearance, stigma and social behavior: The Ontario Symposium* (Vol. 3). Hillsdale, NJ: Erlbaum.

Chaiken, S. (in press). The heuristic model of persuasion. In M. P. Zanna, J. M. Olson, & C. P. Herman (Eds.), *Social Influence: The Ontario symposium* (Vol. 5). Hillsdale, NJ: Erlbaum.

Chaiken, S., & Baldwin, M. W. (1981). Affective-cognitive consistency and the effect of salient behavioral information on the self-perception of attitudes. *Journal of Personality and Social Psychology, 41,* 1-12.

Chaiken, S., & Eagly, A. H. (1976). Communication modality as a determinant of message persuasivensess and message comprehensibility. *Journal of Personality and Social Psychology, 34,* 605-614.

Chaiken, S., & Eagly, A. H. (1983). Communication modality as a determinant of persuasion: The role of communicator salience. *Journal of Personality and Social Psychology, 45,* 241-256.

Chaiken, S., & Yates, S. (1985). Affective-cognitive consistency and thought-induced attitude polarization. *Journal of Personality and Social Psychology, 49,* 1470-1481.

Cialdini, R. B. (1984). Principles of automatic influence. In J. Jacoby & C. S. Craig (Eds.), *Personal selling: Theory, research, and practice.* Lexington, MA: D. C. Heath.

Cialdini, R. B. (1985). *Influence: Science and practice.* Glenview, IL: Scott-Foresman.

Cialdini, R. B., Levy, A., Herman, P., & Evenbeck, S. (1973). Attitudinal politics: The strategy of moderation. *Journal of Personality and Social Psychology, 25,* 100-108.

Cialdini, R. B., Levy, A., Herman, P., Kozlowski, L., & Petty, R. E. (1976). Elastic shifts of opinion: Determinants of direction and durability. *Journal of Personality and Social Psychology, 34,* 663-672.

Cialdini, R. B., & Petty, R. E. (1981). Anticipatory opinion effects. In R. Petty, T. Ostrom, & T. Brock (Eds.) *Cognitive respones in persuasion* (pp. 217-235). Hillsdale, NJ: Erlbaum.

Cialdini, R. B., Petty, R. E., & Cacioppo, J. T. (1981). Attitude and attitude change. *Annual Review of Psychology, 32,* 357-404.

Clark, M. S., & Fiske, S. T. (Eds.). (1982). *Affect and cognition: The seventeenth annual Carnegie symposium on cognition.* Hillsdale, NJ: Erlbaum.

Clark, M. S., & Isen, A. M. (1982). Toward understanding the relationship between feeling states and social behavior. In A. Hastorf and A. Isen (Eds.), *Cognitive social psychology.* New York: Elsevier-North Holland.

Cohen, A. (1957). Need for cognition and order of communication as determinants of opinion change. In C. Hovland et al. (Eds.), *The order of presentation in persuasion.* New Haven, CT: Yale University Press.

Cohen, A., Stotland, E., & Wolfe, D. (1955). An experimental investigation of need for cognition. *Journal of Abnormal and Social Psychology, 51,* 291-294.

Cook, T. D., & Flay, B. (1978). The temporal persistence of experimentally induced attitude change: An evaluative review. In L. Berkowitz (Ed.), *Advances in experimental social psychology* (Vol. 11). New York: Academic Press.

Cook, T. D., Gruder, C., Hennigan, K., & Flay, B. (1979). History of the sleeper effect:

Some logical pitfalls in accepting the null hypothesis. *Psychological Bulletin, 86,* 662–679.

Cooper, H. M. (1979). Statistically combining independent studies: Meta-analysis of sex differences in conformity research. *Journal of Personality and Social Psychology, 37,* 131–146.

Cooper, J., & Croyle, R. T. (1984). Attitudes and attitude change. *Annual Review of Psychology, 35,* 395–426.

Cooper, J., & Fazio, R. H. (1984). A new look at dissonance theory. In L. Berkowitz (Ed.), *Advances in experimental social psychology* (Vol. 17). New York: Academic Press.

Cooper, J., & Jones, R. A. (1970). Self-esteem and consistency as determinants of anticipatory opinion change. *Journal of Personality and Social Psychology, 14,* 312–320.

Corballis, M. C. (1980). Laterality and myth. *American Psychologist, 35,* 284–295.

Corlett, W. C. (1984). *Central or peripheral routes to attitude change: The role of repetition in television commercial wearout.* Unpublished doctoral dissertation, University of Iowa, Iowa City, IA.

Craik, F. I. M. (1979). Human memory. *Annual Review of Psychology, 30,* 63–102.

Craik, F. I. M., & Lockhart, R. S. (1972). Levels of processing: A framework for memory research. *Journal of Verbal Learning and Verbal Behavior, 11,* 671–684.

Craik, F. I. M., & Tulving, E. (1975). Depth of processing and the retention of words in episodic memory. *Journal of Experimental Psychology: General, 104,* 268–294.

Craik, F. I. M., & Watkins, M. J. (1973). The role of rehearsal in short-term memory. *Journal of Verbal Learning and Verbal Behavior, 12,* 599–607.

Crocker, J., Fiske, S. T., & Taylor, S. E. (1984). Schematic bases of belief change. In R. Eiser (Ed.), *Attitudinal judgment.* New York: Springer-Verlag.

Darwin, C. E. (1965). *The expression of the emotions in man and animals.* Chicago: University of Chicago Press. (Original work published 1872).

Das, J. P., Roth, R., & Stagner, D. (1955). Understanding versus suggestion in the judgment of literary passages. *Journal of Abnormal and Social Pscyhology, 51,* 624–628.

Davidson, A. R., Yantis, S., Norwood, M., & Montano, D. E. (1985). Amount of information about the attitude object and attitude-behavior consistency. *Journal of Personaltiy and Social Psychology, 49,* 1184–1198.

Davidson, R. J., Schwartz, G. E., Saron, C., Bennett, J., & Goleman, D. (1979). Frontal versus parietal EEG asymmetry during positive and negative affect (Abstract). *Psychophysiology, 16,* 202–203.

Deaux, K. (1984). From individual differences to social categories: Analysis of a decade's research on gender. *American Psychologist, 39,* 105–116.

Deci, E. L. (1975). *Intrinsic motivation.* New York: Plenum Press.

Deci, E. L., & Ryan, R. M. (1980). The empirical exploration of intrinsic motivational processes. In L. Berkowitz (Ed.), *Advances in experimental social psychology* (Vol. 13). New York: Academic Press.

DePaulo, B. M., Zuckerman, M., & Rosenthal, R. (1980). The deceptions of everyday life. *Journal of Communication, 30,* 216–218.

Dinner, S. H., Lewkowicz, B. E., & Cooper, J. (1972). Anticipatory attitude change as a function of self-esteem and issue familiarity. *Journal of Personality and Social Psycholgoy, 24,* 407–412.

Eagly, A. H. (1967). Involvement as a determinant of response to favorable and unfavorable information. *Journal of Personality and Social Psychology Monograph, 7* (3 Pt. 2).

Eagly, A. H. (1974). Comprehensibility of persuasive arguments as a determinant of opinion change. *Journal of Personality and Social Psychology, 29,* 758–773.

Eagly, A. H. (1978). Sex differences in influenceability. *Psychological Bulletin, 85,* 86–116.

Eagly, A. H. (in press). Social influence research: New approaches to enduring issues. In M. Zanna, J. Olson, & C. Herman (Eds.), *Social influence: The Ontario symposium* (Vol. 5). Hillsdale, NJ: Erlbaum.

Eagly, A. H., & Carli, L. (1983). Sex of researchers and sex-typed communications as determinants of sex differences in influenceability. *Psychological Bulletin, 90,* 1–20.

Eagly, A. H., & Chaiken, S. (1984). Cognitive theories of persuasion. In L. Berkowitz (Ed.), *Advances in experimental social psychology* (Vol. 17). New York: Academic Press.

Eagly, A. H., Chaiken, S., & Wood, W. (1978). An attributional analysis of persuasion. In J. Harvey, W. Ickes, & R. Kidd (Eds.), *New directions in attribution research* (Vol. 3). Hillsdale, NJ: Erlbaum.

Eagly, A. H., & Himmelfarb, S. (1974). Current trends in attitude theory and research. In S. Himmelfarb & A. Eagly (Eds.), *Readings in attitude change.* New York: Wiley.

Eagly, A. H., & Himmelfarb, S. (1978). Attitudes and opinions. *Annual Review of Psychology, 29,* 517–554.

Eagly, A. H., & Manis, M. (1966). Evaluation of message and communication as a function of involvement. *Journal of Personality and Social Psychology, 3,* 483–485.

Eagly, A. H., & Warren, R. (1976). Intelligence, comprehension, and opinion change. *Journal of Personality, 44,* 226–242.

Eagly, A. H., Wood, W., & Chaiken, S. (1978). Causal inferences about communicators and their effect on opinion change. *Journal of Personality and Social Psychology, 36,* 424–435.

Eibl-Eibesfeldt, I. (1972). Similarities and differences between cultures in expressive movement. In R. A. Hinde (Ed.), *Nonverbal communication.* Cambridge: Cambridge University Press.

Ekman, P., & Friesen, W. V. (1975). *Umasking the face.* Englewood Cliffs, NJ: Prentice-Hall.

Ekman, P., & Friesen, W. V. (1978). *Facial action coding system (FACS): A technique for the measurement of facial actions.* Palo Alto, CA: Consulting Psychologists Press.

Ekstrom, R. B., French, J. W., & Harman, H. H. (1962). *Kit of factor referenced cognitive tests.* Princeton: Educational Testing Service.

Elms, A. C. (1966). Influence of fantasy ability on attitude change through role-playing. *Journal of Personality and Social Psychology, 4,* 36–43.

Fazio, R. H. (1985). How do attitudes guide behavior? In R. M. Sorrentino & E. T. Higgins (Eds.), *The handbook of motivation and cognition: Foundations of social behavior.* New York: Guilford.

Fazio, R. H., Chen, J., McDonel, E., & Sherman, S. J. (1982). Attitude accessiblity, attitude-behavior consistency, and the strength of the object-evaluation association. *Journal of Experimental Social Psychology, 18,* 339–357.

Fazio, R. H., Sanbonmatsu, D. M., Powell, M. C., & Kardes, F. R. (1986). On the automatic activation of attitudes. *Journal of Personality and Social Psychology, 50,* 229–238.

Fazio, R. H., & Williams, C. (1985). *Attitude accessibility as a moderator of the attitude-perception and attitude-behavior relations: An investigation of the 1984 presidential election.* Unpublished manuscript, Indiana University, Bloomington, IN.

Fazio, R. H., & Zanna, M. P. (1981). Direct experience and attitude behavior consistency. In L. Berkowitz (Ed.), *Advances in experimental social psychology,* (Vol. 14, pp. 161–202). New York: Academic Press.

Fazio, R. H., Zanna, M. P., & Cooper, J. (1977). Dissonance and self-perception: An integrative view of each theory's proper domain of application. *Journal of Experimental Social Psychology, 13,* 464-479.

Festinger, L. (1950). Informal social communication. *Psychological Review, 57,* 271-282.

Festinger, L. (1954). A theory of social comparison processes. *Human Relations, 7,* 117-140.

Festinger, L. (1957). *A theory of cognitive dissonance.* Stanford, CA: Stanford University Press.

Festinger, L., & Maccoby, N. (1964). On resistance to persuasive communications. *Journal of Abnormal and Social Psychology, 68,* 359-366.

Fishbein, M. (1980). A theory of reasoned action: Some applications and implications. In H. Howe & M. Page (Eds.), *Nebraska symposium on motivation, 1979.* Lincoln: University of Nebraska Press.

Fishbein, M., & Ajzen, I. (1972). Attitudes and opinions. *Annual Review of Psychology, 23,* 487-544.

Fishbein, M., & Ajzen, I. (1975). *Belief, attitude, intention, and behavior: An introduction to theory and research.* Reading, MA: Addison-Wesley.

Fishbein, M., & Ajzen, I. (1981). Acceptance, yielding and impact: Cognitive processes in persuasion. In R. Petty, T. Ostrom, & T. Brock (Eds.), *Cognitive responses in persuasion.* Hillsdale, NJ: Erlbaum.

Fiske, S. T. (1981). Social cognition and affect. In J. H. Harvey (Ed.), *Cognition, social behavior, and the environment.* Hillsdale, NJ: Erlbaum.

Fiske, S. T., Kinder, D. R., & Larter, W. M. (1983). The novice and the expert: Knowledge-based strategies in political cognition. *Journal of Experimental Social Psychology, 19,* 381-400.

Fiske, S.T., & Taylor, S.E. (1984). *Social cognition.* Reading, MA: Addison-Wesley.

Folkes, V. (1985). Mindlessness or mindfulness: A partial replication and extension of Langer, Blank and Chanowitz. *Journal of Personality and Social Psychology, 48,* 600-604.

Forer, B. (1949). The fallacy of personal validation. *Journal of Abnormal and Social Psychology, 44,* 118-123.

Frank, J. D. (1963). *Persuasion and healing.* New York: Schocken Books.

Freedman, J. L. (1964). Involvement, discrepancy, and change. *Journal of Abnormal and Social Psychology, 69,* 290-295.

Freedman, J. L., & Sears, D. O. (1965). Warning, distraction and resistance to influence. *Journal of Personality and Social Psychology, 1,* 262-266.

Freedman, J. L., Sears. D. O., & O'Conner, E. F. (1964). The effects of anticiapted debate and commitment on the polarization of audience opinion. *Public Opinion Quarterly, 28,* 615-627.

Fridlund, A. J., & Izard, C. E. (1983). Electromyographic studies of facial expressions of emotions and patterns of emotions. In J. T. Cacioppo & R. E. Petty (Eds.), *Social psychophysiology: A sourcebook.* New York: Guilford.

Fridlund, A. J., Schwartz, G. E., & Fowler, S. C. (in press). Facial electromyography and emotion: Implementation of multivariate pattern-classification strategies. *Psychophysiology.*

Fukada, H. (1986). Psychological processes mediating the persuasion inhibiting effect of forewarning in fear arousing communication. *Psychological Reports, 58,* 87-90.

Furguson, M., Chung, M., & Weigold, M. (1985). Need for cognition and the medium dependency components of reliance and exposure. Paper presented at the International Communication Association Meeting, Honolulu, Hawaii.

Gorn, G. (1982). The effects of music in advertising on choice behavior: A classical conditioning approach. *Journal of Marketing Research, 46* 94–101.

Gorn, G., & Goldberg, M. (1980). Children's responses to repetitive TV commercials. *Journal of Consumer Research, 6,* 421–425.

Greenwald, A. G. (1968). Cognitive learning, cognitive response to persuasion, and attitude change. In A. Greenwald, T. Brock, & T. Ostrom (Eds.), *Psychological foundations of attitudes* (pp. 148–170). New York: Academic Press.

Greenwald, A. G. (1975). On the inconclusiveness of "crucial" cognitive tests of dissonance versus self-perception theories. *Journal of Experimental Social Psycholgy, 11,* 490–499.

Greenwald, A. G. (1980). The totalitarian ego: Fabrication and revision of personal history. *American Psychologist, 35,* 603–618.

Greenwald, A. G. (1981). Ego task analysis: An integration of research on ego-involvement. In A. Hastorf & A. Isen (Eds.), *Cognitive social psychology.* New York: Elsevier.

Greenwald, A. G., & Albert, R. (1968). Acceptance and recall of improvised arguments. *Journal of Personality and Social Psychology, 8,* 31–34.

Griffit, W., & Veitch, R. (1971). Hot and crowded: Influences of population density and temperature on interpersonal affective behavior. *Journal of Personality and Social Psychology, 17,* 92–98.

Gruder, C. L., Cook, T. D., Hennigan, K. M., Flay, B. R., Alessi, C., & Halamaj, J. (1978). Empirical tests of the absolute sleeper effect predicted from the discounting cue hypothesis, *Journal of Personality and Social Psychology, 36,* 1061–1074.

Grush, J. E. (1976). Attitude formation and mere exposure phenomena: A nonartifactual explanation of empirical findings. *Journal of Personality and Social Psychology, 33,* 281–290.

Harkins, S. G., Latane, B., & Williams, K. D. (1980). Social loafing: Allocating effort or taking it easy. *Journal of Experimental Social Psychology, 16,* 457–465.

Harkins, S. G., & Petty, R. E. (1981a). The effects of source magnification of cognitive effort on attitudes: An information processing view. *Journal of Personality and Social Psychology, 40,* 401–413.

Harkins, S. G., & Petty, R. E. (1981b). The multiple source effect in persuasion: The effects of distraction. *Personality and Social Psychology Bulletin, 7,* 627–635.

Harkins, S. G., & Petty, R. E. (1982). The effects of task difficulty and task uniqueness on social loafing. *Journal of Personality and Social Psychology, 43,* 1214–1229.

Harkins, S. G., & Petty, R. E. (1983). Social context effects in persuasion: The effects of multiple sources and multiple targets In P. Paulus (Ed.), *Basic group processes.* New York: Springer-Verlag.

Harkins, S. G., & Petty, R. E. (in press). Information utility and the multiple source effect. *Journal of Personality and Social Psychology.*

Harrison, A. A. (1977). Mere exposure. In L. Berkowitz (Ed.), *Advances in experimental social psychology* (Vol.10). New York: Academic Press.

Harvey, O. J., Hunt, D. E., & Schroder, H. M. (1961). *Conceptual systems and personality organization.* New York: Wiley.

Hasher, L., Goldstein D., & Toppino, T. (1977). Frequency and the conference of referential validity. *Journal of Verbal Learning and Verbal Behavior, 16,* 107–112.

Hass, R. G. (1981). Effects of source characteristics on cognitive responses and pesuasion. In R. Petty, T. Ostrom, & T. Brock (Eds.), *Cognitive responses in persuasion.* Hillsdale, NJ: Erlbaum.

Hass, R. G., & Grady, K. (1975). Temporal delay, type of forewarning, and resistance to influence. *Journal of Experimental Social Psychology, 11,* 459–469.

Haugtvedt, C., Petty, R. E., & Cacioppo, J. T. (1986). *Need for cognition and the use of peripheral cues.* Paper presented at the Midwestern Psychological Association, Chicago, IL.

Heesacker, M. H. (in press). A critique of the need for cognition scale. In D. J. Keyser & R. C. Sweetland (Eds.), *Test critiques* (Vol. 3). Kansas City, MO: Test Corp. of America.

Heesacker, M. H. (1986). Counseling pretreatment and the Elaboration Likelihood Model of attitude change. *Journal of Counseling Psychology, 33,* 107–114.

Heesacker, M., Petty, R. E., & Cacioppo, J. T. (1983). Field dependence and attitude change: Source credibility can alter persuasion by affecting message-relevant thinking. *Journal of Personality, 51,* 653–666.

Heider, F. (1946). Attitudes and cognitive organization. *Journal of Psychology, 21,* 107–112.

Heider, F. (1958). *The psychology of interpersonal relations.* New York; Wiley.

Heppner, P. P., & Dixon, D. M. (1981). A review of the interpersonal influence process in counseling. *Personnel and Guidance Journal, 59,* 542–550.

Heppner, P. P., Reeder, L., & Larson, L. M. (1983). Cognitive variables associated with personal problem-solving appraisal: Implications for counseling. *Journal of Counseling Psychology, 30,* 537–545.

Higgins, T., Herman, C. P., & Zanna, M. P. (1981). (Eds.), *Social cognition: The Ontario symposium* (Vol. 1). Hillsdale, NJ: Erlbaum.

Himmelfarb, S., & Eagly, A. H. (1974). Orientations to the study of attitudes and their change. In S. Himmelfarb & A. Eagly (Eds.), *Readings in attitude change.* New York: Wiley.

Hirt, E. R., & Sherman, S. J. (1985). The role of prior knowledge in explaining hypothetical events. *Journal of Experimental Social Psychology, 21,* 519–543.

Holtz, R., & Miller, N. (1985). Assumed similarity and opinion certainty. *Journal of Personality and Social Psychology, 48,* 890–898.

Hovland, C. I., Harvey, O. J., & Sherif, M. (1957). Assimilation and contrast effects in reactions to communications and attitude change. *Journal of Abnormal and Social Psychology, 55,* 244–252.

Hovland, C. I., Janis, I., & Kelley, H. H. (1953). *Communication and persuasion.* New Haven, CT: Yale University Press.

Hovland, C. I., Lumsdaine, A., & Sheffield, F. (1949). *Experiments on mass communication.* Princeton, NJ: Princeton University Press.

Hovland, C. I., & Weiss, W. (1951). The influence of source credibility on communication effectiveness. *Public Opinion Quarterly, 15,* 635–650.

Huddleston, B. M. (1985). *An experimental investigation of the influence deceptive nonverbal cues exert on persuasive processes.* Unpublished doctoral dissertation, Department of Communication, University of Missouri-Columbia, MO.

Ingham, A., Levinger, G., Graves, J., & Peckham, V. (1974). The Ringelmann effect: Studies of group size and group performance. *Journal of Experimental Social Psychology, 10,* 371–384.

Insko, C. A. (1964). Primacy versus recency in persuasion as a function of the timing of arguments and measures. *Journal of Personality and Social Psychology, 69,* 381–391.

Insko, C. A. (1967). *Theories of attitude change.* New York: Appleton-Century-Crofts.

Insko, C. A. (1981). Balance theory and phenomenonology. In R. Petty, T. Ostrom & T. Brock (Eds.), *Cognitive responses in persuasion.* Hillsdale, NJ: Erlbaum.

Insko, C. A. (1984). Balance theory, the Jordan paradigm, and the Wiest tetrahedron. In L. Berkowitz (Ed.), *Advances in experimental social psychology* (Vol. 18). New York: Academic Press.

Insko, C. A., Lind, E. A., & LaTour, S. (1976). Persuasion, recall, and thoughts. *Representative Research in Social Psychology, 7,* 66–78.

Insko, C. A., Turnbull, W., & Yandell, B. (1974). Facilitating and inhibiting effects of distraction on attitude change. *Sociometry, 37,* 508–528.

Izard, E. C. (1971). *The face of emotion.* New York: Appleton-Century-Crofts.

Izard, E. C. (1977). *Human emotions.* New York: Plenum Press.

Janis, I. L., & Gilmore, J. B. (1965). The influence of incentive conditions on the success of role playing in modifying attitudes. *Journal of Personality and Social Psychology, 1,* 17-27.

Janis, I. L., Kaye, D., & Kirschner, P. (1965). Facilitating effects of "eating while reading" on responsiveness to persuasive communications. *Journal of Personality and Social Psychology, 1,* 181-186.

Janis, I. L., & Rife, D. (1959). Persuasibility and emotional disorder. In C. Hovland, & I. Janis (Eds.), *Personality and persuasibility.* New Haven, CT: Yale University Press.

Jellison, J., & Arkin, R. (1977). Social comparison of abilities: A self-presentation approach to decision making in groups. In J. Suls & R. Miller (Eds.), *Social comparison processes: Theoretical and empirical perspectives.* Washington, D. C.: Hemisphere.

Johnson, H. H., & Scileppi, J. A. (1969). Effects of ego-involvement conditions on attitude change to high and low credibility communicators. *Journal of Personality and Social Psychology, 13,* 31-36.

Johnson, H. H., & Watkins, T. A. (1971). The effects of message repetitions on immediate and delayed attitude change. *Psychonomic Science, 22,* 101-103.

Jones, E. E., & Aneshansel, J. (1956). The learning and utilization of contravalent material. *Journal of Abnormal and Social Psychology, 53,* 27-33.

Jones, E. E., & Kohler, R. (1958). The effects of plausibility on the learning of controversial statements. *Journal of Abnormal and Social Psychology, 57,* 315-320.

Judd, C. M., & Lusk, C. M. (1984). Knowledge structures and evaluative judgments: Effects of structural variables on judgmental extremity. *Journal of Personality and Social Psychology, 46,* 1193-1207.

Kahle, L. R., & Homer, P. M. (1985). Physical attractiveness of the celebrity endorser: A social adaptation perspective. *Journal of Consumer Research, 11,* 954-961.

Kahneman, D. (1973). *Attention and effort.* Englewood Cliffs, NJ: Prentice-Hall.

Kahnemen, D., Slovic, P., & Tversky, A. (Eds.). (1982). *Judgment under uncertainty: Heuristics and biases.* New York: Cambridge University Press.

Kallgren, C. A., & Wood, W. (1985). *Access to attitude-relevant information in memory as a determinant of attitude-behavior consistency.* Unpublished manuscript, Texas A & M University, College Station, Texas.

Karabenick, S. A. (1983). Sex-relevance of content and influenceability: Sistrunk and McDavid revisited. *Personality and Social Psychology Bulletin, 9,* 243-252.

Kassarjian, H. H. (1982). Consumer psychology. *Annual review of psychology, 33,* 619-649.

Katz, D. (1960). The functional approach to the study of attitudes. *Public Opinion Quarterly, 24,* 163-204.

Keating, J. P., & Brock, T. C. (1974). Acceptance of persuasion and the inhibition of counterargumentation under various distraction tasks. *Journal of Experimental Social Psychology, 10,* 301-309.

Kelley, H. H. (1967). Attribution theory in social psychology. In D. Levine (Ed.), *Nebraska symposium on motivation* (Vol. 15). Lincoln: University of Nebraska Press.

Kelman, H. C. (1958). Compliance, identification, and internalization: Three processes of attitude change. *Journal of Conflict Resolution, 2,* 51-60.

Kelman, H. C. (1961). Processes of opinion change. *Public Opinion Quarterly, 25,* 57-78.

Kelman, H. C., & Eagly, A. H. (1965). Attitude toward the communicator, perception of communication content, and attitude change. *Journal of Personality and Social Psychology, 1,* 63-78.

Kelman, H. C., & Hovland, C. I. (1953). Reinstatement of the communicator in

delayed measurement of opinion change. *Journal Abnormal and Social Psychology,*
48, 327–335.

Kerr, N., & Bruun, S. (1981). Ringelmann revisited: Alternative explanations for the
social loafing effect. *Personality and Social Psychology Bulletin, 7,* 224–231.

Kessler, J. B. (1973). An empirical study of six- and twelve-member jury de-
cisionmaking processes. *University of Michigan Journal of Law Reform, 6,* 712–734.

Kiesler, C. A. (1971). *The psychology of commitment.* New York: Academic Press.

Kiesler, C. A., Collins, B., & Miller, N. (1969). *Attitude change: A critical analysis of*
theoretical approaches. New York: Wiley.

Kiesler, C. A., & Kiesler, S. (1964). Role of forewarning in persuasive communications. *Journal of Abnormal and Social Psychology, 68,* 547–549.

Kiesler, C. A., & Munson, P. A. (1975). Attitudes and opinions. *Annual Review of*
Psychology, 26, 415–456.

Kiesler, S. B., & Mathog R. (1968). The distraction hypothesis in attitude change.
Psychological Reports, 23, 1123–1133.

Kohlberg, L. (1963). The development of children's orientations toward a moral
order. I. Sequence in the development of moral thought. *Vita Humana, 6,* 11–33.

King, B. T., & Janis, I. L. (1956). Comparison of the effectiveness of improvised versus
nonimprovised role-playing in producing opinion change. *Human Relations, 9,*
177–186.

Kleinhesselink, R. R., & Edwards, R. E. (1975). Seeking and avoiding belief-
discrepant information as a function of its perceived refutability. *Journal of*
Personality and Social Psychology, 31, 787–790.

Krugman, H. E. (1980). Point of view: Sustained viewing of television. *Journal of*
Advertising Research, 20, 65–68.

Kunst-Wilson, W. R., & Zajonc, R. B. (1980). Affective discrimination of stimuli that
cannot be recognized. *Science, 207,* 557–558.

LeBerge, D., & Samuels, S. J. (1974). Toward a theory of automatic information
processing in reading. *Cognitive Psychology, 6,* 293–323.

Lacey, B. C., & Lacey, J. I. (1974). Studies of heart rate and other bodily processes in
sensorimotor behavior. In P. Obrist, A. Black, J. Brener, & L. DiCara (Eds.),
Cardiovascular psychophysiology. Chicago: Aldine.

Lacey, J. I. Kagan, J., Lacey, B., & Moss. H. A. (1963). The visceral level: Situational
determinants and behavioral correlates of autonomic response patterns. In P. H.
Knapp (Ed.), *Expression of the emotions in man.* New York: International
Universities Press.

Lammers, H. B., & Becker, L. A. (1980). Distraction: Effects on the perceived
extremity of a communication and on cognitive responses. *Personality and Social*
Psychology Bulletin, 6, 261–266.

Landman, J., & Manis, M. (1983). Social cognition: Some historical and theoretical
perspectives. In L. Berkowitz (Ed.), *Advances in experimental social psychology* (Vol.
16). New York: Academic Press.

Langer, E. J. (1975). The illusion of control. *Journal of Personality and Social*
Psychology, 32, 311–328.

Langer, E. (1978). Rethinking the role of thought in social interaction. In J. Harvey,
W. Ickes, & R. Kidd (Eds.), *New directions in attribution research* (Vol. 2). Hillsdale,
NJ: Erlbaum.

Langer, E. J. (1982). *Minding matters: The mindlessness/mindfulness theory of cognitive*
activity. Paper presented at the meeting of the Society of Experimental Social
Psychology, Nashville, Indiana.

Langer, E., Blank, A., & Chanowitz, B. (1978). The mindlessness of ostensibly
thoughtful action. *Journal of Personality and Social Psychology, 36,* 635–642.

Langer, E. J., Chanowitz, B., & Blank, A. (1985). Mindlessness-mindfulness in perspective: A reply to Valerie Folkes. *Journal of Personality and Social Psychology, 48,* 605–607.

Lastovicka, J., & Gardner, D. (1979). Components of involvement. In J. Maloney & B. Silverman (Eds.), *Attitude research plays for high stakes.* Chicago: American Marketing Association.

Latane, B., & Dabbs, J. (1975). Sex, group size, and helping in three cities. *Sociometry, 38,* 180–194.

Latane, B, & Darley, J. (1970). *The unresponsive bystander: Why doesn't he help?* New York: Appleton-Century-Crofts.

Latane, B., Williams, K., & Harkins, S G. (1979). Many hands make light the work: The causes and consequences of social loafing. *Journal of Personality and Social Psychology, 37,* 822–832.

Latane, B., & Wolf, S. (1981). The social impact of majorities and minorities. *Psychological Review, 88,* 438–453.

Leippe, M. R., & Elkin, R. A. (in press). When motives clash: Issue involvement and response involvement as determinants of persuasion. *Journal of Personality and Social Psychology.*

Lemon, N. (1973). *Attitudes and their measurement.* New York: Wiley.

Lepper, M. R., Greene, D., & Nisbett, R. E. (1973). Undermining children's intrinsic interest with extrinsic reward: A test of the "overjustification" hypothesis. *Journal of Personality and Social Psychology, 28,* 129–137.

Liebhart, E. H. (1979). Information search and attribution: Cognitive processes mediating the effect of false autonomic feedback. *European Journal of Social Psychology, 9,* 19–37.

Likert, R. (1932). A technique for the measurement of attitudes. *Archives of Psychology, 140,* 1–55.

Lingle, J. H., & Ostrom, T. M. (1981). Principles of memory and cognition in attitude formation. In R. E. Petty, T. Ostrom, & T. Brock (Eds.), *Cognitive responses in persuasion.* Hillsdale, NJ: Erlbaum.

Linville, P. (1982). The complexity-extremity effect and age-based stereotyping. *Journal of Personality and Social Psychology, 42,* 193–210.

Lord, C. G., Ross, L., & Lepper, M. R. (1979). Biased assimilation and attitude polarization: The effects of prior theories on subsequently considered evidence. *Journal of Personality and Social Psychology, 37,* 2098–2109.

Love, R. E., & Greenwald, A. G. (1978). Cognitive responses to persuasion as mediators of opinion change. *Journal of Social Psychology, 104,* 231–241.

Lowin, A. (1967). Approach and avoidance as alternate modes of selective exposure to information. *Journal of Personality and Social Psychology, 6,* 1–9.

Lutz, R. J., MacKenzie, S. B., & Belch, G. E. (1983). Attitude toward the ad as a mediator of advertising effectiveness: Determinants and consequences. *Advances in Consumer Research, 10,* 532–539.

Maass, A., & Clark, R. D. (1984). Hidden impact of minorities: Fifteen years of minority influence research. *Psychological Bulletin, 95,* 428–450.

Maddux, J. E., & Rogers, R. W. (1980). Effects of source expertness, physical attractiveness, and supporting arguments on persuasion: A case of brains over beauty. *Journal of Personality and Social Psychology, 38,* 235–244.

Markus, H. (1977). Self-schemata and processing information about the self. *Journal of Personality and Social Psychology, 35,* 63–78.

McCullough, J. L., & Ostrom, T. M. (1974). Repetition of highly similar messages. *Journal of Applied Social Psychology, 59,* 395–397.

McDavid, J. (1959). Personality and situational determinants of conformity. *Journal of Abnormal and Social Psychology, 58,* 241–246.

McGinley, H., LeFevre, R., & McGinley, P. (1975). The influence of a communicator's body position on opinion change in others. *Journal of Personality and Social Psychology, 31,* 686–690.

McGuigan, F. J. (1970). Covert oral behavior during the silent performance of language tasks. *Psychological Bulletin, 74,* 309–326.

McGuigan, F. J. (1978). *Cognitive psychophysiology: Principles of covert behavior.* New York: Appleton-Century-Crofts.

McGuire, W. J. (1964). Inducing resistance to persuasion: Some contemporary approaches. In L. Berkowitz (Ed.), *Advances in experimental social psychology* (Vol. 1). New York: Academic Press.

McGuire, W. J. (1968). Personality and attitude change: An information-processing theory. In A. Greenwald, T. Brock, & T. Ostrom (Eds.), *Psychological foundations of attitudes.* New York: Academic Press.

McGuire, W. J. (1969). The nature of attitudes and attitude change. In G. Lindzey & E. Aronson (Eds.), *The handbook of social psychology* (2nd ed., Vol. 3). Reading, MA: Addison-Wesley.

McGuire, W. J. (1981). The probabilogical model of cognitive structure and attitude change. In R. E. Petty, T. M. Ostrom, & T. C. Brock (Eds.), *Cognitive responses in persuasion.* Hillsdale, NJ: Erlbaum.

McGuire, W. J. (1983). A contextualist theory of knowledge: Its implications for innovation and reform in psychological research. In L. Berkowitz (Ed.), *Advances in experimental social psychology* (Vol. 16). New York: Academic Press.

McGuire, W. J. (1985). Attitudes and attitude change. In G. Lindzey & E. Aronson (Eds.), *Handbook of social psychology* (3rd ed., Vol. 2). New York: Random House.

McGuire, W. J., & Papageorgis, D. (1961). The relative efficacy of various types of prior belief-defense in producing resistance to persuasion. *Public Opinion Quarterly, 62,* 327–337.

McGuire, W. J., & Papageorgis, D. (1962). Effectiveness of forewarning in developing resistance to persuasion. *Public Opinion Quarterly, 26,* 24–34.

McHugo, G., Lanzetta, J. T., Sullivan, D. G., Masters, R. D., & Englis, B. (1985). Emotional reactions to a political leader's expressive displays. *Journal of Personality and Social Psychology, 49,* 1513–1529.

Mehrabian, A. (1981). *Silent messages: Emplicit communication of emotions and attitudes.* Belmont, CA: Wadsworth.

Millar, M. G., & Tesser, A. (1984). *Thought-induced attitude change: The effects of schema structure and commitment.* Unpublished manuscript, University of Georgia, Athens, GA.

Miller, N. (1965). Involvement and dogmatism as inhibitors of attitude change. *Journal of Experimental Social Psychology, 1,* 121–132.

Miller, N., & Baron, R. S. (1968). *Distraction, communicator credibility and attitude change.* Unpublished manuscript, University of Iowa, Iowa City, Iowa.

Miller, N., & Baron, R. S. (1973). On measuring counterarguing. *Journal for the Theory of Social Behavior, 3,* 101–118.

Miller, N., & Campbell, D. T. (1959). Recency and primacy in persuasion as a function of the timing of speeches and measurements. *Journal of Abnormal and Social Psychology, 59,* 1–9.

Miller, N., & Colman, D. (1981). Methodological issues in analyzing the cognitive mediation of persuasion. In R. E. Petty, T. M. Ostrom, & T. C. Brock (Eds.), *Cognitive responses in persuasion.* Hillsdale, NJ: Erlbaum.

Miller, N., Maruyama, G., Beaber, R., Valone, K. (1976). Speed of speech and persuasion. *Journal of Personality and Social Psychology, 34,* 615–625.

Miller, R. L. (1976). Mere exposure, psychological reactance, and attitude change. *Public Opinion Quarterly, 40,* 229–233.

Miller, R. L., Brickman, P., & Bolen, D. (1975). Attribution versus persuasion as a means for modifying behavior. *Journal of Personality and Social Psychology, 31,* 430–441.

Mills, J., & Aronson, E. (1965). Opinion change as a function of the communicator's attractiveness and desire to influence. *Journal of Personality and Social Psychology, 1,* 173–177.

Mills, J., & Harvey, J. H. (1972). Opinion change as a function of when information about the communicator is received and whether he is attractive or expert. *Journal of Personality and Social Psychology, 21,* 52–55.

Mitnick, L., & McGinnies, E. (1958). Influencing ethnocentrism in small discussion groups through a film communication. *Journal of Abnormal and Social Psychology, 56,* 82–92.

Moreland, R. I., & Zajonc, R. B. (1976). A strong test of the exposure effect. *Journal of Experimental Social Psychology, 12,* 170–178.

Morris, K., Bachman, E., Bromwell, G., & Sterling, S. (1982). *The need for cognition: Relationship to other personality factors.* Unpublished manuscript, University of Iowa, Iowa City, IA.

Moscovici, S. (1980). Toward a theory of conversion behavior. In L. Berkowitz (Ed.), *Advances in experimental social psychology* (Vol. 13). New York: Academic Press.

Nemeth, C. (1986). Differential contributions of majority and minority influence. *Psychological Review, 93,* 23–32.

Newcombe, N., & Arnkoff, D. B. (1979). Effects of speech style and sex of speaker on person perception. *Journal of Personality and Social Psychology, 37,* 1293–1303.

Nisbett, R. E., & Wilson, T. D. (1977). Telling more than we can know: Verbal reports on mental processes. *Psychological Review, 84,* 231–259.

Norman, R. (1975). Affective-cognitive consistency, attitudes, conformity, and behavior. *Journal of personality and Social Psychology, 32,* 83–91.

Olson, K., Camp, C., & Fuller, D. (1984). Curiosity and need for cognition. *Psychological Reports, 54,* 71–74.

Osgood, C. E., Suci, G. J., & Tannenbaum, P. H. (1957). *The measurement of meaning.* Urbana, IL: University of Illinois Press.

Osgood, C. E., & Tannenbaum, P. H. (1955). The principle of congruity in the prediction of attitude change. *Psychological Review, 62,* 42–55.

Osterhouse, R. A., & Brock, T. C. (1970). Distraction increases yielding to propaganda by inhibiting counterarguing. *Journal of Personality and Social Psychology, 15,* 344–358.

Ostrom, T. M., & Brock, T. C. (1968). A cognitive model of attitudinal involvement. In R. Abelson et al. (Eds.), *Theories of cognitive consistency: A sourcebook.* Chicago: Rand McNally.

Pallak, M. S., Mueller, M., Dollar, K., & Pallak, J. (1972). Effect of commitment on responsiveness to an extreme consonant communication. *Journal of Personality and Social Psychology, 23,* 429–436.

Pallak, S. S., Murroni, E., & Koch, J. (1983). Communicator attractiveness and expertise, emotional versus rational appeals, and persuasion. *Social Cognition, 2,* 122–141.

Palmerino, M., Langer, E., & McGillis, D. (1984). Attitudes and attitude change: Mindlessness-mindfulness perspective. In J. R. Eiser (Ed.), *Attitudinal judgment.* New York: Springer-Verlag.

Papageorgis, D. (1963). Bartlett effect and the persistence of induced attitude change. *Journal of Abnormal and Social Psychology, 67,* 61–67.

Papageorgis, D. (1968). Warning and persuasion. *Psychological Bulletin, 70,* 271–282.

Park, C. W., & Young, S. M. (1986). Consumer response to television commercials: The impact of involvement and background music on brand attitude formation. *Journal of Marketing Research, 23,* 11–24.

Perloff, R. M., & Brock, T. C. (1980). And thinking makes it so: Cognitive responses to persuasion. In M. Roloff & G. Miller (Eds.), *Persuasion: New directions in theory and research*. Beverly Hills: Sage.

Petty, R. E. (1977). *A cognitive response analysis of the temporal persistence of attitude changes induced by persuasive communications*. Unpublished doctoral dissertation, Ohio State University, Columbus, OH.

Petty, R. E., & Brock, T. C. (1976). Effects of responding or not responding to hecklers on audience agreement with a speaker. *Journal of Applied Social Psychology, 6,* 1–17.

Petty, R. E., & Brock, T. C. (1979). Effects of "Barnum" personality assessments on cognitive behavior. *Journal of Consulting and Clinical Psychology, 47,* 201–203.

Petty, R. E., & Brock, T. C. (1981). Thought disruption and persuasion: Assessing the validity of attitude change experiments. In R. Petty, T. Ostrom, & T. Brock (Eds.), *Cognitive responses in persuasion* (pp. 55–79). Hillsdale, NJ: Erlbaum.

Petty, R. E., & Cacioppo, J. T. (1977). Forewarning, cognitive responding, and resistance to persuasion. *Journal of Personality and Social Psychology, 35,* 645–655.

Petty, R. E., & Cacioppo, J. T. (1978). *A cognitive response approach to attitudinal persistence*. Presented at the annual meeting of the American Psychological Association, Toronto, Canada.

Petty, R. E., & Cacioppo, J. T. (1979a). Effects of forewarning of persuasive intent and involvement on cognitive responses and persuasion. *Personality and Social Psychology Bulletin, 5,* 173–176.

Petty, R. E., & Cacioppo, J. T. (1979b). Issue-involvement can increase or decrease persuasion by enhancing message-relevant cognitive responses. *Journal of Personality and Social Psychology, 37,* 1915–1926.

Petty, R. E., & Cacioppo, J. T. (1981a). *Attitudes and persuasion: Classic and contemporary approaches*. Dubuque, IA: Wm. C. Brown.

Petty, R. E., & Cacioppo, J. T. (1981b). Issue involvement as a moderator of the effects on attitude of advertising content and context. *Advances in Consumer Research, 8,* 20–24.

Petty, R. E., & Cacioppo, J. T. (1983a). Central and peripheral routes to persuasion: Application to advertising. In L. Percy & A. Woodside (Eds.), *Advertising and consumer psychology* (pp. 3–23). Lexington, MA: Lexington Books, D.C. Heath.

Petty, R. E., & Cacioppo, J. T. (1983b). The role of bodily responses in attitude measurement and change. In J. T. Cacioppo & R. E. Petty (Eds.), *Social psychophysiology: A sourcebook*. New York: Guilford.

Petty, R. E., & Cacioppo, J. T. (1984a). The effects of involvement on responses to argument quantity and quality: Central and peripheral routes to persuasion. *Journal of Personality and Social Psychology, 46,* 69–81.

Petty, R. E., & Cacioppo, J. T. (1984b). Motivational factors in consumer response to advertisements. In R. Geen, W. Beatty, & R. Arkin, *Human motivation: Physiological, behavioral, and social approaches* (pp. 418–454). Boston: Allyn & Bacon.

Petty, R. E., & Cacioppo, J. T. (1984c). Source factors and the Elaboration Likelihood Model of persuasion. *Advances in Consumer Research, 11,* 668–672.

Petty, R. E., & Cacioppo, J. T. (1986). The Elaboration Likelihood Model of persuasion. In L. Berkowitz (Ed.), *Advances in Experimental Social Psychology* (Vol. 19). New York: Academic Press.

Petty, R. E., Cacioppo, J. T., & Goldman, R. (1981). Personal involvement as a determinant of argument-based persuasion. *Journal of Personality and Social Psychology, 41*, 847–855.

Petty, R. E., Cacioppo, J. T., & Harkins, S. G. (1983). Group size effects on cognitive effort and attitude change. In H. Blumberg, A. Hare, V. Kent, & M. Davies (Eds.), *Small groups and social interaction* (Vol. 1, pp. 165–181). London: John Wiley.

Petty, R. E., Cacioppo, J. T., Haugtvedt, C., & Heesacker, M. (1986). *Consequences of the route to persuasion: Persistence and resistance of attitude changes.* Unpublished manuscript, University of Missouri, Columbia, MO.

Petty, R. E., Cacioppo, J. T., & Heesacker, M. (1981). The use of rhetorical questions in persuasion: A cognitive response analysis. *Journal of Personality and Social Psychology, 40*, 432–440.

Petty, R. E., Cacioppo, J. T., & Heesacker, M. (1984). Central and peripheral routes to persuasion: Application to counseling. In R. McGlynn, J. Maddux, C. Stoltenberg, & J. Harvey (Eds.), *Social perception in clinical and counseling psychology* (pp. 59–89). Lubbock, TX: Texas Tech Press.

Petty, R. E., Cacioppo, J. T., & Kasmer, J. (1985). *Effects of need for cognition on social loafing.* Presented at the Midwestern Psychological Association meeting, Chicago, IL.

Petty, R. E., Cacioppo, J. T., & Schumann, D. (1983). Central and peripheral routes to advertising effectiveness: The moderating role of involvement. *Journal of Consumer Research, 10*, 134–148.

Petty, R. E., Cacioppo, J. T., & Schumann, D. (1984). Attitude change and personal selling. In J. Jacoby & S. Craig (Eds.), *Personal selling: Theory, research, and practice* (pp. 29–55). Lexington, MA: D. C. Heath.

Petty, R. E., Harkins, S. G., & Williams, K. D. (1980). The effects of group diffusion of cognitive effort on attitudes: An information processing view. *Journal of Personality and Social Psychology, 38*, 81–92.

Petty, R. E., Harkins, S. G., Williams, K. D., & Latane, B. (1977). The effects of group size on cognitive effort and evaluation. *Personality and Social Psychology Bulletin, 3*, 579–582.

Petty, R. E., Ostrom, T. M., & Brock, T. C. (Eds.) (1981a). *Cognitive responses in persuasion.* Hillsdale, NJ: Erlbaum.

Petty, R. E., Ostrom, T. M., & Brock, T. C. (1981b). Historical foundations of the cognitive response approach to attitudes and persuasion. In R. E. Petty, T. M. Ostrom, & T. C. Brock (Eds.), *Cognitive responses in persuasion.* Hillsdale, NJ: Erlbaum.

Petty, R. E., Wells, G. L., & Brock, T. C. (1976). Distraction can enhance or reduce yielding to propaganda: Thought disruption versus effort justification. *Journal of Personality and Social Psychology, 34*, 874–884.

Petty, R. E., Wells, G. L., Heesacker, M., Brock, T., & Cacioppo, J. T. (1983). The effects of recipient posture on persuasion: A cognitive response analysis. *Personality and Social Psychology Bulletin, 9*, 209–222.

Pieters, R. G. M. (1986). *The external and moderating effect of need for cognition on attitude-belief and attitude-intention consistency: A field study.* Unpublished manuscript, Erasmus University, Rotterdam, The Netherlands.

Poffenberger, A. T. (1925). *Psychology in advertising.* New York: Shaw.

Posner, M. I., & Snyder, C. R. (1975). Attention and cognitive control. In R. L. Solso (Ed.), *Information processing and cognition: The Loyola symposium.* Hillsdale, NJ: Erlbaum.

Pratkanis, A. R., & Greenwald, A. G. (1985). A reliable sleeper effect in persuasion: Implications for opinion change theory and research. In L. Alwitt & A. Mitchell (Eds.), *Psychological processes and advertising effects: Theory, research, and application.* Hillsdale, NJ: Erlbaum.

Pryor, B., & Steinfatt, T. M. (1978). The effects of initial belief level on inoculation theory and its proposed mechanisms. *Human Communication Research, 4*, 217–230.

Puckett, J., Petty, R. E., Cacioppo, J. T., & Fisher, D. (1983). The relative impact of age and attractiveness stereotypes on persuasion. *Journal of Gerontology, 38*, 340–343.

Regan, D. T., & Cheng, J. B. (1973). Distraction and attitude change: A resolution. *Journal of Experimental Social Psychology, 9*, 138–147.

Regan, D. T., & Fazio, R. (1977). On the consistency between attitude and behavior: Look to the method of attitude formation. *Journal of Experimental Social Psychology, 13*, 28–45.

Rhine, R., & Severance, L. (1970). Ego-involvement, discrepancy, source credibility, and attitude change. *Journal of Personality and Social Psychology, 16*, 175–190.

Rogers, R. (1983). Cognitive and physiological processes in fear appeals and attitude change: A revised theory of protection motivation. In J. T. Cacioppo & R. E. Petty (Eds.), *Social psychophysiology: A sourcebook*. New York: Guilford Press.

Romer, D. (1979). Distraction, counterarguing, and the internalization of attitude change. *European Journal of Social Psychology, 9*, 1–17.

Ronis, D. L., Baumgardner, M., Leippe, M., Cacioppo, J. T., & Greenwald, A. G. (1977). In search of reliable persuasion effects: I. A single session procedure for studying persistence of persuasion. *Journal of Personality and Social Psychology, 35*, 548–569.

Rosen, E. (1963). Need for cognition: Measurement and some correlates. *Psychological Reports, 13*, 408.

Rosen, E. (1964). Factor analysis of the need for cognition. *Psychological Reports, 15*, 619–625.

Rosen, E., Siegelman, E., & Teeter, B. (1964). A dimension of cognitive motivation: Need to know the known vs. the unknown. *Psychological Reports, 13*, 703–706.

Rosenberg, M. (1956). Cognitive structure and attitudinal affect. *Journal of Abnormal and Social Psychology, 53*, 367–372.

Rosenberg, M. (1960). An analysis of affective-cognitive consistency. In M. J. Rosenberg, C. I. Hovland, W. J. McGuire, R. P. Abelson, & J. W. Brehm, (Eds.), *Attitude organization and change*. New Haven, CT: Yale University Press.

Ross, E. A. (1908). *Social psychology: An outline and a sourcebook*. New York: Macmillan.

Ross, L. (1981). The "intuitive scientist" formulation and its developmental implications. In J. H. Flavell & L. Ross (Eds.), *Social cognitive development: Frontiers and possible futures*. Cambridge: Cambridge University Press.

Ross, L., Lepper, M., & Hubbard, M. (1975). Perseverance in self-perception and social perception: Biased attributional processes in the debriefing paradigm. *Journal of Personality and Social Psychology, 32*, 880–892.

Ryan, E. B., & Giles, H. (Eds.), (1982). *Attitudes toward language variation: Social and applied contexts*. London: Arnold.

Rydell, S. T., & Rosen, E. (1966). Measurement and some correlates of need-cognition. *Psychological Reports, 19*, 139–165.

Sadler, O., & Tesser, A. (1973). Some effects of salience and time upon interpersonal hostility and attraction during social isolation. *Sociometry, 36*, 99–112.

Salancik, G. R., & Conway, M. (1975). Attitude inferences from salient and relevant cognitive content about behavior. *Journal of Personality and Social Psychology, 32*, 829–840.

Sandelands, L. E., & Larson, J. R. (1985). When measurement causes task attitudes: A note from the laboratory. *Journal of Applied Psychology, 70*, 116–121.

Sarason, I. G. (1972). Experimental approaches to test anxiety: Attention and the uses of information. In C. D. Spielberger (Ed.), *Anxiety: Current trend in theory and research* (Vol. 2). New York: Academic Press.

Sawyer, A. G. (1981). Repetition, cognitive responses and persuasion. In R. Petty, T. Ostrom, & T. Brock (Eds.), *Cognitive responses in persuasion* (pp. 237–261). Hillsdale, NJ: Erlbaum.

Scheier, M. F., Carver, C. S., & Matthews, K. (1983). Attentional factors in the perception of bodily states. In J. T. Cacioppo & R. E. Petty (Eds.), *Social psychophysiology: A sourcebook*. New York: Guilford.

Schlenker, B. R. (1980). *Impression management: The self-concept, social identity, and interpersonal relation*. Monterey, CA: Brooks/Cole.

Schneider, W., & Shiffrin, R. M. (1977). Controlled and automatic human information processing: I. Detection, search and attention. *Psychological Review, 84,* 1–66.

Schumann, D., Petty, R. E., & Cacioppo, J. T. (1966). *Effects of involvement, repetition, and variation on responses to advertisements*. Unpublished manuscript, University of Missouri, Columbia, MO.

Schwartz, G. E. (1975). Biofeedback, self-regulation, and the patterning of physiological processes. *American Scientist, 63,* 314–324.

Schwartz, G. E., Fair, P. L., Salt, P., Mandel, M. R., & Klerman, G. L. (1976). Facial muscle patterning to affective imagery in depressed and nondepressed subjects. *Science, 192,* 489–491.

Scott, C. A., & Yalch, R. F. (1978). A test of the self-percepton explanation of the effects of rewards on intrinsic interest. *Journal of Experimental Social Psychology, 14,* 180–192.

Sherif, C. W., Kelly, M., Rodgers, H. L., Sarup, G., & Tittler, B. (1973). Personal involvement, social judgment, and action. *Journal of Personality and Social Psychology, 27,* 311–327.

Sherif, C. W., Sherif, M., & Nebergall, R. E. (1965). *Attitude and attitude change: The social judgment-involvement approach*. Philadelphia, PA: W. B. Saunders Co.

Sherif, M. (1977). Crisis in social psychology: Some remarks towards breaking through the crisis. *Personality and Social Psychology Bulletin, 3,* 368–382.

Sherif, M., & Hovland, C. I. (1961). *Social judgment: Assimilation and contrast effects in communication and attitude change*. New Haven, CT: Yale University Press.

Sherif, M., & Sherif, C. W. (1967). Attitude as the individual's own categories: The social judgment-involvement approach to attitude and attitude change. In C. W. Sherif & M. Sherif (Eds.), *Attitude, ego-involvement, and change*. New York: Wiley.

Sherman, S. J. (in press). Cognitive processes in the formation, change, and expression of attitudes. In M. Zanna, J. Olson, and C. Herman (Eds.), *Social influence: The Ontario Symposium* (Vol. 5). Hillsdale, NJ: Erlbaum.

Sherman, S. J., & Fazio, R. H. (1983). Parallels between attitudes and traits as predictors of behavior. *Journal of Personality, 51,* 308–345.

Shiffrin, R. M., & Schneider, W. (1977). Controlled and automatic information processing: II. Perceptual learning, automatic attending, and a general theory. *Psychological Review, 84,* 127–190.

Shipley, W. C. (1940). *Shipley-Hartford scale: Manual of directions*. Hartford, CT: Neuro-Psychiatric Institute of the Hartford Retreat.

Sidera, J. A. (1983). *The effects of need for cognition on latitudes of acceptance, noncommitment, and rejection of issues and attraction to similar and dissimilar strangers*. Unpublished doctoral dissertation, University of Notre Dame, South Bend, Indiana.

Sistrunk, F., & McDavid, J. W. (1971). Sex variable in conforming behavior. *Journal of Personality and Social Psychology, 17,* 200–207.

Sivacek, J., & Crano, W. D. (1982). Vested interest as a moderator of attitude-behavior consistency. *Journal of Personality and Social Psychology, 43,* 210–221.

Slamecka, N. J., & Graf, P. (1978). The generation effect: Delineation of a phenomenon. *Journal of Experimental Psychology: Human Learning and Memory, 4,* 592–604.

Sloan, L. R., Love, R. E., & Ostrom, T. M. (1974). The political heckler: Who really loses. *Journal of Personality and Social Psychology, 30,* 518–528.

Smith, B. L., Lasswell, H. D., & Casey, R. D. (1946). *Propaganda, communication, and public opinion.* Princeton, NJ: Princeton University Press.

Smith, M. B., Bruner, J. S., & White, R. W. (1956). *Opinions and personality.* New York: Wiley.

Smith, M. J. (1982). *Persuasion and human action.* Belmont, CA: Wadsworth.

Snyder, M. (1974). The self-monitoring of expressive behavior. *Journal of Personality and Social Psychology, 30,* 526–537.

Snyder, M. (1979). Self-monitoring processes. In L. Berkowitz (Ed.), *Advances in experimental social psychology* (Vol. 12). New York: Academic Press.

Snyder, M., & DeBono, K. G. (1985). Appeals to image and claims about quality: Understanding the psychology of advertising. *Journal of Personality and Social Psychology, 49,* 586–597.

Sokolov, A. N. (1972). *Inner speech and thought.* New York: Plenum Press.

Srull, T. K. (1983a). Affect and memory: The impact of affective reactions in advertising on the representation of product information in memory. *Advances in Consumer Research, 10,* 520–525.

Srull, T. K. (1983b). The role of prior knowledge in the acquisition, retention, and use of new information. *Advances in Consumer Research, 10,* 572–576.

Srull, T. K., Lichtenstein, M., & Rothbart, M. (1985). Associative storage and retrieval processes. *Journal of Experimental Psychology: Learning, Memory, and Cognition, 11,* 316–345.

Staats, A. W., & Staats, C. K.(1958). Attitudes established by classical conditioning. *Journal of Abnormal and Social Psychology, 57,* 37–40.

Staats, C. K., & Staats, A. W. (1957). Meaning established by classical conditioning. *Journal of Experimental Psychology, 54,* 74–80.

Stang, D. J. (1974). Methodological factors in mere exposure research. *Psychological Bulletin, 81,* 1014–1025.

Stang, D. J. (1975). The effects of mere exposure on learning and affect. *Journal of Personality and Social Psychology, 31,* 7–13.

Steiner, I. (1972). *Group process and productivity.* New York: Academic Press.

Sternthal, B., Dholakia, R., & Leavitt, C. (1978). The persuasive effect of source credibility: A test of cognitive response analysis. *Journal of Consumer Research, 4,* 252–260.

Stoltenberg, C. D., & Davis, C. S. (in press). Career and study skills information: Who says what can alter message processing. *Journal of Social and Clinical Psychology.*

Strong, E. K. (1925). *The psychology of selling and advertising.* New York: McGraw-Hill.

Strong, S. R. (1968). Counseling: An interpersonal influence. *Journal of Counseling Psychology, 15,* 215–224.

Suedfeld, P., Borrie, R. A. (1978). Sensory deprivation, attitude change, and defense against persuasion. *Canadian Journal of Behavioral Science, 10,* 16–27.

Swasy, J. L., & Munch, J. M. (1985). Examining the target of receiver elaborations: Rhetorical question effects on source processing and persuasion. *Journal of Consumer Research, 11,* 877–886.

Taylor, S. E. (1975). On inferring one's attitude from one's behavior: Some delimiting conditions. *Journal of Personality and Social Psychology, 31,* 126–131.

Taylor, S. E. (1981). The interface of cognitive and social psychology. In J. H. Harvey (Ed.), *Cognition, social behavior, and the environment.* Hillsdale, NJ: Erlbaum.

Taylor, S. E., & Fiske, S. (1978). Salience, attention, and attributions: Top of the head phenomena. In L. Berkowitz (Ed.), *Advances in experimental social psychology* (Vol. 11). New York: Academic Press.

Tesser, A. (1976). Thought and reality constraints as determinants of attitude polarization. *Journal of Research in Personality, 10,* 183–194.

Tesser, A. (1978). Self-generated attitude change. In L. Berkowitz (Ed.), *Advances in experimental social psychology* (Vol. 11). New York: Academic Press.

Tesser, A., & Conlee, M. C. (1975). Some effects of time and thought on attitude polarization. *Journal of Personality and Social Psychology, 31,* 262–270.

Tesser, A., & Leone, C. (1977). Cognitive schemas and thought as determinants of attitude change. *Journal of Experimental Social Psychology, 13,* 340–356.

Thurstone, L. L. (1928). Attitudes can be measured. *American Journal of Sociology, 33,* 529–544.

Tompkins, S. S. (1962). *Affect, imagery, consciousness: The positive affects* (Vol. 1). New York: Springer-Verlag.

Tompkins, S. S. (1963). *Affect, imagery, consciousness; The negative affects* (Vol. 2). New York: Springer-Verlag.

Tsal, Y. (1984). *The role of attention in processing information from advertisements.* Unpublished manuscript, Cornell University, Ithaca, NY.

Tucker, D. M. (1981). Lateral brain function, emotion, and conceptualization. *Psychological Bulletin, 89,* 19–46.

Tucker, D. M., Stenslie, C. E., Roth, R. S., & Shearer, S. L. (1981). Right frontal lobe activation and the right hemisphere performance during a depressed mood. *Archives of General Psychiatry, 38,* 169–174.

Tyler, S. W., Hertel, P. T., McCallum, M., & Ellis, H. C. (1979). Cognitive effort and memory. *Journal of Experimental Psychology: Human Learning and Memory, 5,* 607–617.

Valenti, A., & Downing, L. (1975). Differential effects of jury size on verdicts following deliberations as a function of the apparent guilt of a defendant. *Journal of Personality and Social Psychology, 32,* 655–663.

Valins, S. (1966). Cognitive effects of false heart rate feedback. *Journal of Personality and Social Psychology, 4,* 400–408.

Vinokur, A., & Burnstein, E. (1974). The effects of partially shared persuasive arguments on group-induced shifts: A group problem solving approach. *Journal of Personality and Social Psychology, 29,* 305–315.

Ware, P. D., & Tucker, R. K. (1974). Heckling as distraction: An experimental study of its effect on source credibility. *Speech Monographs, 41,* 185–188.

Watson, C., & Klett, W. (1986). Prediction of WAIS IQs from the Shipley-Hartford, the Army General Classification Test, and the Revised Beta Examination. *Journal of Clinical Psychology, 24,* 338–341.

Watts, W. A. (1967). Relative persistence of opinion change induced by active compared to passive participation. *Journal of Personality and Social Psychology, 5,* 4–15.

Watts, W. A., & Holt, L. E. (1979). Persistence of opinion change induced under conditions of forewarning and distraction. *Journal of Personality and Social Psychology, 37,* 778–789.

Watts, W. A., & McGuire, W. J. (1964). Persistence of induced opinion change and retention of inducing message content. *Journal of Abnormal and Social Psychology, 68,* 223–241.

Weber, S. J. (1972). *Opinion change is a function of the associative learning of content and source factors.* Unpublished doctoral dissertation, Northwestern University.

Wegner, D. M., & Giuliano, T. (1980). Arousal-induced attention to the self. *Journal of Personality and Social Psychology, 38,* 719–726.

Weldon, E., & Gargano, G. M. (1985). Cognitive effort in additive task groups: The effects of shared responsibility on the quality of multiattribute judgments. *Organizational Behavior and Human Decision Processes, 36,* 348–361.

Wells, G. L., & Petty, R. E. (1980). The effects of overt headmovements on persuasion: Compatibility and incompatibility of responses. *Basic and Applied Social Psychology, 1,* 219–230.

White, G. L. (1975). Contextual determinants of opinion judgments: Field experimental probes of judgmental relativity boundary conditions. *Journal of Personality and Social Psychology, 32,* 1047–1054.

White, R. W. (1959). Motivation reconsidered: The concept of competence *Psychological Review, 66,* 297–333.

Wicker, A. (1971). An examination of the "other variable" explanation of attitude-behavior inconsistency. *Journal of Personality and Social Psychology, 19,* 18–30.

Wiens, A., & Banaka, W. (1960). Estimating WAIS IQ from Shipley-Hartford scores: A cross validation. *Journal of Clinical Psychology, 16,* 452.

Wilder, D. (1977). Perception of groups, size of opposition, and social influence. *Journal of Experimental Social Psychology, 13,* 253–268.

Williams, K. D., Harkins, S., & Latane, B. (1981). Identifiability as a deterrent to social loafing: Two cheering experiments. *Journal of Personality and Social Psychology, 40,* 303–311.

Wilson, T. D. (1986). *Self-analysis and the cognitivation of attitudes.* Proposal submitted to the National Science Foundation, University of Virginia, Charlottesville, Va.

Wilson, T. D., Dunn, D., Bybee, J., Hyman, D., & Rotondo, J. (1984). Effects of analyzing reasons on attitude-behavior consistency. *Journal of Personality and Social Psychology, 47,* 5–16.

Witkin, H. A., Goodenough, D. R., & Oltman, P. K. (1979). Psychological differentiation: Current status. *Journal of Personality and Social Psychology, 37,* 1127–1145.

Witt, W. (1976). Effects of quantification in scientific writing. *Journal of Communication, 26,* 67–69.

Wood, W. (1982). Retrieval of attitude-relevant information from memory: Effects on susceptibility to persuasion and on intrinsic motivation. *Journal of Personality and Social Psychology, 42,* 798–810.

Wood, W., Kallgren, C., & Priesler, R. (1985). Access to attitude relevant information in memory as a determinant of persuasion. *Journal of Experimental Social Psychology, 21,* 73–85.

Wright, P. L. (1981). Cognitive responses to mass media advocacy. In R. E. Petty, T. M. Ostrom, & T. C. Brock (Eds.), *Cognitive responses in persuasion.* Hillsdale, NJ: Erlbaum.

Wyer, R. S., & Srull, T. (1984). *The handbook of social cognition.* Hillsdale, NJ: Erlbaum.

Yalch, R. F., & Elmore-Yalch, R. (1984). The effect of numbers on the route to persuasion. *Journal of Consumer Research, 11,* 522–527.

Zacks, R. T., Hasher, L., Sanft, H., & Rose, K. (1983). Encoding effort and recall: A cautionary note. *Journal of Experimental Psychology: Learning, Memory & Cognition, 9,* 747–756.

Zajonc, R. B. (1968). Attitudinal effects of mere exposure. *Journal of Personality and Social Psychology Monograph Supplement, 9,* 1–27.

Zajonc, R. B. (1980). Feeling and thinking: Preferences need no inferences. *American Psychologist, 35,* 151–175.

Zajonc, R. B., & Markus, H. (1982). Affective and cognitive factors in preferences. *Journal of Consumer Research, 9,* 123–131.

Zajonc, R. B., Shaver, P., Tavris, C., & VanKreveld, D. (1972). Exposure, satiation, and stimulus discriminability. *Journal of Personality and Social Psychology, 21,* 270–280.

Zanna, M. P., Kiesler, C. A., & Pilkonis, P. A. (1970). Positive and negative attitudinal affect established by classical conditioning. *Journal of Personality and Social Psychology, 14,* 321–328.

Zillmann, D. (1972). Rhetorical elicitation of agreement in persuasion. *Journal of Personality and Social Psychology, 21,* 159–165.

Zimbardo, P. G. (1960). Involvement and communication dicrepancy as determinants of opinion conformity. *Journal of Abnormal and Social Psychology, 60,* 86–94.

Zimbardo, P. G. (1970). The human choice: Individuation, reason, and order, versus deindividaution, impulse, and chaos. In W. Arnold & D. Levine (Eds.), *Nebraska symposium on motivaton, 1969* (Vol. 17). Lincoln, NE: University of Nebraska Press.

Zimbardo, P. G., Snyder, M., Thomas, J., Gold, A., & Gurwitz, S. (1970). Modifying the impact of persuasive communications with external distraction. *Journal of Personality and Social Psychology, 16,* 669–680.

Zuckerman, M., DePaulo, B. M., & Rosenthal, R. (1981). Verbal and nonverbal communication of deception. In L. Berkowitz (Ed.), *Advances in experimental social psychology* (Vol. 11). New York: Academic Press.

Author Index

Subject Index

Springer Series in Social Psychology

Attention and Self-Regulation: A Control-Theory Approach to Human Behavior
Charles S. Carver/Michael F. Scheier

Gender and Nonverbal Behavior
Clara Mayo/Nancy M. Henley (Editors)

Personality, Roles, and Social Behavior
William Ickes/Eric S. Knowles (Editors)

Toward Transformation in Social Knowledge
Kenneth J. Gergen

The Ethics of Social Research: Surveys and Experiments
Joan E. Sieber (Editor)

The Ethics of Social Research: Fieldwork, Regulation, and Publication
Joan E. Sieber (Editor)

Anger and Aggression: An Essay on Emotion
James R. Averill

The Social Psychology of Creativity
Teresa M. Amabile

Sports Violence
Jeffrey H. Goldstein (Editor)

Nonverbal Behavior: A Functional Perspective
Miles L. Patterson

Basic Group Processes
Paul B. Paulus (Editor)

Attitudinal Judgment
J. Richard Eiser (Editor)

Social Psychology of Aggression: From Individual Behavior to Social Interaction
Amélie Mummendey (Editor)

Directions in Soviet Social Psychology
Lloyd H. Strickland (Editor)

Sociophysiology
William M. Waid (Editor)

Compatible and Incompatible Relationships
William Ickes (Editor)

Facet Theory: Approaches to Social Research
David Canter (Editor)

Action Control: From Cognition to Behavior
Julius Kuhl/Jürgen Beckmann (Editors)

Springer Series in Social Psychology